F.D.R.'s UNDECLARED WAR

F.D.R.'s
UNDECLARED
WAR

1939 to 1941

by

T. R. Fehrenbach

DAVID McKAY COMPANY, INC.

New York

F.D.R.'s UNDECLARED WAR

Library of Congress Catalog Card Number: 67-13415

MANUFACTURED IN THE UNITED STATES OF AMERICA

VAN REES PRESS • NEW YORK

The history of . . . war shows that modern war must be fought on three fronts: the military front, the economic front, and the propaganda front.

HAROLD D. LASSWELL

Contents

1.

The Undeclared War

---

*When foreign affairs are ruled by democracies the danger of war
will be in mistaken beliefs.*   Elihu Root.

On a steamy late July day in the brooding summer of 1939,
President Franklin D. Roosevelt requested several key Senators to appear at the White House. Both Democrats and Republicans arrived: Charles McNary, from Oregon and the
number one Republican in the Senate, and his New England
colleague, Warren Austin, and genial Alben Barkley of Ken-
tucky, the Democratic Majority Leader. Seventy-four-year-old
William Edgar Borah, the independent and irascible war-horse
from Idaho, who had deserted his party for Bryan and then
jumped back again, and who was a power unto himself, came
also. Dapper Key Pittman, the southern gentleman who had
gone West and represented the mining interests of Nevada
so well that he had become head of the Foreign Relations
Committee, arrived and sat gingerly on his chair.

President Roosevelt was in his usual wheelchair, flanked by
White House Secretary Steve Early and soft-spoken Cordell
Hull, his Secretary of State. John Nance Garner, the Texan
Vice President, sat in the background, smoking his inevitable
cigar.

1

Roosevelt got quickly down to business. The summer was sultry; both the country and the Congress were in the doldrums, but in Europe things were happening. The State Department had handed F.D.R. a series of gloomy advices. Nazi Germany had mobilized two million men. Other nations had called their reserves to the colors. Army divisions from one end of Europe to the other were marching on frontiers, and gas masks were being issued to civilians. They were practicing air raid drills in Paris. Ambassador Davies in Belgium—who had developed secret, key sources of information not even available to British intelligence—predicted war. The President himself, adding it all up, thought a European war was imminent.

Of course, there had been war or rumors of war for more than a year, ever since Hitler had marched into Austria, then browbeat France and Britain into the surrender of Czechoslovakia at Munich. The 1938 crisis had seemed worse. There had been an electric sort of fear then; now there was a fatalistic feeling that somehow, someway, everything would be all right. This opinion Roosevelt himself, with his State Department, did not share. They were worried, and had in fact been worried ever since the days of Munich.

F.D.R. told the senators that war was coming, and when it did, the Neutrality Acts of 1935—which required the United States to stay entirely clear of any foreign conflict—tied too many strings to his freedom of action. The Neutrality Acts, joint resolutions of the Congress, forbade the export of arms, ammunition, or any implement of war to any belligerent, either direct or through transhipment. As amended in 1937, they not only required American ships and citizens to stay out of war zones, but made it unlawful for any American citizen to book passage on the vessels of any belligerent nation. Munitions makers in the United States had been licensed, and the "Cash and Carry" principle—made popular in the United States by the Great Depression—applied to all buying of raw materials

2

by foreign powers. Further, there was the Johnson Act of 1934, which prohibited loans to any nation that was behind on its World War I debt, which meant every friendly country except Finland.

Roosevelt said he could not deal with the current world situation under such handicaps. World peace was being threatened by a handful of "relentless men" seeking power for themselves in Europe. The German and Italian dictators were armed; their nations had been rearming for years. Now, the American export embargo worked against the rearmament of the democratic countries, France and Britain, who needed to buy arms and matériel in the United States. F.D.R. wanted repeal, or at least, significant amendment of the Neutrality Acts, so that he could at least discriminate between a totalitarian aggressor and its democratic victim.

Old Senator Borah snorted in his seat. Freedom of action was exactly what he had no intention of ever allowing the President. He did not trust Roosevelt, and above all, he did not trust Roosevelt's growing taste for involving himself in international affairs. He was, in 1939, by no means alone; there was a whole school in Congress and in the nation that thought the same. It was as much an emotional reaction as an intellectual one.

To Borah, foreign politics were "Power Politics" and all power politics were bad. The United States had nothing to gain by sticking its nose in abroad, and a lot to lose. The mood of this school, or at least the intelligent and informed people of it, was shown clearly in the summer of 1939 by *Time*. That magazine worried over "Roosevelt's bent for international power politics" and even carried foreign news under the heading "Power Politics." The connotation was always bad, in the opinion of *Time*'s editors as well as of Senator Borah.

Borah did not have any use for Hitler, or Mussolini, or any strutting dictator. But he didn't have any use for the English, or the French, either. Getting involved in the European cess-

3

pool again would be a mistake. Getting in the first war in 1917 had been a mistake. The boys had gone overseas to "make the world safe for democracy" and to "end all wars." Many of them had gotten killed, and it hadn't solved anything, except perhaps to pull England's fat out of the fire.

William Edgar Borah, along with Hiram Johnson of California, Burton Wheeler of Montana, Gerald Nye of North Dakota, and Arthur Vandenberg of Michigan, had sat on the old Senate Munitions Committee of 1934-1935, which had investigated the causes, actions, and results of American intervention in Europe in 1917. The committee had dug deeply into the dark corners of World War I. It had studied the activities of the so-called "merchants of death," the munitions makers who had made millions selling arms to Allied governments; it had explored the deliberate and brilliant propaganda issued by the British over the German occupation of Belgium, that had so turned American opinion against the Kaiser. And with the slaughter of millions of young men always in their minds, the senators had investigated the vengeful Peace of Versailles, that watered down all of Woodrow Wilson's hopes and fine ideals and showed Americans that the European powers in World War I had only been playing the old nationalistic power game.

Significantly for the future, no United States senator who sat on the Munitions Committee remained unaffected. They had developed a profound cynicism toward war, replacing the earlier American idealism, and in both Senate and the public at large the investigations produced a deepening turn toward isolationism.

If Borah had anything to say about it, American boys would never go into European trenches again, for any reason.

The arms embargo laws of the mid-thirties were a direct outgrowth of Congress' growing cynicism toward foreign intervention. They were designed and passed specifically to prevent any future President from getting the United States into a

4

foreign entanglement step by step, as Wilson had in 1916-1917.

A President who could neither sell nor give arms to any side during a foreign war, it was felt, would be hard put to drag the United States into it. Like Borah, many key members of the Senate felt that the initial mistake in World War I had been taking sides. It was impossible to favor the Allies in spirit, sell them arms, and in the long run remain neutral. The only hope of noninvolvement, to Borah and his colleagues, lay in complete neutrality, no matter who won or lost. Thus Borah's battle lines were drawn years before President Roosevelt called him to the White House in 1939—and Roosevelt himself could look back ruefully to those years when, occupied with the Depression and domestic problems, he had failed even to oppose the Neutrality Acts when they came before the Congress.

But now, Borah, who had as deep a distrust for Roosevelt as he had once had for Morgan and Company, the world bankers, and "Eastern interventionalists," did not oppose the President directly. He chose to mount a flanking attack.

He told F.D.R. that there wasn't going to be any European war.

He said he had his own sources of information, and he also studied foreign media and events closely. He saw no signs that war was imminent.

This was too much for Cordell Hull. The Secretary of State, in his soft Tennessee drawl, asked if the Senator meant to say his own intelligence sources were superior to those of the Department?

Borah, one of those oratorical, completely courageous and utterly opinionated senators who, like Hiram Johnson or Wayne Morse, ride periodically out of the American West, said no. But his face told Hull what he thought of the Department's sources of information. In the corner, John Garner, who by this time disagreed with Roosevelt on almost everything, grinned and pulled on his cigar.

More to the point, the other Republicans, McNary and Austin, indicated no desire to increase the President's powers on the international scene. They represented the mainstream of their party's thought, which had no belief in appeasement but took a general isolationist tone.

And the Republicans were not really Roosevelt's problem. Key Pittman indicated that the isolationist question cut across party lines. If most Republicans could be counted on to oppose anything F.D.R. wanted on general principles, Burton Wheeler, Dennis Chavez and others, all New Deal Democrats, were just as opposed. The liberal group in the Senate was strongly against any involvement in a foreign war, and while they didn't care to oppose F.D.R. openly on anything, some of them were exceedingly dubious of his turning outward toward the world. New Deal programs, further domestic reform, dear to their hearts, both were bound to suffer if the United States looked outward instead of concentrating on its own problems.

Since the first war crisis in Europe in 1938 there were definite signs that F.D.R.'s attention was being increasingly drawn overseas, just at a time when domestic opposition to further New Deal reform was hardening. Ironically, for diametrically opposed reasons, both liberals and conservatives were alarmed at Roosevelt's interest in the world.

There was a newfound, still uneasy, but powerful alliance between Northern Republicans and Southern Democrats in the Congress. The two wings of this coalition, which were ideologically close but separated into opposed parties by an accident of history, first discovered they were the real balance of power in the Congress in 1938. The liberals were afraid that further reform would be abandoned through inattention or foreign involvement. Conservatives, who generally disliked F.D.R. on principle, were against anything he wanted. They were also fearful of getting in any foreign war—because war could bring social unrest, greater governmental control, and more reform.

Now, Pittman told Roosevelt that there was no chance of repealing or even amending the Neutrality Act. F.D.R. didn't have the votes.

When old Hiram Johnson of California had said recently: "The people of this country can thank God they have a Congress that hasn't made the mistake thus far of intervening in present affairs in China or of being the ally of anybody," most senators had secretly agreed with him. Congress read the mood of the country, and the country was profoundly isolationist.

The meeting between the President, Secretary of State, and Senate leaders broke up on a slightly sour note. F.D.R. was angry and disappointed. He was deeply concerned with the situation abroad, deeply worried over the coming war. He felt that America's security was at stake, and that America's future hung on the outcome of events now taking place far away.

He was eager to guide the United States into world action and to do something effective in the foreign field. F.D.R. was far ahead of his time, or at least his country. He had already succumbed to the logic of great power politics by 1939, but 90 percent of the American people hardly even realized the United States was not only a great nation, but a great power with a definite place in the power structure of the world.

But since Woodrow Wilson's terrible rebuff on the League of Nations, and since Congress rejected America's acceptance of the World Court after World War I, no President had seriously attempted to make America effective in the world. There was no evidence that Harding, Coolidge, or Hoover felt the game was worth trying; they were as thoroughly insular and isolationist as their people. Calvin Coolidge had said the business of the United States was business, and the corollary was that it had no business prying into politics overseas. From all evidence, the whole spectrum of American political thought thoroughly agreed.

7

The experience of 1917-1919, when the United States entered World War I as a great crusade, had brought the sobering realization that the world had not been made safe for democracy and the war to end all wars had done nothing of the kind. Rather, it had soured the American people on foreign adventures. The disillusion and bitterness ran all the way from Left to Right. It solidified in real political opposition to any further involvement overseas, and in a folk-feeling that the boys should never again be sent overseas, to die in some forgotten Flanders Fields. The world was in bad shape, true. But there was too much to take care of, too much to be done, here at home.

This fervent desire to avoid trouble, entanglement, and foreign bloodshed was not peculiarly American. It was universal, decent, and sprang from the human heart. Seen only from inside America, it seemed laudable. America had no designs on anybody, and wanted only to be left alone. If John Donne had written that no man was an island, Americans wanted to live on one; if the Bible had left the question of whether Cain was his brother's keeper unanswered, Americans were prepared to answer it now, in the negative. But translated into foreign policy, these emotions made sense only to statesmen and citizens who failed to see or understand the structure of the twentieth-century world and the place of the democratic commercial nations in it.

If Harding and Hoover had had a certain humanitarian interest in the world at large but rejected any enduring American ties to the world political order, Franklin Roosevelt had entered the White House thinking exactly the same. The combination of a certain cultural interest in the world with a failure to recognize any American responsibilities in or for it was a remarkable characteristic of the entire American educated class prior to 1940.

At most only 10 percent of the people were interested in, or paid any attention to, affairs abroad. The others were desperately concerned with the here and now, making a living, getting ahead, avoiding bankruptcy. What happened overseas seemed to have no meaning, or effect, on their lives. The few who were interested, or studied foreign affairs, seemed to be convinced that America had developed moral and legal concepts of great value to the world—but they were disillusioned and unhappy over the fact that other nations and peoples continually rejected them. These men and women continually advised the world to scrap its armaments, quit power politics, and live under the rule of international law.

Because the democratic societies, particularly the United States, had been able to achieve the transfer of wealth, status, power, and prestige among citizens without manning the barricades or chopping off heads, most educated Americans saw no reason why these same practices could not be extended everywhere, between nations. The fact that nations and peoples were very different, and had utterly diverging dominant ethics, was not driven home in American schools or colleges. At any rate, American concern rarely went beyond the giving of advice. Once the United States, either through private agencies or its government, had advised the other nations on legality, decency, and morality as seen by Americans, there its responsibility ended.

Ironically, during the 1930's, very few Americans realized that, by refusing any responsibility for world order and by insisting on the observance of a nonexistent "international law," they did their part to assure a truly jungle world. At almost the same time that the United States' major diplomatic drive was directed toward getting all nations to sign the Kellogg Pact, or Pact of Paris, in 1929—a pledge to renounce the use of war as an instrument of national policy—Adolf Hitler was writing with murderous truth that any pact, alliance, or law that was not intended to be upheld in the end by force was no pact, alliance, or law at all.

Americans did not understand that there was no law with-

9

out effective government, and no government without effective consensus and a monopoly of force. These things did not exist across national boundaries. Furthermore, Americans even in government were extremely slow to see the breaking up of the industrial world into two hostile camps, and the beginnings of a genuine revolution against the Anglo-French-American political, commercial, and cultural order that had grown up across the North Atlantic.

For reasons of education, sentiment, and political bias most Americans denied that such an order even existed. And it was tenuous—its real shape became clear only after it had been destroyed under Hitlerian attack.

There is no evidence to show that President Roosevelt understood the real world any better than most Americans of his class in 1933. He certainly approved of President Hoover's rejection of the British bid for a united front against Japanese aggression in Manchuria in 1931. His Administration in no way recognized Manchuria as a fatal milestone on the path to world collapse. The problem was, Roosevelt came to power at a time of severe economic crisis. In 1933, the deepening Depression occupied his attention almost exclusively; he did not recognize that the international economic depression itself was a symptom of disorder in the industrial world.

The business of America had been business, but domestically it was apparent that the structure had broken down. F.D.R.'s great concern was to break the Great Depression and get the country moving again. And his major political aims and attentions were not directed toward the world community —they were engaged in the forming of that enormous political alliance between the American underprivileged voters, various non-Anglo-Saxon ethnic groups, and the rural South which he now made the dominant factor in United States Presidential politics. He changed the middle-class nature of Woodrow Wilson's party, and almost overnight broke the long, historic chain of Republican domination of the country.

10

F.D.R.'s New Deal was in no way a revolution in America —which most business leaders eventually came to realize. It was, in effect, a new stabilization, and the reforms and the stabilization were both indicative of the great strength of American institutions and democratic experience. Ironically, however, as all but a few of the most emotionally committed historians and economists were to admit, the Roosevelt New Deal failed in its express purpose: it did not end the world Depression, nor did it effectively end massive unemployment. The vast Federal budgets aimed at fostering prosperity were mere palliatives that never touched the root causes of the problem, and they remained the basis of strong democratic disagreement within America. The social and financial reforms of the New Deal, however, undeniably made life seem more secure and more comfortable for millions of Americans, and they were accepted into the fabric of United States society, even by groups and classes that did not materially benefit from them. Not social reforms, but fiscal policy, remained the great controversy of New Deal politics.

But the immense problems of the Depression, unemployment, and political consensus captured all of F.D.R.'s attention at the exact time that democratic world order was cracking to pieces in Europe and Asia. In his first inaugural address F.D.R. did not so much as mention foreign affairs.

He accepted and continued the strong trade barriers against the rest of the democratic industrial world that had sprung up under Herbert Hoover. These tariffs were, of course, defensive, and they were a phenomenon of the 1920's. All countries adopted and enforced them, France and Britain as well as the United States. The industrial establishment in every nation demanded them, and the result was a form of industrial and commercial war that many economists came to believe was the real cause of the Great Depression of 1929.

The United States was the world's greatest financial and industrial nation after 1918, and under F.D.R.'s leadership

11

it was as responsible as any nation for the worldwide economic breakdown and monetary collapse. Roosevelt torpedoed British efforts to stabilize the world financial crisis in the early 1930's without hesitation. His revaluation of gold from twenty to thirty-five dollars an ounce was made for purely domestic reasons, in an attempt to foster monetary inflation and thus prosperity, with no thought whatever of the crisis this move created in gold-standard France.

With the greatest financial power playing a unilateral game, the immediate result was world monetary chaos. If the Great Depression, which spread like wildfire on the heels of the collapse of Atlantic trade, hurt America and the democracies badly, its result in Germany was disastrous.

Almost all political observers agree that the Great Depression in Germany, with its complete economic collapse and its more than ten million unemployed, opened the door for the Nazi march to power. F.D.R. himself could not be held personally responsible for his domestic actions to alleviate the Depression and their long-term effects. He made each of them with a firm consensus of advisor support, and with no opposition from the public. The vital connection between German prosperity, Japanese trade, and American national security was not seen or understood, by anyone in a position of influence or power.

Roosevelt made no moves in support of the faltering League of Nations, either. He stayed as aloof as Harding, if not as hostile. He did, with much controversy, restore diplomatic relations with Communist Russia. But this act was not done with any regard to strengthening world order, but for a hoped-for American advantage.

It is probable that the President could not have done much to change the supremely isolationist mood of America in the Depression years; he had no fulcrum to apply. But what is interesting is that Roosevelt's own mood was just as isolationist, and he saw no reason to try. He did not oppose passage of the Johnson Act of 1934, which cut off future funds or aid to former American allies. He did nothing to prevent the initial passage of the Neutrality Acts of 1935—which, significantly, were the American reaction to Mussolini's grab of Ethiopia in the summer of 1935. Instead of trying to prevent the collapse of world order, the country's desire, and the President's, was to remove itself so far as possible from the coming disorder.

Roosevelt's first misgivings, and his interest in foreign affairs occurred during his second administration. The Japanese gambit in Manchuria had been allowed to succeed by default; Mussolini's bluff over Ethiopia had worked. Mussolini and Italy were not a real threat to world peace; Italy simply lacked the resources of national power to threaten France or England. But Mussolini's example, and what the invasion of Ethiopia had revealed about the state of the democratic world, convinced the new German dictator, Hitler, of his opportunity. He abrogated the punitive disarmament clauses of the Treaty of Versailles. He ordered troops into the Rhineland in 1936.

The Japanese created a war with China in 1937 and began a systematic invasion of that country. Japan announced that it was determined to create a new political and economic order in East Asia, one that would inevitably bring it into confrontation with the United States and the European powers.

In Europe, Hitler annexed Austria through military invasion in the spring of 1938. A few months later he demanded the return of the German Sudetenland, which meant the dismemberment of the democratic state of Czechoslovakia. By this time, Hitler had built the most powerful army, and above all, the greatest air force in Europe or the world. Visibly frightened, but quite obviously hoping for a détente with Hitler that might turn him against the Soviet Union, France and Britain agreed to German terms at Munich. By selling out a remote but democratic and friendly people, the Western democracies hoped to buy peace in their time.

13

It is very clear, in retrospect, that Franklin Roosevelt and his closest advisers saw the meeting at Munich for the geopolitical defeat that it was. Not only were two million armed Czech soldiers lost for a potential showdown with an aggressive Germany, along with a central European bastion and an advanced industrial state—Munich was a moral disaster. It convinced Hitler, fatally, that the Western powers were too weak, too wrapped in their own conflicts and concerns, and too pacifist to fight. Up to Munich Hitler had played shrewdly upon the aura of his time. He had played off fears of the gigantic Bolshevist Soviet Union against Western hopes that he would contain Communism. He had demanded revision of the unfair provisions of Versailles at the point of a gun, and got them. Statesmen with guilty consciences were easy enough to push.

In five years Hitler took Germany from collapse and national impotence to the position of dominant power upon the European continent. He gained each of Germany's legitimate foreign aims. But after Munich, where his threats and browbeating achieved a complete Western moral collapse, Hitler was no longer shrewd or rational. After Munich, Hitler became nihilistic, messianic, and blinded by visions of German world domination. He saw nothing to stop him.

Ironically, only two men of world stature saw this. They were Roosevelt and Winston Churchill. Churchill was out of favor and out of power, and distrusted by almost the entire English upper economic class. Roosevelt was the head of a great nation, but it was a nation completely uninterested and unconcerned with events in Europe, and it was a country which had no rationale for effective intervention. And while Roosevelt had made himself the most powerful peacetime President the United States had ever had, he had no real freedom of action overseas. Foreign affairs were the President's responsibility, under the Constitution, but only with the advice and consent of the Senate.

Roosevelt headed a democratic society, where all final

power still resided in the hands of the people, variously organized. He was bound by Abraham Lincoln's famous dictum: "With public support, you can do anything. Without public support, you can do nothing."

Interestingly enough, while Churchill, a mere member of Parliament, rose and in speech after speech blasted the settlement at Munich as a disastrous sellout and a guaranty of war, Roosevelt took the tack of sending personal messages to the dictators. F.D.R. did have a belief, which he never completely lost, in the efficacy of personal transactions at the highest level.

But he also was aware that Churchill's efforts were having little effect. The immediate result of telling the British public unpleasant truths was that Churchill became anathema. His Conservative Party attacked him. The public scorned him, as they had since his early warnings about the Hitlerian danger. He did not succeed in getting effective British rearmament.

In the spring of 1939 Hitler completely repudiated his promises at Munich—that he had no further designs on Czechoslovakia—by invading and occupying the rest of the country. Only then did British opinion on Churchill change. He was, and continued to be, unpalatable to the reigning Tory hierarchy, who violently opposed Churchill's entry into the Chamberlain Cabinet. And as late as June, 1939, when it was obvious to all European publics that war was at hand, and that the democracies were going to have to fight or surrender to a madman, only slightly more than half of the British public wanted Churchill to have a place in the British government. Winston Churchill was a farseeing statesman, and a great moral leader, but he was never a fully effective politician.

Roosevelt, however, was an adroit politician. Unlike Churchill, he advanced his opinions in different ways. Roosevelt knew how to take a moral stand, and felt deeply compelled to do so. But his political instincts never permitted him to take a politically dangerous stand with the magnificent abandon Churchill employed. Churchill had spent a great part of his life out of office, a voice crying in the wind, right or wrong, but unpopular. Roosevelt's whole success lay in being, like every successful American President, an advocate of consensus. He could not afford, in his own estimation, to be unpopular, even while the world went to hell. He would work, not like Winston Churchill, but in his own ways.

In 1938 he sent personal messages to Hitler and Mussolini, requesting them to refrain from war. He asked them to pledge not to attack the democracies. These appeals got a contemptuous answer from each dictator, which in the reality of world politics they probably deserved, for they were gratuitous advice. But they did do one thing which F.D.R. obviously intended: they did not change the course of history but had the propaganda effect of putting the United States on record.

The enormous difference between 1914 and 1939 was that in 1914 the United States, with the exception of small segments of the anglophile East, was genuinely neutral. Woodrow Wilson had called for "complete impartiality" when the guns of August boomed. F.D.R. had abandoned any pretense of neutrality. This dichotomy in the President and the United States government, committed in spirit but neutral by law and public demand, was to cause the national schizophrenia of the coming years.

In 1938, and through 1939, F.D.R. continued to do the one thing he felt he could, and must, do—put the United States on record. He condemned armed aggression and the aggressor leaders. The condemnations had no visible or practical effect on the condemned, and probably F.D.R. was not so naïve as to think they would. He was speaking not only to them but to the American people.

Not all people were aware that leadership was implicit in democratic government in 1939. Most people understood that democratic society was being directly challenged by totalitarian revolution, and that for almost a decade, democratic

16

beliefs and solutions had been in a state of crisis. The "efficiency of dictatorship" was both admired and feared.

The problem of the United States, in the complex and collapsing world of 1939, was one of leadership. It had become the peculiar and personal problem of Franklin Roosevelt.

His meeting with Congressional leaders in July, 1939, went unnoticed by the public. But it marked the beginning of a war. It was a war that would engage the American Presidency and the Congress and the Cabinet. At times it would be between the Congress and the President, the Congress and the people, and even the people and the President. It would finally include action in the North Atlantic between the navies of Germany and the United States. Unlike the shooting war in Europe, it would never be declared.

This conflict would continue for two-and-one-half years. It would not be ended, but submerged when the Japanese warplanes flew out of the sun at Pearl Harbor.

2.

The Tyranny of Gallup

Is the Roosevelt Administration neutral? Certainly not. Is there any chance of the United States to stay out of another world war? Practically none. Will the Roosevelt program of liberal reform go on in the event of a general war? It will not. Would the outbreak of war mean a third term for President Roosevelt? Probably. Kenneth Crawford in *The Nation*, September, 1939.

This Nation will remain a neutral nation.... President Franklin D. Roosevelt, September 3, 1939.

On August 22, 1939, a short, dark-haired, palefaced man with unforgettable burning eyes addressed a convocation of the commanders of the German forces. Gold braid glittered from shoulder loops and light flashed from ceremonial daggers in front of him; he was surrounded by field-gray tunics and Luftwaffe blue. Listening to him were the leaders of the greatest concentration of military might anywhere in the world: Keitel, the Hanoverian who was more Prussian than the Prussians, and who would make a religion out of loyalty; Bock, who would twice make the cover of *Time;* Raeder, who would almost win the war but would retire in deep disgrace and thus avoid Dönitz' fate.

More than one *Generaloberst* or *Grossadmiral,* more than

one cold, brilliant brain behind an icy face hated the man with the burning eyes. In this throng, dripping with symbols of status and power, he wore only a simple gray tunic without sign of rank, adorned only with the 1914-1918 Prussian Iron Cross, Second Class. On his service record an Imperial German army officer had once written: *This man is unfit to command other men,* but Adolf Hitler, Führer of the German Reich, had understood the logic of his times.

Until this moment he had played upon them with superb skill. There had been nothing like him since Napoleon.

He had come out of the Central European gutter knowing only a few truths, all of them unpalatable, few of them understood in his time. He had written that the big lie was always more believable than the little one, that the man in the street paid no attention to public affairs until it was too late, and that the only way to get something through a people's collective head was to say it many times. He was an historical accident, a product of the crisis of European civilization that brought the holocaust of 1914, and a result of those forces, errors, and beliefs which afterward made 1939 inevitable. He was not a monster; he was a human being. He would be recognizable to future historians as an unpleasant, but completely logical, manifestation of his times.

He had appeared into a European world that had shot up all its ideals and faiths, along with its blood and treasure, in the trenches. He offered a nonsensical mythology, but sold it with charismatic skill. He said unpleasant things, but he raised roaring passions, because he told Germans things that in some dark places of their souls they longed to hear. To a society which feared God was dead, he appeared to be a new messiah.

The old social order, the aristocrats, judges, professors, and upper middle class, had backed the Empire, and with the Empire had gone down to discredit and defeat. The Allies at Versailles, still hating Prussiandom, did not understand the wounds that by indirection they would inflict upon themselves.

19

When the German state in 1918 collapsed in revolution and ruin, they had only felt a somber satisfaction.

"Let dog eat dog," Winston Churchill said. But when dog ate dog, anywhere in the world, no one could say for sure who might be eaten in the end.

The industrial technology everywhere, even in Britain and America, was creating social changes and tensions that only the strongest and most stable societies could absorb. German society barely survived the hideous attrition and sacrifices of 1914-1918; the German home front in World War I was much more involved, and suffered more, for example, than civilians in Britain. The humiliation of defeat, the destruction of former institutions in the revolution that ended the Empire, and the disastrous inflation that eroded the social position of the entire middle classes were all dangerous blows to German society. The Great Depression, which came in 1929 and left deep but invisible scars elsewhere, cut a raw wound across Germany. British and American institutions survived the economic crises because of a long tradition and basic social strength in both countries. In Germany, however, both tradition and strength had already decayed, and the terrible problem of mass unemployment created new tensions on top of older ones. Unemployment—the new social disease that made human beings both useless and desperate—was far worse in Weimar Germany than in either America or Britain.

The characteristic reaction of the twentieth century everywhere to too-rapid change and to severe economic crisis was some form of corporate state or totalitarianism.

Burgeoning democratic orders in Latin America, especially in Brazil and Chile and Argentina, succumbed at this time. Japan went through somewhat the same ordeal. In every case, the new totalitarianism was supported by the economically fragile middle classes in their almost hysterical search for security, and by major industrial forces fearful of another modern "solution" to economic stress—Marxism.

20

The new crop of dictators, whether relatively mild like Brazil's Vargas, or ferocious like the messianic Hitler, sprang from similar sources, and rode like forces of unrest and change. But where new totalitarian drives in Argentina or Brazil could have small effect on the world beyond their borders, nations like Italy, Japan, and above all, Germany, were, or had the potential to be, world powers.

The world could frown on the fascist ideology of Brazilian marshals and Argentinian admirals and Eastern European strong men, but it could also ignore these men. Fascism or national socialism in major industrial powers, with its inherent bent toward revising the entire commercial structure of the world, could not be ignored, as the democratic order found to its sorrow.

All the new strong men of the 1930's were adept at playing different groups and domestic forces within nations off, one against the other. Mussolini showed the way, but Hitler proved himself the real genius at the game. First, Hitler rose to German power; then he rose to world power, playing group against group, and finally, nation against nation.

German bankers, army officers, and industrialists saw Hitler's rise as an effective counterpoise to the thing they feared most—Bolshevism. This Hitler understood. He seemed to cater to them. They did not understand him at all, until much too late. What some men of democratic persuasion and experience never understood, about Germans under Hitler, or Russians under Stalin, is that there could be an underground, but never an opposition, in a totalitarian state.

But the tension, despair, and social malaise of Hitler's era were not purely German. They were European, if not worldwide. If German bigwigs derided Hitler's brown-shirted hoodlums but trusted they could be used for a good purpose, French and British industrialists, frightened by the Russian Revolution, hoped Hitler could serve a purpose, too. The new Nazi and older Soviet states professed undying hatred for each other, and in this everyone who hated Communism saw some good.

The thirties were years of social unrest and ideological tension beyond anything before or since. The specter of the U.S.S.R. haunted the 1918-1938 generation in a way Khrushchev's later rockets never could. The Comintern seemed hideously effective, about to undermine all Western ideals and institutions from within. Communism was new, and still virulent, and praise for the U.S.S.R. from gentlemen of the democratic Left only impelled the equally blind men of the Right to seek a way to live with Hitler.

The Conservative government of Great Britain, the one real order-keeping power in the world, was too intent upon the threatened social revolution to see the imminent national revolt Hitler's Germany was mounting against the democratic world. Hitlerian Germany could have been a counterpoise against the national and revolutionary ambitions of the Soviet Union. But Hitler was too much an opportunist. After the mad intoxication of Munich, when he stood at last predominant in Europe, he could not stop. He planned to finish off world Communism. But he was equally eager to dominate the West.

As late as 1938, members of the French General Staff and British leaders said privately, "Why doesn't that Czech politician, Beneš, get out of the way and let Hitler go about his business to the East?" They were angry when the Czechs, under pressure, called for help, and for fulfillment of French treaty obligations. General Weygand, like retired General Pétain, had no use for Germans. But he hated Bolshevism worse than anything else in the world. It did not seem a moral defeat but some kind of victory to sell Czechoslovakia short.

French and British leadership, unsure at home, governing but not leading, kept hoping up till 1939, as German industrialists hoped in 1933, that somehow, some way, a deal could be made. To the generation that had been through 1918, anything seemed better than another war. Democrats, eager for détente, did not see that Hitler was unappeasable.

Now, in August, 1939, Hitler had played off West and East to rare perfection. He had made Germany the world's greatest military power at the expense of and with no opposition from the West. He had frightened Russia into a nonaggression pact. Hitler recognized seven great powers in the world. Italy and Japan were friendly, with aims that converged with his. Russia now was neutralized. America did not count.

Hitler had his divisions poised along the Polish corridor, air armies ready in the east. He had made demands on Poland that could not be met. All that remained to be seen was if Britain and France, each of whom had a military alliance with Poland, would fight at last.

He hold the assembled German commanders:

> I shall give a propagandist reason for starting the war. No matter if it is believed or not. The winner will not be asked if he told the truth. When you start a war, it does not matter who is right, but who wins.
>
> Close your hearts to pity. Act with brutality. Eighty million Germans must get what is their due. Their existence must be made secure. The stronger man is in the right.

The struggle for the world had begun.

Throughout the summer of 1939 the United States took no effective diplomatic action relative to the coming war, one way or the other. It was understandable that the Germans, who were well aware of the potentialities of American production and remembered what American entry in World War I had cost them, ruled the United States out as a factor in the coming struggle.

In the 1930's the United States had three broad lines of foreign policy. These were: 1. In the Orient, an undefinable generalization called the Open Door, which really meant the United States wanted no one power to dominate there and

23

freeze the others out; 2. In the Western Hemisphere, and particularly the Caribbean, predominance, which F.D.R. continued but ameliorated by changing the Large Policy with its incessant Marine interventions into the Good Neighbor Policy which spawned a rash of dictators; 3. In Europe, nonintervention and neutrality, which, however, as all European chancelleries were aware, did not exclude the continual giving of advice.

The British Foreign Office was particularly cynical of American actions in the field of foreign policy. Each time a sticky situation developed, threatening trouble, the United States rushed into it at once with free advice. All parties were asked to talk it over, to pledge not to fight, to guarantee human rights, and were bombarded with similar abstractions or moral generalizations.

These actions were extremely irritating to statesmen with real problems, here and now, who had to discuss and deal with specific issues, like Danzig or the Sudetenland. For the American proposals never offered the faintest hint of a solution, or set up any guidelines as to how wealth, populations, and boundaries might be altered peacefully. The European power struggle in the 1930's was colored by fear, anger, insecurity, and a growing German arrogance and ambition. It could not be settled simply by getting everyone to sit down around a table, or having them sign pledges to sin no more. Yet this is exactly what the American policymakers of that generation proposed, and in each case they got a kind of half-hearted response from all parties.

No government, even Hitler's, wanted to come out openly for sin. Yet all these professions of high moral principle that Americans like Frank Kellogg and Cordell Hull insisted upon —and that they tried to represent to the American public as positive actions—did not in even one case prevent each European regime from doing what it wanted to do, or slow the slide toward war.

24

Cordell Hull, many of the men in the State Department, and Roosevelt himself held a completely misplaced confidence in the power of something called "public opinion" to influence foreign governments. Public opinion was important in the United States; Roosevelt's office and power rested upon it. But Hitler's, and to a lesser extent, most European governments', did not. Hitler controlled what his own public was allowed to think, and he cared nothing for what any other public thought. In fact, "international public opinion" was something of an American myth, though it was sincerely held and believed. In actuality all foreign governments, including the democracies, were influenced only by their sense of, or lack of, responsibility, or the fear of consequences.

In the view of the British Foreign Office, the United States government rushed into each approaching crisis, offering hasty advice on general and moral terms. It *never* proposed specific solutions: any means for European nations to change their politics, enrich themselves, protect their trade, gain a place in the sun, or work out a suitable compromise. It *never* threw or offered to throw its power, real or potential, behind any proposal or solution, or against *any* nation's aggressions. Each demand or aggression by Hitler, Mussolini, and later Japan, was roundly condemned in moral and legal terms. Not once, in the 1930's, did the United States government so much as hint that it would oppose any of them with sanctions or force.

In fact, when the situation did not yield to moral platitudes or turned really bad, the immediate American reaction was to wash its hands and withdraw. If the proverb "talk is cheap" was American, the reality was painfully brought home to the French and British in the years before the war.

The basic problem for the United States was twofold, particularly as the fascist world revolution took a form discernible in high levels of American government. The first prong was that the American public was profoundly uninterested in foreign developments, determined not to get caught up in them,

25

and both innocently and willfully blind to the fact that the squabbles in Europe and Asia were not mere arguments over the exchange of a few people, or the movement or boundaries. Most Americans, as late as 1939, still refused to accept the notion that the Axis aggressions were a determined effort to change the structure of the world and to make a new world order in which the United States' place and privileges would be greatly altered.

Most Americans saw the troubles in Asia and Europe as a continuation of the stupid power struggles of 1914, in which the United States had dabbled in 1917 without any lasting effect.

Actually, the French generals in 1939 were not the only ones prepared to fight the last war—the American public thought history was repeating itself, but this time they were determined not to get sucked in.

The other prong of the problem was that by 1939 Franklin Roosevelt, much of the State Department, and the key members of his Cabinet saw the world revolution in its real shape, but they had no rationale or even a precedent for coping with it, particularly in a complete vacuum of public support. A whole new foreign policy of intervention—if there was to be intervention—had to be devised. The country, and particularly the Congress, had to be convinced that the Administration knew what it was talking about, and that it knew what to do. Here Roosevelt ran into extremely difficult terrain.

Roosevelt had become the most powerful peacetime President in history. He had been able to forge a huge consensus inside the United States for his domestic policies. His partisans on domestic issues dominated Congress completely, at least until 1938. He had not had to explore new avenues of Presidential power; he could always get Congress to acquiesce to each Federal extension. When he needed, or wanted, new powers, Congress gave them to him. It did not always do this willingly, but sometimes in fear of the public opinion within

26

the United States that F.D.R. was able to arouse and exploit.

But the consensus behind Roosevelt in the 1930's stopped abruptly at the water's edge. The huge coalition of ethnic groups and underprivileged that was the base of his political power was, ironically, the very body of Americans least interested in foreign affairs.

The Congress, which could only slow him down on domestic policy, had few fears or scruples of blocking him completely overseas. With the Neutrality Acts of 1935 and 1937 it had tied his hands. Roosevelt could not offer to use power of any sort against the dictators because he was not empowered to use any kind of power under American law and custom. Only Congress could declare war. Congress made it very clear it not only would not declare war, but would oppose any active form of American participation in European political affairs.

Roosevelt's great problem in 1939, seen from his viewpoint, was that of building a new American consensus on foreign policy that would allow him to oppose the growing danger— or failing that, to find ways for effective Executive action around the Congress, and if necessary, in the teeth of public opinion.

Here, an immense watershed in the long history of American constitutional government was at hand. Roosevelt over the next two years would create striking precedents in the use of Presidential power, which would last far beyond his own time.

In this atmosphere, influenced by both his own Congressional restrictions and his own mythology, Roosevelt's actions to try to prevent the European war consisted of sending urgent appeals abroad. Again, as before Munich, he asked Hitler for a personal pledge not to attack Poland.

Adolf A. Berle, the Assistant Secretary of State, remarked bitterly that these appeals "would have about the same effect as a valentine sent to someone's mother-in-law out of season; and they have all that quality of naïvete which is the prerogative alone of the United States." Berle knew—he had helped

27

draft them. He was hardly sanguine about the effect of invoking American morality in the face of German armor. But even Berle thought it was proper that they should be sent. Few Americans of F.D.R.'s generation, even educated and knowledgeable men like Berle, or F.D.R. himself, would acknowledge that "public opinion" was not an effective instrument of policy, nor could they keep from issuing statements of principle.

F.D.R. was happy with his appeals, however. He told his aides they "put the bee on Germany." If war came, he wanted it clearly established that Nazi Germany had started it.

The war came. Freed from the danger of a two-front war by his Nonaggression Pact with Stalin—which shocked both the Western and the Communist world—Hitler marched his Wehrmacht into Poland on September 1, 1939. The attack was deliberate, well-planned, and murderously executed. Hitler, as he had told the German staff, shouted propaganda about Polish atrocities and provocations, which no one believed.

The Polish state, under dictator Smigly-Rydz, was no democracy. It was, at the time, backward, agricultural, and even anti-Semitic, though not officially so, like Germany. Twenty million Poles, badly organized and without a modern military force, were no match for armored columns and the Luftwaffe. There was no question that Hitler would win—and there was now no question that Hitler was bent not just on predominance in Europe, but an armed hegemony based on the conquest of his neighbors.

France had a military treaty with Poland. With great reluctance, the French government saw no choice, this time, but to fight.

The Chamberlain government in Britain, which had been willing a year before to sell out a democratic Czechoslovakia in a final hope of appeasing Hitler, at last had no choice but to recall the words Sir Edward Grey, British Foreign Secretary, said to United States Ambassador Walter Hines Page on August 4, 1914: "It is upon solemn compacts that civilization rests. England would be forever contemptible if it should sit by . . . there will be war." The question was not the fate of Poland, but the fabric of the world.

Great Britain sent Germany an ultimatum to withdraw from Poland. It was ignored. Britain declared war.

At the age of sixty-five, when most men are clearing their desks for retirement and oblivion, Winston Churchill was vindicated at last. He had argued for six years that while the U.S.S.R. was a menace, Hitler was a more immediate one. He had called the settlement at Munich, which not only the Cabinet but most Englishmen wanted, a moral disgrace, and for years he had been regarded by his own countrymen as a calamity.

Englishmen had distrusted him because he was "not predictable." His first speech in Parliament, in 1903, had been in praise of the South African Boers, who had put a price on his head, but for whom he demanded a generous and honorable settlement. Actually, Churchill was always predictable, if his vision were seen and understood. To Churchill the great world was never simple, it was always changing—but the great things, races, and peoples, and morality, were eternal. To a time which had forgotten these things, but hoped that maps, alliances, and philosophies would somehow cease to be ephemeral, Churchill was disturbing and incomprehensible. Now, he would return to the British government, but ironically only because his vision of Hitler had been the right one—not because his vision of an eternal mankind was understood.

September 1, 1939, President Roosevelt held his 575th press conference. Here Phelps Adams of the New York *Sun* asked the big question: "Can we stay out of it?"

Roosevelt, even then, had great and sincere doubts that the security and interests of the United States would permit neutrality. But he paused for a long moment, then replied:

> I not only sincerely hope so, but I believe we can, and
> every effort will be made by this Administration to do so.

No one at the conference doubted his sincerity, though all knew his obvious and expressed sympathy with the French-British cause. In retrospect, a certain hypocrisy and confusion colored Roosevelt's public statements about the war and the United States role. This was not always intentional, though his detractors swore it was, then and later.

F.D.R. had a coherent philosophy about the war, which was that the Allies had to win, because it was in the interests of the United States and world order that they win. But he had evolved no coherent plan of action. His political instincts, and his advisers in the Democratic Party, told him it was much too early to besiege the public with harsh or unpleasant facts. The American public's major fear, when Hitler marched, was not that Germany would conquer Europe and the world, but that the United States would get in the war.

Some of the complacency, of course, was caused by the fact that Anglo-French weaknesses were not understood. In the American mind, Britain still ruled the waves, and probably always would, and the French Army "was the best in the world." The Allies could handle Hitler, and anyway, it was their job.

There was an old American political proverb, told at many meetings in smoke-filled rooms, that no politician could be a statesman unless he were first elected. With America's emergence as a great power in the twentieth century, and finally, as the only power standing between the world and a complete collapse of democratic order, this joke took on a bitter relevancy.

Franklin Roosevelt could not become a great wartime leader if he failed to be reelected in 1940. The war had now made his reelection to an unprecedented third term, in his own and supporters' eyes, not only urgent but feasible. He needed to pursue a calm and temperate course.

For this reason, when two days later, Sunday, September 3, he went on national radio with a report to the country about the war this speech was relatively cautious. It was filled with platitudes, like the call for unity, but it also marked the beginning of an effort to get the United States to think in terms of a world struggle that must, one way or another, affect the American future:

> It is, of course, impossible to predict the future . . . you are, I believe the most enlightened and best-informed people in all the world at this moment. You are subjected to no censorship of news, and I want to add that your Government has no information which it has any thought of withholding from you. . . .

At the time, this was true. Later, Roosevelt was to find open discussion of all policy unworkable.

> It is easy for you and me to shrug our shoulders and say that conflicts taking place thousands of miles from the continental United States, and indeed, the whole American hemisphere, do not seriously affect the Americans, and that all the United States had to do is ignore them and go about our own business.
>
> Passionately though we may desire detachment, we are forced to realize that every word that comes through the air, every ship that sails the sea, every battle that is fought, does affect the American future.

But Roosevelt did not open the door too far. He stated:

> Let no man or woman thoughtlessly or falsely talk of America sending its armies to European fields.

He did not, however, say that American boys would not go overseas, until it was all over over there.

Then he said:

> This nation will remain a neutral nation, but I cannot ask that every American remain neutral in thought as well. Even a neutral cannot be asked to close his mind and conscience.

F.D.R. was not thinking ahead to sending troops abroad. He had no power to do that, in the theory of government then held, and he had no wish to. He was thinking ahead to the necessity of aiding the Allies.

The President now sent wires to all belligerents, asking them to refrain from the bombing of civilians or open cities. It was a typically American message again, with "all that quality of naïvete" Berle had pointed out. Each warring power answered that it would not begin the bombing of civilians unless the other side did so first, which was a typical reply to American moral pronunciamentos.

A war map was strung in the executive office of the White House, so that F.D.R. could follow the action on the ground. And he made his first "war moves": at White House instigation United States Customs in New York delayed the sailing of the German liner *Bremen* to allow the British cruiser *Berwick* to race down from the north to intercept it.

Then, as he was required by law, Roosevelt proclaimed United States neutrality, marked Europe as a war zone, declared the arms embargo, and ordered United States nonintervention in all respects. He delayed doing this as long as possible to let considerable war material be rushed over the border into Canada.

There was never any question of the United States being neutral in spirit in this war. On September 3, sermons from pulpits all over the country blasted Hitler for beginning it. A poll taken during the first week of fighting showed that 82 percent of the public blamed Hitler for the war. However, there was still widespread suspicion, particularly in the American middle west, of all the European powers. There was an even stronger, understandable, and selfish desire to keep out of war, no matter who had started it.

32

But the image of Hitler, who on September 3 preached his own sermon about "the plutocratic upper crust which desires to see in all other peoples only slaves" and included America in that group, kept 1939 from any real resemblance to 1914.

The United States in 1914 had been neutral in spirit as a whole. The attitude changed under German provocations and British propaganda.

In 1939 it was almost impossible for any American who gave the matter real thought to be completely neutral. The fascist states had flagrantly violated treaties; they openly sneered at all existing international conventions. They oppressed ethnic and political minorities, and they preached and carried out virulent racism and nationalism. They pursued deliberate policies of armed territorial aggression, and they made no bones about remaking the world in their fascist image, with themselves on top. No one disputed this.

But the confusion, and the problem that made it almost impossible for the American government to follow any coherent line in the months ahead was shown by the results of a *Fortune* poll taken a few days after the war began. Eighty-three percent of all Americans interviewed—and these were generally well-educated, well-informed leaders of business and industry—wanted the Allies to defeat Germany; only 1 percent hoped Germany would win. But only 20 percent thought the United States should help by all means short of war, and only 17 percent said that America had a moral right to get in the war, or should send troops to fight. Eight-three percent of the "most enlightened and best-informed people in all the world" at the moment wanted no part in the war. Initially, their view prevailed.

3.

Peace Bloc

Beware the words "We cannot keep out," "Our entry in the war is inevitable." "We must fight to preserve democracy," and all the Devil's messages we heard twenty years ago. Senator Hiram Johnson, California.

I frankly question whether we can become an arsenal for one belligerent without being the target for the other. Senator Arthur Vandenberg, Michigan.

"We cannot escape part in it if war comes to Europe." Why does this thought persist and grow? Norway, Denmark Holland, Switzerland, and Spain stayed out of the last war. Senator Gerald Nye, North Dakota.

There are two worlds. One must succumb. Every people eating from democracy will die of it. Adolf Hitler.

After officially declaring the United States neutral, as required by the Neutrality Acts, President Roosevelt made two significant moves. One was to shore up hemisphere defense.

Sumner Welles, Undersecretary of State, and the workhorse of the Department, departed for a conference of the Latin American states Washington called at Panama. Here he proposed Resolution XIV, which was called the Declaration of Panama. This created a neutral zone extending 300 miles to sea around the entire hemisphere, excluding Canada and the European possessions in America, which were already legally at war. This zone was to be kept "clear of all belligerents and warlike actions." The patrolling and enforcement would be by all of the American states, through mutual agreement—which meant, in effect, that the United States, the only naval power in the hemisphere, would assume the main burden.

Surprisingly, there was no legal or other argument to the proposal, which was a tribute to American diplomacy in Latin America. The idea that the United States was responsible for hemispheric defense was not new; it went back to the Monroe Doctrine; but now it was firmly implanted again.

When Roosevelt stated that the United States would defend its "territorial waters" from belligerent action—which implied German action—he was asked at a press conference how far United States territorial waters reached out.

He replied, "As far as United States interests require them to go."

Someone asked: "Does that reach the Rhine, Mr. President?" Roosevelt laughed.

The second move by the Administration was to call Congress into special session and demand repeal of the Neutrality Acts.

The Administration viewpoint had now hardened into something like this: conditions that had existed in 1914 could not be compared to the world of 1939. The Allies were fighting for the preservation of democratic world order against a fascist world revolution, not another imperialistic quarrel over boundaries in Europe. The United States could not be completely neutral in such a war. The arms embargo gave Hitler the equivalent of an Atlantic fleet, since it barred France and Britain from obtaining arms and munitions in America. A state of quasi-war already existed, or should exist, between the United States and Nazi Germany.

35

The proposals, and the world view, were immediately subject to violent Congressional counterattack.

The war in Europe did not establish new battle lines in Congress; these had been drawn four years before. There was a substantial body of Congressional opinion, reflecting an even larger public viewpoint—that the United States had no responsibility for world order, and certainly none to France or England. The United States was safe behind its oceans. Hitler might be a monster, but he had no navy, and therefore no real threat to the Americas existed.

The first polls taken after September 1 showed that the United States public had a deep-seated desire to remain at peace, but that few people really thought it could. There was considerable fatalism that the nature of wars being what they were, the United States would inevitably be drawn in. This feeling was strongest among those groups which were most opposed to Germany, either intellectually or emotionally. A great distaste for fascism and armed aggression existed side by side with a hatred of war—just as it had among the publics of France and Britain during Hitler's march to world power.

In fact, the feeling still lasted in Europe. In Britain, while Poland was being demolished by the German Wehrmacht, many intellectuals still begged for peace after thirty days of war. George Bernard Shaw called for "tabling English-German grievances" and for "negotiations." J. B. S. Haldane insisted that there be "peace negotiations now," followed by "free elections everywhere to determine the earth's destiny." A British poll revealed that a full quarter of the British public was against fighting the war. In France, as it would be revealed the next spring, the malaise was even deeper.

Intellectual and geopolitical arguments about the incompatibility of aggressive fascism and a stable democratic world —or even the continued existence of a democratic world— clashed with the all-pervading fear and distaste for war itself that was a characteristic of all Western civilization. The argu-

36

ment of Churchill and many others, now that the issues of the war were plain, that it was a war of civilization against a new barbarism, was widely protested. There was a very good reason for this. The 1914-1918 war had been sold, and accepted, on those terms, when it had been no such thing at all. The after taste of "holy" war was very sour.

Even the German people, with real and imagined grievances that Hitler had propagandized for years, were apathetic in 1939. A kind of gloom pervaded Berlin. The German public would not have voted in favor of a war in 1939, though of course it had no choice in the matter.

But the fatalistic feeling that the United States would sooner or later get in the war was badly battered by the Congressional attack on the Administration's premises about the war and the world.

Senator Johnson of California, who was isolationist and anti-foreign by nature, threw up 1917 and all the disillusion of 1919 again and again. He scoffed that the Allies were fighting for "democracy," and denied with a deep personal conviction that such a thing as a "world order" existed. He warned about insidious British propaganda that would get the United States to pull foreign governments' chestnuts out of the fire. He touched deep American suspicions.

Nye of North Dakota was bitter about "planted propaganda," partly by the Allies, partly by the Administration. All of it was aimed at getting the United States into a shooting war.

Senator Borah went on network radio to try to offset the President's September 3 speech. He argued with clarity, force, and great persuasion that repeal of the arms embargo, no matter what name was put on it, meant taking sides, and therefore, involvement. He said: "We cannot enter the struggle in part and stay out in part. Our boys would follow the guns into the trenches." He was the best speaker of the anti-war group, and he assumed a sort of leadership of it, although he was seventy-four years old. With enormous insight—domestic insight—Borah called his group the "Peace Bloc."

Vandenberg of Michigan also played on the fear of war. He stated that supplying arms to the Allies would inevitably bring German reprisal, for it would be no neutrality at all. He doubted seriously if the United States could remain "half-in, half-out" just as much as Borah.

He argued further that the first step was the fatal one: "Arms repeal would be like taking the first drink of whiskey." His passion was to keep America out of other people's wars.

The entire attack was emotional. It dealt very little with world politics or world reality. It took as its watchword "Peace," and this, not theoretical arguments about world order, or American security, was the argument that carried. By late September, a majority of American newspapers editorially agreed with Senator Borah.

The influential men outside the Administration arguing for intervention or arms repeal—Frank Knox, Henry Stimson, and Nicholas Murray Butler—did not have the same ability to rouse apprehension or play upon American emotions.

Against the fear of sending American troops abroad, and the call for peace, statements like James Conant's of Harvard —that if West Europe fell, free institutions as a basis for modern industrial civilization would be jeopardized—were obscured. Conant publicly argued that the case for repealing the Neutrality Acts and for sending arms to the Allies had to be examined on its merits, and not on an emotional basis of "peace" versus "war." He said that if the United States could not argue the question on practical merits, then war, or the fear of war, had already defeated American democracy. It was an entirely valid, but intellectual, argument, which did not much affect the public.

The Peace Bloc cut across party lines. If some of its leading spokesmen were Republicans who could be counted on to oppose anything F.D.R. wanted, there were enough good

Democrats in it thoroughly to confuse things. This fact gave James Byrnes of South Carolina, who had been chosen to carry the Administration's battle in the Senate, considerable trouble. The Administration held a two-thirds majority in the Senate, but Party loyalty could only be invoked behind the scenes. As debate lengthened, and action lagged, Byrnes informed F.D.R. that he was in trouble.

The extended Senate debate—there were far fewer statesmen in the House, which had no Constitutional prerogative over foreign policy, and far fewer men who felt independent enough to speak nationally, or for that matter, to oppose the President—showed that by September 1939, two attitudes had become dominant in the country. A large majority wanted to supply the Allies with arms. An even larger majority wanted the aid to stop there, or somewhere short of war. Thus the country both agreed and disagreed with the Peace Bloc.

A certain schizophrenia was being transmitted to the Congress, and Congress was transmitting a feedback of it, too. Each of the Peace Bloc senators had a philosophy, but there was no coherent philosophy for the whole. Individual members of the Senate could become immensely powerful from time to time, as Borah was now powerful. But historically, every attempt of influential Congressmen or Senators to assume positions of national leadership failed. This was inherent in any parliamentary system. It was why the Founding Fathers of the American Constitution created a powerful Presidency and made it coequal with, not a servant of, the Congress and the courts.

The Congress, by nature, followed rather than created a national consensus. Under the Constitution Congress was the servant, not the ruler, of the American body politic. Because few Congressmen dared go down any chosen path faster or farther than their particular constituency was ready, it was impossible for many Senators to have, or to employ, anything like a consistent world vision, unless the entire public had it,

39

too. In 1939 the Senate was a representative body, not particularly overawed by Franklin Roosevelt. It could keep him from being a Caesar. But it was subject to the same troubles and failures every legislative or representative body, made up of equals, had experienced from the days of the Roman Republic to the English Parliament of 1776.

The Congress represented special interests, but so did every branch of government, the Presidency not excepted. Domestically the Senate stood as much for the guaranty of American traditions, laws, and rights as the Judiciary, because it reflected and had to reflect current opinion. The United States in a uniquely pragmatic, decent way combined the rule of law with the rule by pressure group.

The real crisis, once America had become a great power and had been thrust willy-nilly into the great power world, was that collective national interests, national destiny, or the inescapable logic of world politics were all real but intangible, forces having no local constituencies. Roosevelt—or anyone in the President's chair—was logically subject to them. Anyone who had to keep in close contact with a particular and local spot of American earth, particularly in the hinterland, was not. All the Peace Bloc Senators, from Borah of Idaho to Walsh of Massachusetts, were reflecting local attitudes, and each went roaring down his own particular path.

It was up to Roosevelt to create a new national consensus on foreign policy, just as his domestic power stemmed from the powerful consensus he had created for domestic reform. The problem was that Roosevelt was not able, or in the face of emotional opposition, did not dare to do it. Without such a national consensus to prod Congress, it was illogical to expect Congress to be intellectually amenable to his high-level arguments.

Yet many intelligent people expected exactly this, and the denigration of Congress in the minds of many otherwise far-seeing and clear-thinking Americans began at this time. Most

40

Americans—and they were many, though in an intellectual minority—who were concerned with American security and world order and the survival of reasonably free institutions not only in America but abroad, became disgusted with Congress and began to look to the Presidency for all action.

As the British had to relearn several times, all actions—even those of a democracy—taken overseas must be Executive actions, nor can such actions be influenced wholly by domestic desires of politics. The United States, over a long isolationist period, had not developed any Executive rationale for foreign policy, anymore than it had developed a Senatorial rationale. It was already obvious to the Administration, by 1939, that more power had to be afforded the President—that every foreign move could not be debated with the Senator's due deliberation.

Yet any real destruction or denigration of the Congress, even on foreign affairs, always opened the door to possible dictatorship.

In the final analysis, the real problem of every democracy was foreign affairs and how to handle them; as William Sumner wrote: "Political liberty inside any country depends very largely upon its external relations." How to develop a government with supreme power to take action in the nation's interests abroad, as that government might see them, without violating traditional power limitations at home, was a difficult question. Roosevelt was not to solve it in his time.

Beginning with the question of the repeal of the arms embargo, he had three choices: to build a public consensus behind his foreign views and push them through Congress; to avoid the will of Congress if a way could be found, accepting any Constitutional dangers; or to seek a compromise with Congress. The last was the traditional, and most-used practice of Presidents on domestic issues that had large, but not overwhelming, public support.

On the Neutrality Acts, F.D.R. chose to compromise.

41

Aware of the public fear of war, he trimmed his public sails considerably from what he was saying privately in Cabinet or in the State Department to men like Morgenthau or Berle.

Sometime around Munich, F.D.R., Hull, Sumner, Welles, and other key advisors had agreed that the United States would support an Allied war, if it came, recognizing that the United States was a party at interest in such a war. It was agreed that the United States should use economic and political commitments wherever possible. It was also agreed that it would be a great mistake of policy to envision sending troops abroad. But this was not publicly discussed.

Now, to get arms repeal through the Senate, F.D.R. reiterated again and again his "hatred of war," and that his Administration would never get the United States in one. His cohorts in Congress argued that they, too, wanted the United States to remain out of the shooting war—but that one of the best means of doing so was to strengthen the Allies. Once both parties to the argument had agreed that the United States would and must stay neutral, the question became whether neutrality was best served by selling arms to the Allies, or by making the United States an uncommited island, which might help Hitler.

This was a subtle shift, but it carried the day. It conformed with public wishes. Ironically, F.D.R. had adopted some of the isolationist arguments to get his way. The arms embargo was repealed by a comfortable margin—but in order to get it, and the votes of Senators like Chávez of New Mexico or Walsh of Massachusetts, who were anything but anglophile, F.D.R. had to renounce formally the former principle of freedom of the seas. War zones were delineated around Europe, and these were declared off limits to Americans. Thus, a "danger zone" was accepted, in which no American ship or citizen had any business going on private business. There were to be no *Lusitanias* in this war.

Cash and carry, applied to the Allies, gave them a decided

advantage because the British had control of the seas. There had been considerable sentiment for this among American businessmen, to which neither the Congress nor the Administration was insensible. There were still millions of unemployed inside America; the Depression still persisted, and British representatives were waiting in the wings with lucrative arms contracts that would put hundreds of thousands of Americans to work.

Although it was not seen at the time, this was the beginning of the end of the Great Depression in the United States. Armaments—the same means Hitler had used to get Germany running again—would be the final fuel that would prime the United States pump. The initial British orders, mainly for aircraft, had another effect. They started American industry retooling long before this would have come about had the arms embargo not been repealed. This proved to be of inestimable value two years later.

Thus by October 1939, the American government had achieved several important successes, and one pervasive failure. It had not been able to prevent the coming of war—but then it had never tried to do that, unless Roosevelt's and Hull's moral pronouncements could be accepted as viable political action. It had gained acceptance from every state in the hemisphere for its policy of neutrality, and for its leadership within the hemisphere for the future of the war. It had opened the way to permit the embattled Allies to buy, for cash, arms and other aid from the United States. It had barred itself again by law, with the new Neutrality Act of 1939, from active interference in the war zone. It was still not exerting any real influence on the world scene, though there was a great, and privately admitted, awareness within the Administration that the United States was a member of the world community and the loose commonwealth of free nations. That, compared to the atmosphere prior to Munich, was a great advance.

The failure, and President Roosevelt's error, was that he

was not entirely candid with the country. The government sought to avoid a real showdown on the great issues of the war in Europe. Roosevelt found himself hampered by a stubborn, laggard opinion, but he did not mount a massive assault upon it. His statements were cautious, compromising, an attempt to lead the nation step by step.

He adopted the argument that the United States could serve best by staying out, by being the arsenal, but not the arbiter, of democracy. He backed a position that the country could enjoy a reasonable policy of being half-in and half-out of war.

This initial decision was to cause him enormous difficulties later on.

4.

Phony War

Roosevelt is playing politics with World War II.   Senator Lynn Frazier, North Dakota.

Continuation of the war will be catastrophic for the political, social, and economic life of the world. War would bring into this country chaos beyond anybody's dream.   Joseph Kennedy.

Should we think only of our pocketbooks and skins?   Eleanor Roosevelt.

The peculiar course of World War II in the fall and winter of 1939 further hampered the Administration's efforts to bring the American public to think in terms of a world struggle. "Phony War," Senator Borah dubbed it, and the appelation stuck.

When Hitler sent the massive German armies into Poland, the Western European nations had been totally unprepared for war. The German military was a finely honed instrument, lacking only the high polish of battlefield experience, which in Poland it soon got. The Allied forces, with the exception of the British Navy and tiny British Air Force, were in a generally apathetic shape. They were plagued by shortages, and much worse, obsolescence of both machines and mind.

While Hitler's Luftwaffe destroyed the obsolete Polish air

force, then destroyed Warsaw piece by piece, and panzer units put a new word, *blitzkrieg,* in the popular lexicon by cutting the horse-drawn Polish army into shreds, no offensive was mounted against the Germans in the West. This was in contrast to World War I, when at the outset every power had attacked.

Occupied in Poland, the German army was not prepared to fight in the West. Accordingly, Hitler went completely on the defensive along the Rhine. Though Germany's defenses in the West were relatively weak at this time, the evidence of whether an Allied assault on Germany would have saved Poland or failed disastrously is not completely clear, though majority military opinion then and later believed such an Allied offensive must have failed. The French and British armies had simply never planned to mount an attack on Germany; the whole outlook and military policy of both nations was utterly defensive in nature. But what was now of immense significance was that Hitler still held the moral ascendancy in military terms: the Germans were not fighting the West because they were busy elsewhere; the Allies did not fight primarily because they completely lacked the desire to engage.

Even Allied leaders did not yet realize the actual military superiority of the Germans in 1939. The rapid conquest of Poland took them by surprise—which pointed up again the terrible moral failure of refusing to attack on the Rhine. Poland would not be saved by Anglo-French armies in 1939, as Paris had been saved in 1914 by the disastrous Russian offensive into East Prussia, which had diverted vital German arms to the East. Even after war was declared, some Allied leadership still hoped to avoid altogether a protracted struggle along the lines of World War I.

Along the German-French boundary there was little patrolling in 1939, less firing. German troops and French *poilus* moved about on hillsides sometimes in full sight of each other, without danger. There was even some communication, and badinage, across the lines. There was no serious bombing of

German cities, because the Allied governments were fearful of retaliation.

Thus Hitler was allowed to hold both the military and moral initiative: military, because he was freed to overrun Poland and choose his own time to fight in the West, moral, because he was still the only antagonist ready and eager to wage war.

Meanwhile in Poland German arms rewrote the military manuals, from the employment of armor to the coordination of tactical air support and ground operations. The German tactical air force destroyed the obsolescent Polish air arm on the ground, then supported the rapid, incisive dash of German armor deep into Polish territory. The Polish ground forces were split, surrounded, captured or destroyed, without the mass battles and immense bloodletting of 1914-1918.

This military accomplishment did not make sufficient impression at the time in the West, where only the heroic defense of Warsaw and the suffering of its civilians under aerial bombing were watched in horror. This, however, was nothing new. During the Spanish Civil War, where the new Luftwaffe had been shaken down and received its priceless combat testing, the democratic leadership tended to be most impressed by the slaughter of Spanish civilians at Guernica by German bombing. The single most important event of that war, in European terms—the stunning performance of the shiny new German Messerschmitt ME-109—was completely unseen or ignored.

All through the 1930's, in fact, the democratic nations tended to be more bemused by the horrors of war than impressed by its harsh practicalities.

In 1939 the French mobilized a great army of conscripts, marched it into the Maginot Line, and let it sit, although it was a Frenchman who said the only thing you cannot do with bayonets is sit on them. The British, as in 1914, reluctantly sent a small—about two hundred fifty thousand men—expeditionary force to the continent, and relied primarily on a blockade of German ports. The old saw that the Allies, especially the French generals, were perfectly prepared to fight World War I all over again, seems perfectly true, after a study of the evidence.

Because the naval blockade of 1914-1918 had done the German war machine tremendous harm by breaking the German civilian economy, the British put great store in the new blockade. Informed Allied opinion fully expected this kind of economic warfare to bring Hitler to his knees in time.

De Haas, a leading economist at the Harvard Business School, stated that "the relative internal economic strength of Germany is less than that of any other major country."

He was absolutely right. The German economy showed definite signs of decay in 1939, which some theorists think forced Hitler's hand. But what neither economists nor Allied strategists saw was that Allied policy left the Germans free to wander over a rich continent, and while the relative internal strength of Germany was less than that of Britain, Nazidom was disciplined, organized, and fully prepared to take the full risks of its aggression.

Internal strength is not strength unless it is used.

For eight months of war, Great Britain did not fully mobilize. No real war sacrifices were made. The government failed to call for them.

This "phony war" was anything but phony in the Polish east, where a large nation was completely conquered militarily, its government and integrity destroyed. In the latter stages of the campaign, Soviet Russia moved into eastern Poland, and by a secret concordat the former nation was divided between the two totalitarian powers. In both Russian and German zones, now, Polish territory was annexed as a conquered province, and Polish citizens were ruled as a conquered people, without rights of any kind.

But because the focus of American vision was on Western Europe, where no real war was in progress, American public opinion was confused by what was happening. Even F.D.R.'s government remained indecisive. Roosevelt found it impossible to try to sell the European conflict as a war for civilization in which America had a stake, when the Allies on the front lines of that war did not seem to be fighting. There was no effective way in which the United States could aid Poland, except by propaganda and symbolic measures.

The United States refused to recognize the legality of the German conquest of Poland. The old government, now in exile in London, was praised in United States circles. Franklin Roosevelt showed his contempt of Nazi aggression by proclaiming October 11, 1939 "Pulaski Day." It was fine gesture but meant little, even to American Poles.

The Russian seizure of part of Poland, which had been arranged in the secret protocols of the Communist-Nazi non-aggression pact of August, drew another blast, which the Moscow government blithely ignored.

Meanwhile, the British blockade of the continent caused unexpected frictions, much like those which started the War of 1812. No American seamen were impressed, because none was allowed into the war zones, but American goods, in transit to or from neutrals such as Holland or Sweden, were sometimes seized.

All of the neutrals of Europe were trading with Germany, most of them, like the Swedes or Swiss, from sheer necessity. American goods could be, and were, sometimes transhipped on arrival. The British, confiscating suspected goods at sea, were not acting in accord with international law—but they were acting in accord with the much older and more respected law of self-preservation. They were ruthlessly thorough in this search and seizure, and they stepped on more than one American merchant's toes.

Reported in the United States press, these incidents could not help but arouse American anger or hostility, especially when American neutral rights were violated. F.D.R.'s decision, when this problem developed, was to work each case out with

49

the British, and above all not permit the public to become involved. Hull was so informed, and several cases were compromised in complete secrecy, and generally amicably, with the British authorities.

Hull asked Britain for an agreement on shipping practices. The result of this was a system of shipping certificates, called "Navi-Certs," which went into effect on December 1. By this, the United States agreed that any German goods—German-made, German-bound—could be seized by the British, even if they were in transit between one neutral and another, such as Italy and the United States. This was another indication of United States willingness to support the Allies. It did no real damage to American trade.

It was rough on certain neutral trading nations, such as the Dutch, Swiss, and Swedes, each of whom suffered considerable loss.

The Russian attack on Finland in December 1939, created a quick rash of anger in the United States. The President denounced it savagely, but took no other action. Briefly, this did something the Soviet-Nazi nonaggression pact had never quite succeeded in doing; it linked the Soviet and Nazi states in the public mind.

Germany took an acquiescent attitude toward the Soviet invasion, and it appeared that the new aggression was executed within a total Nazi-Communist plan. This was not true. But it was true that the Soviet state was as thoroughly alienated from the democracies as Germany, and as hostile to their order, and had its own ambitions. In this light the Russian demands on Finland were logical. Unfortunately, despite the brief flare of anger in Britain and the United States at the invasion, the deeper meaning behind it all was later quickly forgotten.

There was great admiration for the Finns in America, most of it stemming from the favorable image Finland had created by being the only European nation to repay or stay current on its World War I debt. Actually, the Finnish debt was small, and was owed for economic assistance; Finland had not been a wartime ally in the sense of France or Britain. The Soviet attack worsened the already strained relations between Washington and Moscow, but did not break them. Otherwise, the effect of the attack was no different from the German attack on Poland. The United States disclaimed responsibility and declared neutrality.

Considerably more governmental agony was caused in the chancellories of Europe. The Swedish Army leaders were both angry and frightened; in spite of Sweden's more than one hundred years of neutrality in Europe, the Swedish military staff recommended aid to Finland. Thousands of individual Swedes volunteered to fight.

Richard Sandler, the Swedish Foreign Minister, was in favor of Swedish action on Finland's side. Finland had been a Swedish province for centuries, before it had passed to Russia in 1809. After Finnish independence in 1918, old ties and friendships had been renewed. But Sandler's views did not prevail, and he was forced out of his post because of them. There was a deep sense of shame in Sweden, but the sense of fear was greater—fear of both Russia and Germany, who warned Sweden not to intervene.

The British and French governments were at this time at least as hostile to the U.S.S.R. as they were to Nazi Germany, and they were in a great agony of indecision as to what to do. They felt some action should be taken so they began organizing a one-hundred-thousand-man expeditionary force to fight in Finland.

Permission was asked of the Norwegian and Swedish governments for this force to cross their territory. The northern route was the only means of reaching the Finnish front. But Germany immediately threatened both Scandinavian countries with retaliation if either allowed an Allied army on its soil. The matter bogged down.

In the United States private collections were made for Finnish aid, and war credits were suggested for the Finnish government. But this opened up the question of war credits for France and Britain and the other combatants. The isolationists in the United States, who generally hated the Soviet Union a little more emotionally than they hated Hitler, were in a quandary.

In the end, no nation sent the Finns more than token aid. Nothing could have been more indicative of the complete breakdown of world order under the revisionist assault.

Amazingly, the Finns put up a splendid defense under the direction of old Baron Mannerheim. Waves of attacking Soviet troops were slaughtered, and grave weaknesses were revealed within the Soviet military camp. A new word— "Molotov cocktail" was added to the public dictionary—as the Finns, without heavy equipment, found new ways of destroying Soviet tanks. But the defense was brief. In the end, superior numbers and equipment cracked the Mannerheim Line. The Finns asked for terms.

Despite all the platitudes and words of friendship and admiration spoken elsewhere, the Finns' glory was their own. In retrospect, the Finns won the Russians' respect, which helped them then and again after the war. The original Russian territorial demands on Finland had been defensive in nature, that is, the Soviets wanted to push the border further back from the important city of Leningrad and to seize other defensive terrain. Once the Finnish defense had been broken, and Finland was helpless before an invasion, the Russians did not take a great deal more than they had originally demanded. In 1940, of course, a Russian takeover of Finland would have aroused both Allied and German fears enormously, which was another reason for restraint.

Roosevelt condemned the peace terms in Finland as soon as they had been concluded, in March 1940. Spokesmen for the Labour Party in England stated "great satisfaction that two hundred thousand men had not been sent" to aid Finland. Throughout the entire campaign, both fascist and Communist groups in the West had joined together in condemning any action in assistance to the Finns.

If the Finnish question had further confused the United States, the same trends were still evident in Britain. A British poll showed that almost 40 percent of those interviewed were bewildered by the war, and only slightly less than half were firmly convinced that it should be vigorously prosecuted. A major preoccupation of British financial interests was a fear that this second war in one generation would leave them bankrupt. The London *Economist*'s assertion that the "United States mood was deliberately myopic" about the war and its relation to Americans had an unintentional ironic ring.

The argument about the United States' interest in the war continued. Was it America's concern? H. L. Mencken quipped from Baltimore:

> The Honorable Mr. Roosevelt and his associated wizards are itching to horn in to the great Crusade to save humanity.

Secretary Hull, for once losing his Southern courtesy, snapped to a committee that World War II was "not just another goddam piddling dispute over a boundary line." But a continuing fear that World War II would not reform the world, but probably bring a worse one, continued to paralyze Americans.

"Pray public opinion be informed," wrote columnist Joseph Alsop.

Frank Knox, a prominent Republican who had been Alfred Landon's running mate, published a series of letters in *The New York Times*. He demanded all United States action possible "short of war"—soon to become a famous phrase.

Walter Lippmann wrote that if Hitler won in Europe, "we shall know no peace in our lifetime." He called for complete truth about the situation and true leadership from F.D.R.

The New York Times editorials in the spring of 1940 re-flected a curious mix of anger at America, gloom about the world, and hate for Hitler. But the *Times* did not call for war.

Time magazine, which by April 1940 had slowly come over into the interventionist camp, slowly, reluctantly, but surely, editorialized: *Too often, when policymakers try to hint at the real shape of international affairs, they are not believed.*

Time stated the problem, but *Time*'s choice of words also stated one of its bases. There was a great deal of cautious "hinting" from members of the Administration about the importance of the Allied cause to America, and some frank hostility to Hitler. But hinting, or even calm and judicious words, were not enough to break through the complacency and confusion. The Administration kept up an anti-totalitarian pose, but did not engage in the blunt, hard-hitting language that would have been necessary to sell its views to the public.

When the German Foreign Office published documents captured in Poland which purported to be transcripts of conversations between the United States Ambassador to France, William C. Bullitt, and the former Polish government, these were denied as forgeries. Bullitt, an American socialite and longtime Hitler alarmist, was known to be convinced that the United States had to get in the war in order to assure a German defeat. According to the Germans, these documents revealed that he had told the Poles F.D.R. would pursue the following policy: denounce the fascist nations, accelerate war preparations in the United States, give the Allies moral assurances of American aid, and frustrate any possible compromise—such as another Munich—between the Allies and Germany.

These "papers" true or false, did not reveal anything that was not reasonably well known to insiders. If they proved anything, they proved Mr. Bullitt perhaps talked too much for a diplomat. But United States policy was not clarified for the public in the only way it could have been—by a complete, honest, and many-times repeated declaration of both immediate and long-term American policy aims.

Private parties, and outside sources, such as columnists and letter writers, were permitted to carry most of the burden of informing the public. The interventionists—who now generally agreed on "aid short of war"—were a definite minority, though a very vocal one.

Roosevelt himself almost studiously stood out of it. He resembled a grand marshall giving broad hints and directions as to how he wanted the parade to form, but letting the parade take shape by natural processes before he stepped to the head of it. This, of course, was part of the normal political process of a democratic society—and also it pointed up one reason democratic societies tended to be vacillating all over the world. It was a process of consensus-building which worked reasonably well on domestic issues in any state where there was representative government and the rule of law. The system broke down badly when extended to the logic of power politics overseas.

In a perfectly natural process, public opinion in the United States kept up a continual shifting under the pressure of outside events. Congress and other interested groups, trying to keep an ear to the ground and learn what the people wanted, found no majority with any workable program. It was not the function of public opinion to formulate a cohesive national foreign policy out of its own juices. Historically, no successful policy was ever so formed.

The invasion of Denmark and Norway in April, 1940 provoked only a strong verbal reaction from F.D.R. He stated on April 13: "Force and military aggression are once more on the march against small nations." This had become obvious long before. The United States went on record again in a moral way. The United States' record for doing nothing about anything was also reaffirmed.

Roosevelt's statements and denunciations did not alarm the

country. The invasion of Scandinavia did not produce as much indignation, in fact, as the aggression against Finland. There was almost an apathetic acceptance of the fact that the totalitarians were going to keep on invading somebody.

Denmark was forced to surrender without a fight, and F.D.R. recognized the German conquest. In Norway, brilliant and prodigal expenditure of the small German Navy, plus the now-proven superiority of land-based air power over ships at sea, won the Germans a quick victory. An Allied landing force which was both too small and was mounted too late to be effective met disaster at Narvik. This defeat was a serious blow to the Chamberlain government in England, which now began to falter.

F.D.R. proclaimed neutrality with Norway as he had with Poland and Western Europe. But the Danish possessions of Iceland and Greenland, the latter inside the Western Hemisphere, provided a new problem. The United States could not tolerate a German occupation of these islands either under the Monroe Doctrine or under the declaration of hemisphere neutrality and security proclaimed at Panama in 1939. But the Monroe Doctrine also prohibited British seizure of the same islands, for the same reasons.

The Danish government requested that the United States assume a protectorate over Greenland. Washington backed off from any overt move such as this, but now adopted a stratagem: the United States immediately opened a consulate in Greenland (where there were no American citizens or interests) and this consulate initiated negotiations with the Danish authorities on the island. By mutual agreement, guards and antiaircraft weapons were provided for the vital cryolite mines near Ivigtut. Cryolite, incidentally, found only in Greenland, was used in making soda and especially aluminum, which at this time was in desperately short supply in the aircraft industry.

And when the British seized Iceland in May, 1940—Iceland lay on the North Atlantic convoy run and its occupation by Germany would have been strategically disastrous for Britain—Washington tacitly accepted the move, declaring that the British occupation was temporary. Hull justified this move on the grounds that Germany, not Britain, had started the war, and that a German victory would be dangerous to the best interest of the United States, which was perfectly valid.

While still holding to the absolute theory of neutrality and noninvolvement, the United States was being forced into the practice of great power politics.

The conquest of Norway, however, brought a new worry to the United States public and created a new hysteria. This was a fear of spies, fifth columnists, and saboteurs. The role of German agents in the rapid seizure of vital air fields in Norway, and of misguided men like Vidkun Quisling, who helped the Germans set up a New Norway, was publicized and popularized. A certain mass reaction was produced, and much of the fifth-column fear was translated into anti-alienism. At least seventy bills calling for alien control were submitted in Congress, ranging from complete expulsion of aliens to compulsory registration.

There was no real consensus as to whether the potential fifth column was a Nazi one, trying to subvert for German war aims, or a domestic fascist movement, or a part of the international Communist Comintern conspiracy. Nor was there any agreement as to whether the aim of the conspirators was to get the United States into the war, or keep it out. Author Clarence Budington Kelland said that the real American fifth column "in this country is headed by that fellow in the White House."

Everybody did play politics with the alien subversion question from this time on. This was to be expected.

Then, in early May, John Cudahy, ambassador to Belgium, tapped those American sources of information that had been consistently superior even to British Intelligence, and which had reported the Nazi-Communist pact, the coming of war, and the invasion of Scandinavia before each happened. Cudahy was told that the Germans were going to advance into the Low Countries. He telephoned F.D.R. on May 9, 1940. The President and Secretary Hull immediately tried to alert and alarm the government of France and Britain that a German assault was imminent.

The American information was rejected in each case. The Allies refused to credit it, or be alarmed.

One day later, on May 10, 1940, the "phony war" exploded into the days that shook the West.

5.

Watershed: The Casual Commitments

We will sooner or later get in it, and are being written off as a factor by the Nazis because they expect to win before the United States acts. Portion of cable to Secretary Hull, May 28, 1940, urging war, from United States Chargé d'Affaires Alexander Kirk in Berlin.

It is possible that if Britain should lose and Hitler become master of the seas, he would suddenly become a good boy and covet nothing that belongs to his neighbors. The sun may also fail to rise tomorrow morning. Time, July, 1940.

Keep the U.S. out of war! From a wire to President Roosevelt signed by 1,000 Dartmouth undergraduates, May, 1940.

The masses with their inertia always need a certain time before they are even ready to notice events.... Adolf Hitler.

The Battle of France, the ninety days that shook the West, was an immense but almost unnoticed turning point for the government of the United States. The real meaning of the long Nazi war preparations and the efficacy of blitzkrieg were revealed with crashing effect.

German arms knifed deeply into France, knocked the Low

Countries out of the war, and pinned the British expeditionary force on the continent back on the beaches at Dunkirk. The British troops were evacuated in a remarkable naval and air operation, but they left their arms and heavy equipment behind. Italy entered the war on the German side. France capitulated. The U.S.S.R., almost forgotten amid the thunderous events in the West, seized and absorbed Latvia, Estonia, and Lithuania and extorted territory from Romania.

The defense of the West had shrunk to the British Isles, which were almost unarmed in 1940, and small in comparison with the power Hitler now controlled. There was no longer any hope that economic warfare could bring Hitler down. The question was suddenly, could Britain survive?

Washington was stunned. The real weakness of the Allies had simply not been seen or believed until France fell. For the first time Washington had to face the immediate prospect of an Axis victory, and estimate where the United States might fit into an Axis-dominated world. Roosevelt watched the growing disaster in Europe with despair.

Up until this point, F.D.R. and his foreign-policy advisers had sincerely believed the Allies could win the war with increased American help. They had not contemplated active American entry, or the sending of American troops abroad. A Germany which dominated the European continent was still far away; but a Germany which suddenly fronted on the Atlantic Ocean, and now seemed destined to control that ocean, impinged upon America. The realization that Germany was close to assuming not only European but world power struck F.D.R. and the State Department like a physical blow.

The realization that German power posed great dangers for the continued world position of the United States had been faced long before, at least by the time of Munich. The difference now was that the danger became immediate. If Britain fell, no one stood in the German way. A policy which had in reality been the comfortable one of "fighting until the last Allied soldier fell" suddenly had to be reevaluated.

"Isolation" as practiced by the United States had been a practical policy only so long as a friendly British navy had controlled the Atlantic Ocean. The American people as a whole had never really faced this question; the British had had undisputed hegemony of the seas since 1815, and since 1823 the British government worked in a pragmatic, if not quite openly admitted, policy of cooperation with the United States. The British navy had been the umbrella under which America had enjoyed freedom to expand and prosper.

All this was well understood in Washington, and above all by the President, who was a competent and keen naval historian. But no effort had been made to sell the American people on the fact that Western hemisphere security, and the Monroe Doctrine itself, had for over a century rested on the two premises of Anglo-American cooperation and British control of the seas. The reasons of course were political, emotional, and patriotic, and those who thought distance was the great factor in American isolation were permitted to graduate from school still unenlightened.

The United States Navy had had parity with the British since World War I. But it was Pacific-oriented, on guard against a rising Japan. In 1940, the United States did not have, and had not had in the century, a powerful Atlantic Fleet.

If the French fleet fell into German hands, and the British navy was either sunk, captured, or neutralized, Hitler, with the Italian navy to supplement Nazi sea forces, could muster overwhelming naval power in the Atlantic. Washington was not afraid of an immediate invasion of North America— although, since Canada was a belligerent, Hitler had a perfect right to attack. What was immediately at stake, if Britain fell, was the entire power balance on the North Atlantic, and the peculiar commercial and political relationships of the United States with South America. Nazi penetration of the hemisphere was not only then feasible, but assured. The Germans had already begun to attempt such penetration by 1940.

And German and Italian political theoreticians had already broadcast the fascist philosophy toward the world: that the British Empire and a North American "plutocracy, with their international clients and servants" really controlled the earth —and the totalitarian revolution was going to change all that.

Hitler had proclaimed the war as a struggle between the dominant British Empire and North American monetary and economic interests, and the rest of mankind. In June, 1940, it suddenly seemed that Hitler would be able to organize a high percentage of mankind, or at least all Europe, against the Western hemisphere. What was now in question was whether the United States could continue to exist as a free power with free institutions, and to prosper, in such a world.

The consensus of informed opinion in Washington and in the State Department abroad was that the United States could not. If the coastlines of both the Old World continents were dominated by a hostile power or a coalition of hostile nations, America would be a beleagered island.

The same logic that had caused Britain to oppose actively any single-power hegemony in Europe over the centuries— not wanting to rule the continent but to assure no one else ruled it—now possessed American strategic planners, of whom Franklin Roosevelt was one of the most farseeing. This inexorable logic of power and power relationships, however, was foreign to the American public. While the British themselves were much admired, the traditional British policy of "balance of power" had not been.

In very simple terms, the American public, though it saw the Anglo-French military forces go down with a sense of shock, and became afraid Britain itself might soon go under, was not prepared to go to war in the interests of a "balance of power," or to salvage an international political order—

which a majority of the key men in the United States State Department now wanted to do.

Alexander Kirk, Chargé d'Affaires in Berlin, went to Rome in the days before Italy entered the war and wired Hull that American participation was urgently necessary. Virtually the entire American diplomatic staff in Europe, from ambassadors through secretaries, who had seen the Nazi power at firsthand, and had been subject to the ultrarational drive and momentum of the fascist assault, believed that America was in danger and should join the Allies.

The logic of power, the sense of American danger, the realization of American military weakness, the attitude of the public—which refused to become aroused—and the imminent collapse of France and Britain created in Washington, in Summer Welles' words, a "nightmare of frustration."

The United States had held out great promise of material aid for the Allies; war machines were just starting to come off production lines. But as the Allies collapsed, Americans had nothing on the ground, ready to go.

The entire American army numbered only two hundred and twenty-seven thousand men. Its equipment was not just obsolete—the Army had no equipment, beyond rifles and some machine guns and a few French 75's brought home from the last war. The United States had only a handful of bombers, and no warplanes that could match either the British Spitfire or the German ME-109. It had no employable tanks. All this was being corrected, but so far only on paper—the United States had not yet really begun to rearm.

The titanic battle of France revealed that the German war machine could swallow the entire American Army as easily as it had beaten the British back to Dunkirk. The United States Navy could not strike at Hitler, and even it could hardly be redeployed from the Pacific in time. The United States Air Force as yet did not exist. On United States airfields American P-40's and other fighter planes still carried only two machine guns, synchronized to fire through the propeller—hardly improved from 1918—and these were only prototypes.

The monstrous air battles that had begun in Europe between the Luftwaffe and the R.A.F. gave American planners a chilling shock. They had known about the Luftwaffe all along, but somehow it had not seemed real, till the fall of France.

The proponents of war now understood this American military weakness. Their argument broke down as follows: 1. America would sooner or later get in the war; if Hitler won, sooner or later he would attack the United States. 2. The declaration of war now would put the United States openly on a course it would eventually have to take. 3. The throwing of the immense potential of the United States on the Allied side would be a psychological blow to the Axis. It could prevent Italy from entering the war. 4. The move, even if no help were forthcoming at once, would give the British great heart, and might even keep the faltering French in the war. A United States declaration of war would turn the eventual balance of power back to the West; it might make the Germans—who were well aware of America's decisive role in 1918—back off. 5. Finally, an open American entry on the side to which it was already sentimentally and psychologically committed would unite the people and expedite the rearmament which was now vital to America's future.

To these pressures from advisers in the State Department were added appeals and urgent demands from the sinking Allies in May and June. Churchill, now British Prime Minister, opened direct communication with Roosevelt, and he made no secret of Allied desperation.

He asked F.D.R. to declare a state of "non-belligerency" but active support; he requested the immediate "loan" of forty to fifty destroyers from the United States to the Royal Navy, and the transfer of all available aircraft, even those destined for the United States Army Air Corps, to British hands. The French government, collapsing under German assault in the north and aware that Mussolini's Italy was preparing to attack in the south, begged F.D.R. to dispatch the United States Fleet to Tangier as a show of force to keep Italy out of the war.

The Australian Minister to the United States called on Cordell Hull and pleaded with him to urge the President to declare war.

On June 15, Churchill further informed F.D.R. that a "declaration that the United States will, if necessary, enter the war might save France."

All these requests from friends in deep trouble, to an American government desperately eager to help, caused the agony Welles described.

Here a fateful turning point was reached, although the majority of Americans remained unaware of it at the time. The United States Government now departed from strict neutrality under international law. "Cash and carry"—the supply of arms and matériel to the Allies in American ports in return for payment—had been throughout a private transaction. The British and French governments contracted with private American firms; arms sale was a business deal and not an act of war.

But in May 1940, Roosevelt—almost casually, as one historian remarked—made far-reaching commitments, on a government level, to the Allies. Over strong protest from certain military leaders, vital military equipment was ordered transferred to the British. F.D.R. then promised more.

This was official intervention, and not neutrality, under all concepts of international law. Axis intelligence was aware of these moves, and the Germans marked them down for future retaliation. They were not vehemently protested, because German policy, then and later, was to avoid any flare-up which might bring the United States prematurely into the war. Here, by June 1940 the die was cast.

These moves—the promise of aid, and the transfer of United States Government military equipment—were not made public. *They were classified, and kept completely secret from the people.* This marked the end of the policy F.D.R. had announced in September 1939, "that the Government had no information which it has any thought of withholding from you. . . ."

But these moves, significant as they were, were as far as Roosevelt apparently dared to go. The only official actions of Washington in the critical weeks as France fell and Italy prepared to join in the kill, were a series of appeals to Italy—one even tried to influence King Victor Emmanuel III, over Mussolini's head—on moral grounds to refrain from attacking France. At the same time, the Allies were urged to make certain concessions to Mussolini, to make him less belligerent.

All this long-distance advice and meddling failed, as it had failed now for a decade. Mussolini ignored Roosevelt's appeals with impunity, because he felt the United States would put no force behind them.

A few days before June 1, Mussolini told his war leaders: "I need a few thousand dead so I can attend the peace conference as a belligerent." Mussolini had played the first year of war with exquisite, as he thought, skill and timing. A revisionist power, committed to the totalitarism Axis, he had still failed to declare war in September 1939, on the German side. He waited until, as he thought, German victory was assured.

By June 1940, Mussolini thought the war was over, that Germany had won, and the New Order in Europe for the long-term future was certain of success. He had been for Germany all along; his only concern was not to bring Italy in too early, when it might get hurt, or to make his declaration too late to share in the juicy spoils.

In June 1940, Mussolini's timing was perfect. He put Italy into the war the exact moment it became apparent France could no longer win, that no last-minute Battle of the Marne would turn the German tide. His predictions of everything else, including the mood and fighting ability of his subject Italians, could not have been more wrong. In sealing his eventual fate with calculated cleverness, Benito Mussolini proved again the immense irony of history, and that perhaps there was a certain justice in the world.

Back in America, in spite of urgent pressures within the government, within the State Department and on Cabinet level, F.D.R. did not declare for war. The simple reason was that he felt he could not.

In one way, convinced that the Allies could hold their own with American arms and matériel, F.D.R. had tied his own hands since 1939. The continual official protestations of neutrality, the reassurance that no American armies would this time go "to European fields," and that arms aid would do the job, had done nothing to help prepare a war psychology inside the United States. Ironically, in September 1939, almost no Americans *wanted* war, but polls showed that about 40 percent were prepared to enter it reluctantly in case the Allies lost. The prevailing feeling had been almost one of fatalism: a great many people felt it would be impossible to keep out of the war.

But each month the United States kept out of it, the more the feeling grew that the United States could continue to keep out. This was only a surface paradox; it was perfectly natural. By its actions, the government helped convince most Americans that it was feasible for the United States to keep out. The government had not argued that the United States carried any responsibility.

The fall of France—and the concurrent display of German power—had another effect: it further dampened what eagerness there had been to give the Nazis a whirl. The rapid German advance, the almost bloodless victory—for German arms, not the French—frightened some Americans and gave the urge to isolation and neutrality new impetus.

By the summer of 1940, qualified polls showed that only 7.7 percent of the United States public thought the country should enter the war. An overwhelming consensus believed

67

the United States should not go to war for any reason, except an attack on the North American continent.

The defensive purposes of an overseas commitment, or the geopolitical consequences of a German hegemony, were neither understood nor accepted by any large group of American citizens. Certain men in government, and many observers in England, found this incredible. The British, however, should have been the first to understand: the American approach toward world power and world responsibility in the early 1940's paralleled their own in the 1930's. Britain collectively refused to believe it would have to fight for its past, and for the entire British future, until its exhausted men were backed up on the beaches at Dunkirk. Churchill, with great historic vision and possessing sound strategic instincts, succeeded only in arousing a nervous distrust in the British public by telling it what it did not want to hear. Even Churchill could not reach that deep reservoir of greatness in the freedom-loving British people until their skies were black with Hitler's planes.

Significantly, Churchill, one of the greatest leaders of a free people in all history, was not elected Prime Minister in 1940. In 1939, three months before the German attack on Poland, the question of whether Mr. Churchill should even hold a post in the British Cabinet was a highly controversial one with the public. Polls indicated that only about half of the British people thought he should hold a leadership post, even a minor one. He was appointed to the Chamberlain Cabinet only after the shooting started—at his old Admiralty post—and even then with deep reluctance on the part of some members of the British government. Ironically, Churchill's besetting sin was that he was prepared to wage war and go for the German throat.

He was finally placed in the Prime Minister's job after it became painfully apparent to the various ruling political coalitions of Britain that the Chamberlain government was morally bankrupt and possessed neither war strategy nor a war will.

Fortunately, he came to power when the British nation was both aroused and shaken by the disaster in France, and only then could his splendid talents be put to use. He could offer "blood, sweat and tears" to a people who at last understood their back was to the wall, and that there was no easy way out of their dilemma.

Roosevelt, dependent upon general elections and general public support for Presidential power, faced an entirely different situation from Churchill in 1940. 1940 was an election year, and the American public tended to have ideas and attitudes similar to those of the British people in 1938 and 1939. They were in no mood for involvement or sacrifice. They transmitted those attitudes to the Congress, or at least a large portion of it.

There was almost no chance that Congress would willingly pass an act of war. With its ear to the grass roots, Congress tended to turn even more isolationist when the bloody fighting began. F.D.R. might have taken a Churchillian stand, painted the vital interests of the United States in bold terms, upheld the moral importance of democratic action, and called for intervention. His Cabinet and almost all his close advisers, especially Hopkins and Morgenthau, were convinced the United States must prepare for war. But public opinion lagged too far behind, in F.D.R.'s estimation. He chose a middle course: to begin American rearmament on a vast scale, to aid Britain short of a shooting war, and to trust in events to forge an American consensus which shared his government's urgency.

The German invasion of the Low Countries and the beginning super-battle in France gave him ample excuse to increase his Presidential powers through the declaration of an emergency. There was some Congressional grumbling but no Congressional action at this. On May 16 he sent Congress a message requesting an immense arms program—in the interest of American defense in a crumbling world. The message was not a mere recital of numbers of guns and vehicles needed, but included a clear statement of defense policy as well, with a lucid defense for "offensive" arms:

> Defense cannot be static. Defense must grow and change from day to day. Defense must be dynamic and flexible, an expression of the vital forces of the nation and its resolute will to meet whatever challenge the future may hold. ... A defense which allows an enemy to consolidate his approach without hindrance will lose. A defense which makes no effective efforts to destroy the lines of supplies and communications of the enemy will lose. An effective defense, by its very nature, requires the equipment to attack an aggressor on his route before he can establish strong bases within the territory of American vital interests.

This was, of course, a clear and brilliant delineation of the concept of active defense in the modern world—which could know no territorial limits or restricting boundaries, though Roosevelt held back from spelling this out. His message was a splendid argument for intervention anywhere against a mounting danger, but it was not so taken. American thought, like French thought throughout the 1930's, remained fixed on a defense *in extremis,* and that reluctantly taken. But unlike French strategy, which accepted only 2,000 warplanes as adequate to fight all World War II, he called for 50,000 planes a year.

Initial Congressional complaints at the vast expense—eleven billion prewar dollars—crumbled under enthusiastic acceptance of rearmament as France fell. If the changed position in Europe did not immediately instruct the public on geopolitical necessities it did make it want to lay by a few guns. Polls showed that 93.6 percent of the people were in favor of spending any amount needed to build up the armed forces. The titanic events in France revealed that the United States Army was about as effective as a horde of Boy Scouts armed with BB guns, by 1940 standards. Papers ran pictures of American

70

troops training with broomsticks and rain pipes to simulate machine guns and mortars. That, coupled with newsreels from Europe, was more than enough.

A number of Congressmen who had been against armaments, on the grounds that F.D.R. might use them to get the nation into war, quickly changed position. The notion that arms could guarantee future isolation took sudden currency —an almost complete reversal of the opinion of the 1930's, when it was held that arms carried the seeds of war—and this sentiment for a new Fortress America did much to pull the isolationists' teeth. The idea that with enough arms America could retreat with impunity and watch the world go to hell in safety was immensely appealing to most groups afraid of a foreign war. On May 26, Roosevelt felt constrained to speak out against this opinion:

> There are those among us who were persuaded by minority groups that we could maintain our physical safety by retiring within our continental boundaries—the Atlantic on the East, the Pacific on the West, Canada in the North and Mexico in the South. I illustrated the futility—the impossibility—of that idea in my message to Congress last week. Obviously a defense policy based on that is merely to invite future attack.

But the Fortress America idea did not die. While ironically it helped get Roosevelt's new arms bills through the Congress in 1940, it would remain as a persistent, pleasant, and perilous strategic concept. It was what the French General Staff had called, in the Maginot Line, a *repli Française*. Despite its pervasive popularity, however, no American government then or later seriously thought of adopting a *repli Americaine*.

From 1940 onward, however, a continual dichotomy between popular thought and government policy on "defense" was apparent. This was inevitable between men who had to think in terms of broad strategic interests and men who could not see them in the exigencies or inertia of the moment.

In the second aim, aid to Britain, the President got important help again from private sources. William Allen White, a Midwestern Republican and the nationally respected editor of the Emporia, Kansas, *Gazette*, on May 19 formed the Committee to Defend America by Aiding the Allies. Hundreds of prominent Americans, particularly in the East, came aboard. These included Gene Tunney, ex-boxer and millionaire businessman, President Charles Seymour of Yale, playwright Robert Sherwood, and scientist Harold Urey. The great American game of the formation of private committees and associations to influence public events was thus begun.

William Allen White was for sending bundles including arms to Britain; he was not for intervention in the Battle of Britain, though this was misunderstood by some. One major object of the Committee was to get Churchill the destroyers he needed. General of the Armies Pershing came out for this; George Fielding Eliot, the military writer, agreed. Dean Acheson put together legal briefs showing that the United States could legally transfer arms to Britain in accord with domestic and international law.

The Committee enjoyed great success. On the day that Italy attacked France, some five thousand sympathizers jammed its Manhattan offices, and within sixty days more than three hundred branches had been organized around the country. But the Committee tended to split, between those who wanted aid short of war and those who wanted to go further. The latter, a minority who called themselves the Century Group, came out for war, and their activities on behalf of open war eventually drove White himself to resign from the Committee to Aid the Allies.

A high percentage of intellectuals and liberals—who had generally been isolationist in tone during the 1930's—began to change their minds and plump for British aid. Walter Millis, whose *Road to War* had been almost an isolationist Bible, was one. Lewis Mumford, another well-known liberal, resigned in anger from *The New Republic* because it hesitated in openly favoring arms for the Allies.

By early summer, a *Fortune* poll indicated that 67.5 percent of America's business and intellectual leadership favored increased shipments to the Allied cause. The battle for open aid to Britain had been won.

On June 10, at a speech given at the University of Virginia, President Roosevelt put the commitment into words, in general terms:

> In our American unity, we will pursue two obvious and simultaneous courses: we will extend to the opponents of force the material resources of this nation and, at the same time, we will harness and speed up the use of those resources in order that we ourselves in the Americas may have the equipment and training equal to the task of every emergency and every defense.

This was again a giant step away from neutrality in the sense that Woodrow Wilson had tried to maintain it.

Roosevelt did not make clear, however, his already-made commitments of vital warplanes and other equipment from the United States Army and Navy. Ironically, the two enthusiasms of rearmament and aid to the Allies were running into each other and clashing. The aftereffect of the German victory in France—and the public disclosure that Britain was disarmed and threatened with immediate invasion—had created a considerable American opinion that the Germans were invincible in Europe. Britain was expected by these people momentarily to fall. Even Walter Lippmann and the *New York Herald Tribune*—a Republican-oriented paper which had earlier editorialized for war—wrote the British off, contemplating a Nazi victory. Lippmann, who consistently took an instinctive "fall back and consolidate and not provoke" approach to each developing situation wrote that the United States should abandon ideas or plans to send expeditionary forces abroad and concentrate upon a military policy of denying Hitler control of the Atlantic.

The public approach was more blunt: keep all arms and equipment that might be needed at home at home, and don't risk letting it go to waste.

Roosevelt had to pay attention to this sentiment; at least he could not defy it openly until he was clearly certain that Britain would stand.

Another problem—the "training" that the president referred to in his Charlottesville speech, meaning the training of American boys for possible war, had now arisen and took the stage in the continuing great debate.

6.

Conscience, Cowardice, and Conscription

If we are wise, let us prepare for the worst. George Washington.

You will fight for your democracy only when forced to by invasion, and then it will be too late. Sigrid Undset.

... The Christian Church ... refuses to respond to that form of ..cheap patriotism that has as its slogan "In times of peace prepare for war." Convention of Episcopal Bishops in U.S.A. (1934)

Where are the Americans hiding? David Cohen.

In 1940 only the United States, Canada, Cuba, and a handful of other Latin American republics had no form of compulsory military training. The training of conscripts and their release to the reserve had been a normal European practice for a hundred and fifty years. The traditional continental democracies called their classes to the colors as did the monarchies and dictatorships.

Finland required each male citizen to undergo two years training and remain in the reserve until age fifty-two. Switzerland had a similar system—every citizen was a soldier—and at the outbreak of World War II, although a neutral, had called one fourth of its male population to arms and manned its mountain defenses. But there was a deep and persistent antipathy to compulsory military training in all the English-speaking nations. Great Britain did not use conscript soldiers until deep in World War I.

The United States had resorted to the draft in wartime twice before. In the Civil War both sides used it, but it had resulted in bloody riots in New York and other Northern cities. It had been reinstituted in 1917, not as a universal system, but a lottery where men's names were chosen by chance. After the Armistice, conscription had been quickly abolished, and no Americans had been called to the colors for training since.

The idea of compulsory military service was as old as the Republic; every male had been a member of the militia in colonial times. George Washington had warned the nation to prepare, and had tried to institute a regular draft for training citizen soldiers from the first. But he had failed, and the idea was so unpopular that no President had called for such a practice since.

Two persistent notions kept even Americans willing to serve from favoring the draft in peacetime: one was, that like the colonial militia, Americans had only to take down the traditional musket and muster at arms when danger came. This view was totally ignorant of modern war, or the fact that modern military organizations, such as a trained division with its trained and integrated staff, required two years to make. They could not be assembled out of whole cloth overnight.

Yet Americans, whose professionalism in business and other fields topped the world, stubbornly refused to admit the value of professionalism in military matters. The other problem was, that since American frontiers were not immediately threatened, few Americans felt compelled to serve. There was a tradition that all patriots owed their lives to the country on call—but no tradition whatever that the call could be for a couple of years.

In 1940, Germany, which had been training its citizenry for years, shocked the Allies not only with new tactics, air power, and armor, but with a three-to-one preponderance of trained and hardened infantry. In 1939 the German regular army of eight hundred fifty thousand was slightly less than the combined regular forces of the Polish-French-British Allies. But only Germany had a three-to-one depth in reserve, or three citizen soldiers to step into every regular's place.

The United States Army had stood at about one hundred thousand men for a decade, risen to two hundred and twenty-seven thousand in fiscal 1940. It was totally lacking in trained reserves. In order to fight anyone—in order to beat off an invasion of the hemisphere by *any* great power, once landed—the United States Army required its entire regular strength plus a floating reserve, immediately available, of several million men. There was no notion of matching the immense, three hundred-division-plus ground forces of Nazi Germany or the U.S.S.R.; American strategy, if it came to war, did not contemplate fighting that kind of war.

The United States had already begun to plan a balanced military force which included preponderant naval and air arms, and a reasonably large ground army of up to one hundred divisions. This last caused the real problem. The Navy and Army Air Corps were reasonably popular, the difficulties there lay in making equipment, not securing men. For the Army it was exactly the other way around.

The Army staff saw no hope of creating its floating reserve without a mass conscription and a concurrent call-up of the National Guards of the various states and individual reserve officers trained through the R.O.T.C. program in the colleges. The National Guard could provide both the division frameworks and training cadres for the draftees; the several hundred thousand individual Federal reserve officers would have to serve as the training staff. If the entire regular Army were set to a training mission, which was impossible, it would not be large enough.

General George C. Marshall, the Chief of Staff of the Army, did not visualize a vast standing army in 1940. What he was desperate for was a trained reservoir of manpower that would take two years to create. He was afraid war would come before the United States had it. As he told Congress bluntly in military hearings: "Paper plans will not suffice."

It was all well and good to have standby plans for calling and training men—but Marshall and all skilled professionals knew that such plans could not be implemented overnight, nor could an American army spring up from dragons' teeth, once the whistle blew.

But while the Chief of Staff could formulate war plans, only the Chief Executive could implement them, with the aid of Congress. Recognizing the highly emotional and deeply controversial aspects of calling millions of young Americans to compulsory military service, President Roosevelt did not want to rush into the battle. He followed the course that was by now almost instinctual with him: to decide in favor of a course, to give it encouragement and a nudge here and there behind the scenes, but not to plump for it openly until the tide was running publicly in its favor. This was the Roosevelt strategy that angered his detractors, because he did not give them an opportunity to attack him on an unpopular issue while it was unpopular. It also worried his supporters, most of whom wanted to go much faster, and were eager for him not to manage the battle, but to lead it.

In retrospect, considering the danger his Cabinet agreed upon and the basic decisions he had already made in his own mind, F.D.R. went painfully slow. But considering the mood and political reactions of the nation, he acted with superb political skill. His whole method of operation was that of hinting, stating, urging from the sidelines, while letting a consensus form. He refused to try to lead one before it formed, or to take the country forcibly anywhere it did not want to go.

But once consensus was reached, he was quick to step in front and implement the mass decision with quick, incisive action.

In retrospect, this was democratic politics at its best. But also in retrospect, it was highly dangerous. As George Kennan wrote, history did not forgive folly or wasted time because it could be explained away in terms of the exigencies of domestic politics. Domestic politics, as much as faulty strategy, had sunk France and brought England to the brink.

While Walter Lippmann was writing that a German victory would "mean no peace in our lifetime" and F.D.R. was agreeing with this fear, he still felt he could not provide the complete "truth and leadership" Lippmann also called for, at least not until after reelection.

Again, private parties were allowed to carry the public ball for a draft the government had now decided was vitally necessary for the defense of the nation. When Colonel Julius Ochs Adler of *The New York Times* and Grenville Clark originated and organized a call for military conscription for training, and the *Times* editorialized in favor of it, F.D.R.'s response was to say he "liked the paragraph" in which the call was made.

On June 1, the Gallup Poll showed that opinion for and against calling men for service was exactly half-and-half. By the time France fell, the favorable opinion had shifted to 67 percent. Ironically, and typically, opinion in favor of spending vast sums of money, and of building a huge "two-ocean navy" and fifty thousand-plane air force, far outran that in favor of the draft.

The draft impinged painfully on men's lives, in a Republic where most citizens felt they had better things to do.

Opposition came from many places. As always, it made a very mixed bag of allies. It also made a lot of noise, which was to last all summer. The college generation of 1940 was inclined to assist Great Britain, but it was not inclined to fight.

When General Peyton March called for a "one million-man Army" City College of New York students paraded with placards damning both war and the Reserve Officers Training Program, or R.O.T.C. Student-body leaders at Temple University telegraphed the President to do what he could to "calm the war hysteria" and, specifically, drop the draft.

Harvard Professor Roger Merriam stated angrily that the student antiwar petitions that were pouring in from all across the country "failed to discern the moral issue." Because liberal opinion now tended to rally strongly against Hitler, overcoming previous dubiousness about the morality of war, there was a sharp division between faculties and students on the issue of the draft. But Merriam was proven right, when student leaders against "war hysteria" were interviewed in depth.

Some were pacifist by conviction and honorable in their views. A majority simply refused to believe that somewhere in the world there were powers and forces that meant them harm. The only moral issue these young men saw was whether their lives should be interrupted.

The feeling was not, of course, universal. Other thousands of young men hastened to enlist, and in New York and other areas, three thousand civilians voluntarily entered the C.T.C.A., a volunteer civilian training corps. They drilled for thirty days, without pay, and paid their own costs, amounting to $43.50 per man.

Extreme, or Marxist "liberal" groups in America almost unanimously opposed conscription. The Soviet Union still held great influence with many Americans of far left views, a residue of the 1930's. The Soviet Union's apparent partnership with Hitlerian Germany confused the issue completely for these people. Hitler and fascism had been and were bad, but on the other hand Russia was cooperating with Germany in a cynical balance of power relationship in Europe, and the

80

official Communist line now opposed the Allies. It also instructed American Communists to oppose every American effort toward military preparedness, on the stated grounds that the United States government was now preparing for a dirty capitalist war to salvage the British Empire. The line influenced thousands of fellow travelers besides avowed Marxists.

The great majority of American "liberals" however—those people who generally supported social reform and gave Roosevelt his election victories—kept a better balance. They opposed war, and they tended to oppose the draft on principle. But they were not blinded to the danger of Hitlerian conquest. If forced to choose at this period, certain polls show that Americans who considered themselves liberals would probably have made a Hobson's choice of the U.S.S.R. over Nazi Germany —but in all fairness, the vast majority of American liberal thought tended to dislike both totalitarian societies and all they stood for. If liberal thought made a mistake, it was not seeing Hitler as the greater danger, but in failing to see Russian Communism as an almost equal peril.

An important body of American moral leaders were against conscription, too. Norman Thomas, pacifist Oswald Villard, and Dr. Harry Emerson Fosdick each publicly denounced military training. Prominent clergymen of all faiths felt constrained to speak in opposition. Not all went so far as the preacher who proclaimed over the radio that the draft would mean "Syphilis and Slavery" for young America. Responsible Catholics such as Msgr. Michael J. Ready and Protestant leaders like the Methodist Dr. Charles F. Boos, Jr., pleaded that the use of volunteers, not draftees against their will, was the only American way.

Organized labor was extremely wary. If the government could draft soldiers, labor leaders believed, it could conscript labor for industry, too, as all European powers now were doing. John L. Lewis of the coal miners said that compulsory military service smacked of dictatorship and fascism. "Democracy must offer its own way of life to combat the forces which imperil civilization." But Lewis did not explain his alternate plan.

The American Federation of Labor's William Green stated that he would oppose the draft "until it became necessary to defend, protect, and preserve America" which presumably meant when an invasion force stood on American soil. The Trade Union Committee for Peace, consisting mostly of trade unionist's wives, picketed and lobbied the halls of Congress.

The peace lobby, of all ages, faiths, and persuasions, instinctively came out against the draft. The philosophy seemed to be that if the United States did not draft, then it would not be able to fight. It was a reasonable argument, so far as it went. But it could only be argued so far, and it produced almost a foaming at the mouth in government circles frightened by Hitler's three hundred divisions.

The American Youth Congress, an old liberal organization favored by Eleanor Roosevelt, marched noisily in Washington, D.C. The youths considered the draft undemocratic and unfair. Mrs. Roosevelt criticized them in her widely read column, *My Day:* they were not facing up to the world they lived in. But she herself did not really like the idea of drafting men for war, and obliquely, but not publicly, said so.

The fight was waged in the streets, on campuses, and from pulpits. When the so-called Burke-Wadsworth bill—to draft up to one million youths and call up three hundred ninety-six thousand National Guardsmen and commissioned reservists to train them—was brought up in Congress, the battle shifted to Washington.

With a consensus behind it, the bill should have been easily put through. But the opposition was noisy, well-placed politically, and it was very difficult for individual Congressmen to judge just where sentiment stood—or would solidify, once a popular enthusiasm pro and con had passed. The people who fretted that Congress was cynical in its approach to national security failed to understand what Congress represented and heeded: a collective body of more than 500 men stemming from a quite pluralistic nation, and split four ways between political parties and basic ideologies could defend and protect its constituencies, but it could not lead. The Burke-Wadsworth bill cut across all party and regional lines, and many individual Congressmen were conscientiously opposed to it, on the grounds that it was an abridgment of civil liberties. And so it was, in traditional American thought, but the same processes which made democratic Switzerland stand to arms were now reaching and working across the Atlantic.

When Roosevelt himself refused to back the bill strongly, and only continued to favor it in general terms, Congress bogged down into a long hot summer of acrimony. The isolationist bloc from the West and Midwest had been silenced during the rearmament bills. The consensus for these had been overwhelming; virtually all Americans wanted the two-ocean navy and the immense air force, even if it was going to cost someone eleven billions. But the two million man army did not have this kind of popularity, and Congress in an election year had to be sure. Gradually, the isolationist or peace bloc, and the peace marchers coalesced into a solid, if intellectually incoherent front.

One major feature of the Midwestern isolationists' stand was their belief in a strong, or Fortress America, and most of their Congressional adherents voted for defense. But almost all isolationists by now had a powerful distrust of F.D.R.'s motives toward the war. They were sure he wanted, as H. L. Mencken had said, "to horn in on the great crusade to save mankind."

The American isolationists' great hope was still to avoid war, and the pacifist logic that if the United States did not have trained manpower it could not fight, impressed them deeply. It created a weird inconsistency, however. The men who talked most about making America into an impregnable fortress

83

Hitler would never dare attack were the ones who argued most vehemently against men to man the walls.

Senator Lundeen of Minnesota, for example, was positively belligerent in his professed views as to the defense of the hemisphere. He advocated a United States seizure of all French and British possessions in the New World, which was one way of lessening the isolationists' fear of the war spreading to them. But Lundeen, and others, wanted to do this seizing, and to mount this massive guard, without the draft.

Senators George Norris and Robert La Follette was basically liberal. They despised fascism in any form. But they agreed that American civil liberties would be endangered by an involuntary muster, and maybe even domestic fascism fostered by mobilization.

Despite the arguments used, however, there was a strong sectional, and even an hereditary approach to the question. Those legislators, who like Norris, had voted against entry in World War I and were still around, were most opposed to intervention. They did not agree the world had changed.

Their sons, such as Robert La Follette, Jr., showed the same tendency. Those men, like Michigan's Vandenberg, who had been most disabused in 1919, were still disillusioned with the European power world. And their constituencies at home, in every case, were those least interested in events abroad and most concerned with staying aloof from them. Some of this home sentiment was natural and logical; the Midwest and Rocky Mountain West had been far removed from seaboard affairs for a hundred years. Geography dominated, and made people look inward. But some of the opposition to world events was utterly irrational, too, though completely traditional and American: many people in the Midwest, including those in Congress, were against anything the people in the moneyed, anglophile East seemed to be more and more for.

Not many people in Minnesota, Iowa, Montana, or Illinois

really hated the British Empire—but they did hate the American East and its purported "financial empire."

The feeling that the United States had sent its boys to France in 1917 to save the investments of the House of Morgan and other Wall Street bankers had never died in the Midwest. Henry Ford was one who openly said so. As far as most people from Illinois were concerned in 1940, the great political and mercantile and financial structures of the Atlantic world could collapse—if it was going to take American blood to save them.

The effect of this sentiment on certain highly able Congressmen, such as Everett Dirksen, Republican of Illinois, and Guy Gillette, Democrat of Iowa, was interesting to watch. Neither Gillette nor Dirksen was a stupid man; they were anything but uninformed. But like Arthur Vandenberg, Michigan's able Republican senator, they were extremely able politicians, and they were politicians before they were statesmen. They were the first to admit, wryly, that no American could aspire to statesmanship unless he were first elected, and in this sense, on a local level, they played F.D.R.'s own national game.

Dirksen knew there could be no Fortress America—which he favored—without a draft. But he detected no groundswell for drafting in his district. He was, therefore, opposed to the idea. Gillette was visibly afraid and worried about doing anything his voters wouldn't back. He voted the popular money bills, but argued that the draft ought to wait for "a real emergency"—not the one the people in Iowa did not yet understand.

A good American politician needs a certain amount of indecision and flexibility; he must fear to rush in too soon, and not be afraid to change his mind and rush out. When Senator Joe Robinson of Arkansas once snorted: "Vacuity, vacillation, and Vandenberg!" he was in a sense paying the Senator from Michigan a supreme compliment. Vandenberg, like Dirksen, would not only provide able service over the years, but he would be around a long time. Neither man, when the tide came in, would be afraid to change his mind.

A great many Republicans, however, even those in the more interventionist-minded East, felt constrained to oppose on principle anything President Roosevelt wanted, even if he didn't want it too openly. The idea of a bipartisan foreign policy was an uneasy one, then as later.

It was seriously broached by one Republican senator that the whole idea of conscription was a military plot to make more generals and colonels in the Army. Another Republican, Taft of Ohio, argued that while men were needed, it would show a failure of American democracy if enough could not be made to volunteer.

There were other legislators who were isolationist out of conviction and did not care what their constituencies thought about it. They did not have to care. Borah of Idaho, and Hiram Johnson of California were two of these. Both were crusty old senators, reelected until their voters considered it a habit, unafraid of anything, and exciting local admiration because of it. With this kind of politician even party lines blurred. Many people didn't know what Johnson or Borah was, and in fact they had been known to jump their party more than once. Borah, a Republican, switched to William Jennings Bryan, then just as impudently, switched back again.

Burton K. Wheeler, of Montana, was a liberal, New Deal Democrat, who coincidentally disliked F.D.R. He attacked armaments, drafts, and intervention of any kind, including aid to Britain, with impunity.

These men had no fear of reelection in 1940. Their publics did not elect them because of their foreign policy line. Borah, who was the first and natural leader of the Peace Bloc, died early in 1940, and with the conscription bill the leadership passed more and more to Wheeler. Wheeler began to receive wires and letters from all over the country on his stand. By his admitted count, the opinion was four thousand against, thirty-two for the draft.

Wheeler and the others hauled up Administration leaders before Congress, grilling them for hours in the time-honored way. Sensing they could not win a vote in the summer of 1940, the isolationists anti-drafters sought to delay. The Secretary of War, who was seventy-two, was kept on the witness stand for days. The senators opposed to the draft also took, as a major argument, the line that conscription might possibly be necessary in time, but it shouldn't be enacted hastily or before months of debate.

Secretary Stimson finally snapped back: "All this talk of wait, wait, wait, and we're confronted with an enemy who does not wait!" In Stimson's eyes this was the whole, sad story of the preceding decade; the democracies always did too little and did it too late, from Poland to Norway to France to Britain, and now, seemingly, to the shores of the United States. But his comment only provoked irritation from some who wanted to know "what enemy" he was talking about. The United States was at peace.

Another argument was that the decision should be put off until after the 1940 Presidential election. But when the Republican candidate, Wendell Willkie, stated that he favored the draft as much as Roosevelt, he torpedoed Connecticut Democrat Maloney's moves to postpone the bill until January 1, 1941. While Willkie did not swing a majority of his Republican colleagues in Congress to his view, a number of observers agreed that this was the turning point. Without his statement, the draft would have been postponed; the sentiment to do so —neither reject nor pass but put it aside until the dust settled —was quite strong.

F.D.R. came out publicly for the Burke-Wadsworth bill in August.

Now, the Northern-Midwest Republican-Southern Democrat coalition that had brought the New Deal to a standstill in the year 1938 fell completely apart. The reason was that while Northern Republicans were lukewarm, or opposed to the draft, Southerners of all stripes were almost belligerently for it. This was a regional, not an ideological feeling. The most outspoken Congressmen or Senators for intervention, even war, were Southerners like Alabama's Pepper, whom the "Congress of American Mothers" hanged in effigy more than once.

Southerners, plus Easterners, plus Democrats loyal to F.D.R.'s foreign policy, whether they understood or liked it or not, formed a majority not only in the nation, but in both Houses. It became obvious the draft bill would pass.

By August, 1940, the nation was treated to a new phenomenon: the "beat-the-draft" marriage. Thousands of young people jammed marriage license bureaus. Married men were to be exempt from service, and the sale of marriage licenses broke all records for August.

Congress gave F.D.R. authority to call up the National Guard and Reserves, but still debated voting on the draft. But these were only stalling tactics; passage was assured. On September 2, F.D.R. came out strongly urging Congress to act on the bill, demanding that it be put into effect within two weeks. Several months had already been lost, while General Marshall and others quietly ground their teeth with great restraint.

The bill finally passed the House 266-145, but with a sixty-day delay clause, a last effort amendment by Representative Hamilton Fish of New York. Isolationists voted against it in the main, knocking into a cocked hat their intellectual arguments for a powerful America. In September 1940, the bill carried in the Senate 58-31. The United States had its first "peacetime" draft.

The bill provided for only one year's training for not more than nine hundred thousand draftees. A Selective Service system was set up, under which broad classes of males would register, but only certain categories be called, by lot. The selection of a man to direct this service became a subject of contention; the job paid $10,000 a year and at that time was a considerable political plum. An obscure Army lieutenant colonel named Lewis Hershey was proposed for the post, but there were objections to a military man running the draft. In the end, Hershey got the job of running the system, while a respected political scientist named Clarence Dykstra was appointed to the Directorship.

The American Youth Congress, left-leaning and noisy, refused to acquiesce to the new law of the land. Eventually, this forced Eleanor Roosevelt to withdraw her support of the organization.

Two dozen students at the Union Theological Seminary announced they would refuse to register as required, even though they were certain to be deferred. New York draft director Colonel A. V. McDermott snarled that he would have them jailed. Other people felt this was much too severe.

A minority group, some Mohawk Indians, said they would not register on the grounds that American Indians were not citizens, and anyway had always received bad treatment from the government.

On the appointed day, however, the overwhelming majority of young Americans registered quietly, resignedly, with democratic dignity, and even a certain amount of good cheer.

Most people had always thought they would.

7.

Whose War?

Come three corners of the world in arms
And we shall shock them. Nought shall make us rue
If England to itself do rest but true.
                                                    King John

Never before in human history was so much owed by so many to
so few.   Winston Churchill.

I call on the British Government to abandon the British Isles. . . .
This will end Hitler's ambition for world conquest. I hope this
plan will not be long delayed by futile encouragement to fight on,
because it is conclusively evident that Congress will not authorize
intervention in the European war.   Senator Key Pittman, Nevada,
Chairman of the Foreign Relations Committee.

The outcome of this grim struggle will affect you almost as much
as it will affect us.   Lord Lothian, British Ambassador to the
United States.

In the summer of 1940, the British people saw the whole
world structure as they had envisioned it crumble. British war
strategy, which had put great store on something called "economic warfare" and refused to contemplate sending one hundred or even twenty divisions to hold a British bulwark on the
continent, lay in ruins. They had played "balance of power"
on the soil of Europe, never realizing that they themselves were

90

the only possible balance of power against Hitler—that France and Poland could not do the job merely supported by the Royal Navy. Their diplomacy had ended in utter failure. It had succeeded in bringing about a détente between Germany and the U.S.S.R., the only land power which could hope to offset Hitler's ground divisions.

They were backed up into their small island, fifty millions strong, while their enemy had the resources of a three hundred fifty million-man continent of the most highly skilled people in the world to draw upon. They had no army worthy of the name, and that army had lost all its heavy equipment before Dunkirk. Their projected ground forces for the coming year would equal less than 20 percent of Hitler's, if the arms and equipment could be found.

They did control the seas, but they were only eighteen miles from Hitler's Europe at one point, and their air force was outnumbered approximately four-to-one.

England had vast industry, and enormous resources all around the world. But the British democracy had learned something at last, with its back to the wall and the German military machine preparing to invade. Resources and wealth are comfortable things, but they never historically have been a defense against arms in the hands of an enemy prepared to use them.

The British, waiting for the fateful blow they knew would come, reorganized. They began to build aircraft as they had never realized they could make aircraft before. For the first time in history a democratic public faced total war. They were no longer, as Ambassador Joseph Kennedy reported back to Washington, fighting for something called freedom or democracy. They were fighting for survival, and they knew it.

That they fought so well was due in great part to Winston Churchill. At this time, and only at this time, Churchill was able to reach something in the British soul, to engender that feeling of greatness and historic purpose that more than anything else was to see the British people through. The British had been beaten, in almost every way a nation could be beaten except by invasion and house-to-house conquest, and they were facing that. But Churchill inspired a feeling that historic England still lived, and would never fall.

It was not really realistic, and some of England's best friends abroad said so in worried tones. But courage and greatness in extremity are rarely realistic, which is something historians sifting ruins and records soon forget.

Churchill said, on June 4, after the debacle at Dunkirk, which the British turned into a moral victory:

> I ... have full confidence that if all do their duty ... we shall prove ourselves once again able to defend our Island home ... we shall fight on the seas and oceans, we shall fight with growing confidence and growing strength in the air, we shall defend our Island, whatever the cost may be, we shall fight on the beaches, we shall fight on the landing grounds, we shall fight in the fields and in the streets, we shall fight in the hills; we shall never surrender, and even if, which I do not for a moment believe, this Island or a large part of it were subjugated or starving, then Our Empire beyond the seas, armed and guarded by the British fleet would carry on the struggle, until, in God's good time, the New World, with all its power and might, steps forth to the rescue and liberation of the old.

German soldiers marched into the Channel ports, singing *Wir Fahren Gegen England*. But the German navy did not control the Channel, and German admirals did not pretend it could. Göring's Luftwaffe had lost momentary control of the air above Dunkirk, and they had to gain it back. This was Britain's weakest moment, when every shred of German nerve and muscle sent against it might have prevailed. But the cost would have been horrendous, and Hitler did not believe the cost was worth the gain. He thought he could bring about the fall of Britain in other ways. No more historic, or fatal mistake, was ever made.

German arms moved south, against a collapsing France. The tottering government of old Marshal Pétain, riddled with defeatists and even traitors, capitulated.

Churchill then said:

> ... The battle of France is over. I expect that the Battle of Britain is about to begin. Upon this battle depends the survival of Christian civilization. Upon it depends our British life, and the long continuity of our Empire. The whole fury and might of the enemy must very soon be turned on us. Hitler knows that he will have to break us in this Island or lose the war. If we can stand up to him, all Europe may be free and the life of the world may move forward into broad, sunlit uplands. But if we fail, then the whole world, including the United States, including all that we have known and cared for, will sink into the abyss of a new Dark Age made more sinister, and perhaps more protracted, by the lights of perverted science. Let us therefore brace ourselves to our duties, and so bear ourselves that, if the British Empire and its Commonwealth last for a thousand years, men will still say, "This was their finest hour."

With these words, and the effect of these words, the moral initiative of World War II first passed from Hitler to the Allies, and the leadership of the democratic world came into Winston Churchill's hands.

Churchill had called forth a genuine sense of heroism and greatness in his people. Unrealistic or not, the English were ready to fight.

It was a change that Hitler did not recognize, and it lay at the root of his failure to bring the war to an end. At Munich and beyond he had terrorized the democracies with his air force by holding their cities hostage to bombardment. France was morally and politically defeated before the war. He did not expect much more from England, and based on his experience in the 1930's, he should have been correct in this assumption.

Hitler had been able to take over Europe, first because the free nations could not find the moral courage to oppose him, second, when it came to fighting, because only the German war leaders had understood, experimented with, and prepared for modern war. The British strategists had never understood the vital importance of holding a continental foothold; the British effort that led to Dunkirk had been a token one. But now, with the British pushed back to their island, certain factors changed.

The British could not be terrorized into surrender, although Hitler thought they could. He did not really want to risk invasion. Second, while it was obvious that the highly trained masses of German infantry and armor could not reach across the Channel, there was another German weakness no one had seen. This was in the Luftwaffe itself.

The Luftwaffe had been planned and built as much as a political terror arm as a war machine. It was envisioned that dropping tons of bombs on cities, wiping out whole blocks, would serve an adequate military purpose. In Poland, and again in Rotterdam, this worked. But the German air force had no real concept of, or training for, true strategic bombing, which was now the only thing that could have taken Britain out of the war.

The Battle of Britain began in August, 1940, reached its crescendo in September, and did not end until the next spring. It was a struggle for control of the air over the island, and in the end, though both sides sputtered out in mutual exhaustion, the British won.

There were a variety of reasons. British air power, which had been ineffective over the continent tactically, had been planned and trained for only one mission: defense of the British Isles. It was centrally directed, and had a superb communications system; the R.A.F. could muster aircraft anywhere over the Isles in minutes. The Spitfire fighter, manned by British pilots over British soil, was more than the equal of the aircraft the Germans put in British air space. It was not courage alone that won the Battle of Britain; the R.A.F. was small, but in its own field—air defense—it was the best in the world.

The Luftwaffe had developed no defensive formation flying. The versatility and terrible firepower of the ME-109's was not matched by the German bombers, which were both undergunned and did not carry sufficient bomb loads. The bombers came over England in long strings, letting bombs fall hit-or-miss when they were over English cities. They missed many vital targets, and they were terribly vulnerable to massed fighter attack, which hit them at awkward times, or could harry the strung-out formations almost at will.

Another enormous handicap for the Luftwaffe was that the Germans, normally meticulous, had made no provisions for replacement parts. They did not plan for losses or for the machine fatigue of a protracted campaign. Göring simply could not sustain his thousand-plane effort very long.

The final fatal error again stemmed from the nature of the Luftwaffe and Hitler's lingering misconception that the British would fold. The British aircraft industry in 1940 was exposed and vulnerable to German bombing; up till October it was receiving grave damage and a sustained German effort might easily have knocked it out.

But Hitler was too impatient with this kind of campaign, too politically-minded to comprehend the strategic nature of this air war. Stung by British retaliation in the fall of 1940, he pulled the Luftwaffe off British industry and ordered it to level British towns. The great raids on London, and the destruction of Coventry, were spectacular and seemed important in the news. But they left the production of new Spitfires intact, and actually fanned the British determination to resist.

In March 1941, when the Luftwaffe was transferred to East Europe in preparation for other campaigns, the attempt to conquer Britain from the air had failed. And another important fact was revealed: the German air defense was not able to prevent British bombing in return. The only reason that the R.A.F. did not strike Germany hard was that the British, who had concentrated on air defense, had no strategic air force, either.

If ever a powerful strategic air force were based in Britain, it would be another matter.

Millions of Americans believed that the great watershed of United States policy came at Pearl Harbor, on December 7, 1941—the day Hawaii was attacked and America entered the shooting war. But this was not true. The real change in direction came in the early summer of 1940, when France fell and the Battle of Britain had not yet begun. Here decisions were made in Washington that caused Pearl Harbor not to be a grinding wrench, but only a milestone on the road to war.

Roosevelt's Cabinet jointly agreed with Winston Churchill's view of the Nazi menace, felt that the future security of the United States was in grave danger, and decided the United States must prepare for war. The activists in this decision were Harold Ickes, Secretary of the Interior, Henry Morgenthau, Secretary of the Treasury, Harry Hopkins, who was sometimes in the Cabinet, sometimes serving as a sort of executive secretary and super adviser, Cordell Hull, Secretary of State, and two new Republican members, War and Navy Secretaries Henry L. Stimson and Frank Knox. Chief of Staff George C. Marshall and Admiral H. R. Stark, Chief of Naval Operations, were brought into the decision, and concurred completely. There was no substantial disagreement anywhere in the lower levels of the Executive Branch.

Out of this decision came the tremendous armaments bill of July 1940 and the draft, both of which the country supported.

But another decision was made at the same time—that an understanding should be arrived at with the British. Since British and American interests coincided this made perfect sense. But an American public that was emotionally prepared to rearm was not emotionally or psychologically ready to accept a British alliance, or anything else that seemed likely to push the United States toward a foreign war.

For this reason, from the summer of 1940 till Pearl Harbor, a certain secrecy was clamped over British-American discussions and transactions. There was a certain dissembling by the Cabinet and the President himself. They sometimes talked one way but acted in another. This created confusion, but mostly among those people who wanted to be confused. The direction of United States policy, for anyone who read the still uncensored news, was quite clear.

Roosevelt chose a method of liaison with the British that made sense under the "unofficial" circumstances that prevailed. It was also one that appealed to him personally. F.D.R. never liked nor understood rigid command lines within the Executive Branch of government. The influence or operations of certain Cabinet members never had any real relation to their Constitutional jobs, and Roosevelt was always, in effect, his own Secretary of State. Since 1933 the acquiescent Cordell Hull had not made policy; he followed Roosevelt's lead, and preached against those things F.D.R. decried. This had already made a certain shambles of the structure of the State Department, so when F.D.R. began to use personal emissaries, rather than regular diplomatic channels, in his relations with foreign leaders, there was no great change. Whatever havoc was created by this system of personal messengers and personal relationships between F.D.R. and Churchill and other foreign governments came only after the President's death.

In defense of this system, it can be said that the Executive Branch and the State Department were both too small in 1940-1941, and too loosely structured, to handle a series of vast American commitments around the world. Roosevelt, who turned his whole attention now to foreign affairs, was able to

97

direct things nicely, and to keep everything under control at least for the first two years.

To maintain liaison with the British, and above all, to keep the President informed, an exploratory mission was dispatched to Britain. This was headed by Rear Admiral Robert L. Ghormley, and included United States officers of all arms, such as Major General Delos Emmons and Brigadier General George Strong. Ghormley was instructed to observe the Battle of Britain, and especially to estimate the British chances of survival and their willingness to hold out.

Churchill's government from the first cooperated completely. All doors were opened to the Americans, almost no staff secrets were withheld from them. They were told things the British public, for security reasons, was never told. Churchill, as he indicated in his great 1940 speeches, always hoped for American entry in the war. This angered the isolationists in the United States, of course. But Churchill, who expected Britain to survive, was never so sanguine as to think the British could defeat the German state in the end without American entry in the war. When he reiterated publicly that all Britain desired, or needed, was American industrial aid, not the United States armed forces, this was in deference to American opinion and Roosevelt's position.

Ghormley and his party were shown everything and allowed to talk to anyone they wanted to, and to watch any battle in progress. He reported back to F.D.R. that he was convinced the British would fight, and that they "would not be quickly beaten." No American military opinion really believed the British, unassisted, could win the war. The German lead, the German resources, and the German odds were just too great.

But the belief that the British could hold out made the American policy of vast rearmament and official uninvolvement feasible, however hard it might be on the British themselves.

The British staff, closeted with Admiral Ghormley, wanted

to lead him into a discussion of how United States forces could best be used, if and when. Ghormely shied off from this question. He had no powers to discuss, even hypothetically, this kind of strategy. But he did not slam the door; he told the British the discussion would have to be postponed for a future meeting with Americans who might be so empowered.

From this time on, there was close and special liaison between the British war staff and high American officers. The basis was laid, with approval on the highest level—meaning F.D.R.—for staff discussions to take place at a future date. Ghormley's, and other, special missions, to Britain were made public. What was said and the plans actually laid were not.

The British were encouraged by these missions and private discussions, but both were vastly short of real American participation.

The United States armed forces, with British experience and British secret war discoveries made available to them, were helped tremendously in planning for a coming war. The British, now getting and using American equipment, made specific recommendations as to how it could be improved, and fed their combat experience back into American factories. This enabled American officers and production designers to avoid serious mistakes they would have made without such guidance. The traffic was by no means all one way. The British had learned some bitter lessons in the school of modern combat and were eager to pass them on, in return for American material aid.

Out of this experience, both United States bombers, fighter craft, and naval vessels modified equipment and tactics. The British discoveries in antisubmarine warfare, in which the United States Navy was far behind, were particularly significant in the light of the necessity for democratic control of the Atlantic Ocean.

No serious frictions ever developed during this liaison, which was remarkable considering the fact that many United

States officers had no particular pro-British bias, felt British strategy was wrong in places, and resented the fact that political decisions shipped vital equipment across the Atlantic which they still lacked and preferred to keep at home.

For their part, the British, convinced they were fighting America's war as well as their own, with gentlemanly restraint refrained from asking pointed questions about America's lack of haste in getting in the war. One thing that kept things smooth was policy guidance, from the highest levels on each side, to insure that no such frictions would be permitted to occur. Almost from the first Roosevelt and Churchill understood each other, and this was the firm basis of the eventual Grand Alliance that was to prosecute the war.

On the political and propaganda fronts things were not so smooth.

American isolationism showed its first signs of an eventual anti-British tone. There was still a widespread feeling that the British would surrender, and that further aid would be lost, and worse, give Hitler an excuse to pick a fight with the United States. A certain body of Congressional opinion wanted the United States to take an initiative to end the war—by pressuring the British government into some form of negotiated peace.

The anger and dismay in the Cabinet was intense when Senator Pittman, Chairman of the Foreign Relations Committee, declared that the British government should give up the home islands and retreat to Canada or somewhere in the Commonwealth. Pittman hoped this would satisfy Hitler's ambitions at last. He and others were perfectly willing to leave Hitler in control of Europe, and even the Atlantic, if this avoided a United States-German confrontation and an eventual war.

Pittman made this recommendation in the summer of 1940, without consulting the Administration. He was widely quoted in the press.

Pittman had come to the chair of the Foreign Relations Committee by seniority, and he had no particular knowledge of—and worse—no interest in, foreign affairs. His main concerns were for the silver-mining interests of his home state of Nevada. Under the United States system of government, he did not, and could not speak for United States policy. But all Senators had influence, and overseas the fact that this influence might not be decisive was dimly understood. What the English and others recalled most vividly about the Senate was that it had torpedoed Woodrow Wilson's entrance into the League of Nations, and expressions like Pittman's continued to chill British observers to the bone.

There was also a comfortable illusion that if the British Isles had to be abandoned to German attack, the powerful British fleet would sail West and join in the defense of the New World. This was not only naïve, it was unworthy—but many Americans discussed it as logical.

Lord Lothian, the immensely able British ambassador to Washington, did his best to dispel all such illusions and suspicions. In a speech at Yale University, he said bluntly the British fleet would not abandon its homeland nor would British sailors desert their families and sail westward. If Hitler won, he would either gain control of the British fleet, or he would destroy it in the process—and Lothian said clearly and concisely that either event would be disastrous for American security. "For if Hitler gets our fleet, or destroys it, the whole foundation on which the security of both our countries has rested for one hundred twenty years will have disappeared."

The speech did not go over well with Americans who had never admitted that the security of the United States had rested on Anglo-American cooperation in the Atlantic, or that a pragmatic agreement on the Pacific with the British kept the United States Navy as the mainstay for both countries against Japan.

Lord Lothian had a delicate and difficult course to steer.

101

He understood the sentiments of the Roosevelt government from private conversations, but also its handicaps in pursuing its new course. He himself was always under the gun. A highly respected British aristocrat, he was, at the same time, the very kind of Britisher some Americans detested. He had to be most careful in everything he did, to get the most for his embattled nation while never giving American isolationists too much offense.

He also had to stand between Americans and his own kind. While he propounded Atlantic realities to Ivy League undergraduates who neither understood nor particularly cared, he tried to explain an emerging America to Britons. They could not expect the United States ever to underwrite the British Empire. Americans had a traditional antipathy to empires and the pretensions of empire. But he compared the "island" mentality of the United States to that same mentality in England long before.

After Napoleon, Britain had tried to remain uncommitted on the continent, and to stay clear of all conflicts until a definite menace to its own interests seemed to appear. The British policy had been that the best and cheapest security was to encourage other nations and peoples to fight against a danger that threatened both them and England. The British always assisted with money or subsidies, but only in extremity with arms and troops.

America was selfish, Lothian admitted, but so had Britain been.

He saw that the United States did not aspire to world power; most Americans still wanted isolation and no responsibility toward the world. But Lothian was prophetic in the summer of 1940. He saw and said that world responsibility would be forced on Americans against their will, just as it had been forced on England. American wealth, success, and strength might not make the United States force itself on the world— but they would cause the world to force itself on America.

Hitler, or any other aspirant to world power, simply could not leave the Americas alone.

Meanwhile, the Roosevelt Cabinet had come to another decision, this time a popular one across the country, even in isolationist, Briton-suspicious Chicago. This was on the question of Canada. As a member of the Commonwealth, Canada was at war with Germany, and under the rules of war subject to attack. But the United States could not stand by if Canada was threatened. The mere idea of a German fleet in the St. Lawrence River, or a German army along the undefended northern border was strategically unthinkable.

On August 18, the government authorized secret staff talks with the Canadians, which resulted in the so-called Ogdensburg Agreement. This created a permanent joint board for United States-Canadian defense, and committed the United States to the defense of Canadian territory. This was a weird arrangement in one sense—it formed a defensive alliance between a belligerent and a neutral nation toward the same enemy.

The alliance was made public, however, and there was no deep American dissent. Even the *Chicago Tribune,* which was violently against aid or intervention, approved. The *New York Herald Tribune* agreed that such a pact meant no involvement in the European war.

Even the most dedicated isolationists agreed that if a German army ever reached the New World—even if directed first against Canada or some other Allied possession—the United States would have to fight. The disagreement lay in the fact that the isolationists argued this could never happen, while the interventionists, almost sick with apprehension, were equally convinced it would.

Other diplomatic developments around the world included the seizure of the Baltic States by Russia in August. The United States condemned this roundly, but took no other action. The U.S.S.R. also forced Romania to surrender a province—Bessarabia. Thus the U.S.S.R. was gaining important territory, without the cost of war, while Hitler was preoccupied with France and Britain.

A number of European observers and strategists, now refugees in America, testified that tension between the Germans and Soviets was increasing; Germany could not let control of the Baltic coastline slip away unchallenged. The two monster states had agreed to divide Poland, but other territorial arrangements were not so easily arrived at. Predictions that the Nazis and Soviets might go to war were written off, however, as wishful thinking, and the Communist line derided all such notions.

An original United States concern that the French fleet would fall into Hitler's hands was ended by the British in July. In the Mediterranean, and off the African coast, the British Navy asked the French Navy to surrender itself to England as a defensive move. Some French vessels yielded; General de Gaulle had already founded the Free French in London. Other ships were seized and disarmed. But a sizable part of the French Navy remained loyal to the new French collaborationist regime at Vichy. The British Navy opened fire on this group of vessels and sent many of them to the bottom, together with more than one thousand French seamen.

In the Western Hemisphere the Caribbean island of Martinique remained responsible to Vichy. This posed a certain problem for the United States. Vichy was recognized to be a possible ally of the Germans, or at least subject to German control. But while some vociferous sentiment—including isolationists—was for seizing the island from the French, Washington's policy was more cautious. For one thing, a seizure of the island admitted a final French estrangement and defeat.

An uneasy situation was allowed to continue, with Martinique put under close "surveillance."

There was, also, considerable concern in Washington about possible German subversion in Latin America. The anti-American sentiments of many Latins were well-known, if not publicly admitted. But the Germans were not able to exploit such anti-American sentiments across the Atlantic. Potential German power was far away; the United States was close at hand. Furthermore, the Roosevelt Administration had made great efforts to conciliate and allay Latin suspicions. The result was a real, if ephemeral, diplomatic triumph at a conference at Havana for Cordell Hull and Sumner Welles, who had once been anathema in Cuba and hung in effigy in the Dominican Republic. Latin America acquiesced in United States' control and management of hemisphere defense, though no Latin nation showed any real interest in assuming any of the burden.

The intense preoccupation with an American potential Fifth Column also reached a peak. Congress passed an alien registration bill, and subversive acts legislation, giving the government broad powers of control against espionage, sabotage, or subversion, in spite of vehement opposition by leftist groups.

One thing that fed this worry about subversion was not the evidence of any widespread movements on American ground, but an article published by Col. William Joseph Donovan, who had been sent on a secret mission to Britain for Navy Secretary Knox. Donovan, in collaboration with foreign correspondent Edgar Ansel Mowrer, claimed the Germans had an army of four million foreign agents on which they spent at least two hundred million dollars per year. Spies, secret agents, and the search for them became almost a hobby for Americans as well as the business of the F.B.I.

Spain, which was an Axis friend if not an open Axis ally, announced a status of "non-belligerency"—not neutrality—against England. But Dictator Francisco Franco, to Hitler's disappointment, pointedly refused to attack the British bastion at Gibraltar. Spain was fascist and anti-democratic in spirit, but after almost three years of a protracted civil war that ended

105

in 1939, was in no shape to risk opposing British power. In this sense, Franco was far more realistic than Mussolini.

After an argument in the Cabinet, the United States declared an embargo on aviation gasoline shipped overseas. This was directed at Spain and Japan. Japan, which had always procured at least one half of its raw material and resources for its China war from the United States, protested shrilly. The shipment of scrap iron, however, was continued. Secretary Hull argued that cessation of this trade, or any Japanese trade, put the United States in the position of needlessly irritating Japan.

The 1911 Trade treaty with Japan had been ended by the United States in 1939, largely at the instigation of Senator Vandenberg, and because of feelings aroused by the China War. Walter Lippmann, as well as Cordell Hull, condemned this act because he believed it might lead to war. Lippmann did not want the United States to be put in the position of "challenging a great power" in the Far East. Lippmann, then as before and later, was expert at seeing effects, but rarely reasons or causes.

Thousands of English children began to arrive in the United States, dispatched for reasons of safety from the Battle of Britain "blitz." Some thirty-two thousand in all came in the summer of 1940. This was a token measure, of course, and could not, in any event, save many British children from the very real horrors of war. But the motives of the British government in sending them, and the American government, in dropping quotas and modifying immigration procedures in order to admit them, were partly propaganda. They were visible evidence of Hitler's inhumanity to man.

But as Churchill's Britain prepared to endure its "finest hour" the big news in the United States was not really the war in Europe. It centered on two things: the American Presidential election and rearmament.

106

8.

Rather Right than President

We are likely to have Roosevelt again, whether there is war or not.
Senator Burton K. Wheeler, Montana.

The lower one-third is for you in gratitude for your domestic policies. They don't give a damn about the war. Above all, they don't want their living standards cut, and they will repudiate you if you do. Mayor Ed Kelly of Chicago to President Roosevelt.

In the process of preparing against danger we shall not abandon the great social improvements that have come to America. . . . We need not swap the gain of better living for the gain of better defense. Franklin D. Roosevelt campaign speech, 1940.

The European war, whether admitted by all parties or not, was the crucial question underlying the 1940 election. The Republican candidate, Wendell Willkie, did not and could not have—as a private businessman unconnected with government—the confidence of the American public. That Roosevelt had the confidence of the democratic world was immaterial. While this kind of thing was always brought up in United States elections, then and later, only the American electorate's votes were counted in November.

If the war had not begun in Europe, it is very doubtful if Franklin Roosevelt would, or could, have run for a tradition-breaking third term. There was no groundswell of sentiment for such a term before September 1939. Actually, there was enormous opposition to it in the Democratic Party. But significantly, the Gallup Poll showed that in October 1939, with the war going on, 43 percent of the American public wanted him to run again. Moreover, 52 percent indicated they would vote for him if the war continued through November 1940.

The old American political adage about not changing horses in the middle of the stream held true. Republican barbs on "How did we get in the middle of the stream?" felt flat. F.D.R. was not responsible for the war, but he could not help but be a political beneficiary of it. In times of confusion or danger, the public needed a symbol to rally round. That symbol had to be the Presidency.

The powerful political coalition of lower-income groups, big-city ethnic minorities, and Southerners whom Roosevelt had welded into a dominant majority in the 1930's still held. Even after the ending of reform in 1938, F.D.R. kept the old loyalties alive. On domestic issues F.D.R. was in no trouble. But one of the several ironies of the 1940 election was that the very groups that formed F.D.R.'s voting strength—with the important exception of the South—tended to be those least likely to understand or care about his foreign policy.

F.D.R., like a majority of American Eastern Ivy League-trained individuals from the upper economic class, was instinctively anglophile. He shared attitudes noted again and again by American sociologists: cultural anglophilia (which had nothing to do with approval or disapproval of British power or politics) and a strong tendency to relate America directly to Great Britain and Western Europe in its place in the world society. These attitudes pervaded most American white Anglo-Saxon Protestants, or WASPS, but were strongest in the East.

But the ethnic cores of most large American cities were neither WASP nor culturally anglophile. Americans of Polish,

Italian, Greek, or Eastern European ancestry, as well as Germans and Scandinavians who were prominent in the Middle West, felt no particular sense of crisis at the imminent fall of England. If anything, they were historically anti-British, as were even Americans of British descent who had been several generations in the American interior. Their Americanism, at this time, was expressed most fervently by isolationism from all the furor abroad.

Most Democratic politicians advising F.D.R. conceded that Americans of non-British background in the big cities, and the lower-income groups generally, were those most opposed to the idea of getting in the war. Even the American labor movement, somewhat like the labor groups in England, tended to have an anti-foreign outlook. None of these people really cared for F.D.R.'s emerging foreign policy or shared his concern to aid England. They lacked both the emotional urge and the strategic vision required.

But here, in one of the oddest turns of the campaign, Roosevelt's opponent deliberately failed to capitalize on a Democratic weakness.

The Republican candidate, Wendell Willkie, could call on that 40 percent of the electorate who were almost hereditary Republicans. It was not enough. Probably, Willkie's only chance of election would have been to attack F.D.R.'s foreign policy, and to take a strong isolationist and peace line. This feeling was so strong that the platforms of both parties emerged isolationist, or at least noninterventionist.

But ironically, Willkie was in almost complete agreement with Roosevelt on foreign affairs. It was significant that the German embassy reported to Berlin that if Willkie were elected, no change in direction should be anticipated. Aid to Britain "short of war" would continue.

The draft was an explosive issue in the summer of 1940. But Willkie came out for it, and damped it as an issue. Willkie was for massive assistance to Great Britain. He concurred with the destroyer deal in September 1940. He was for rearmament. He refused to attack F.D.R. on any foreign issues, and based his whole campaign in an area where he was already defeated —the domestic economy. He irritated many powerful men in his own party, particularly in the isolationist Middle West, which had become the Republican ideological heartland. Privately and publicly they criticized him for continually saying, "Me, too!"

But there is no question, his own beliefs aside, that Wendell Willkie put unity of the nation and a certain patriotism first. He honestly did not think it wise, or in the American interest, to drive a wedge between the people on the really explosive issue of peace or war. While this did him damage among those who sincerely wanted to divide the public, ironically it did him no good with those who supported F.D.R.'s ideas. Roosevelt was on record against the Axis, and it was a record he could reiterate from a better platform as President than Willkie had as an aspirant to office.

The newspapers which reported that the Axis wanted F.D.R. defeated did not state the truth. Herbert Matthews wrote from Rome that the Axis hated Roosevelt, which was the truth. But neither the Germans nor Italians saw any hope in Willkie, and said so. F.D.R., however, with keen political sense, took up the idea that the fascists wanted him out. Henry Wallace, the Vice Presidential candiate whom F.D.R. had chosen to replace Jack Garner, stated it again and again from the stump with good effect.

If Willkie, who was of distant German descent, had chosen to pitch an isolationist, anti-war, and anti-draft argument at the Middle West and at the big-city groups least keen on aiding Englishmen, he still might not have become President. But he would have stirred up issues that might have effectively tied F.D.R.'s hands when reelected. He might have created the atmosphere in America that Axis observers hoped might come about, in which the United States washed its hands of European entanglements and withdrew. But Willkie was too good an American for that.

Instead, he seemed to set out to divest himself of all political glamor, and to represent himself as a simple Hoosier who had made good. He stood outside factories, and pitched arguments at men who had already, instinctively, made up their minds. He argued intervention, or at least responsibility and aid, to unresponsive audiencies in Iowa. His arguments, both nationally and internationally, impressed millions of people, but they did not move the masses Willkie had to move to win.

A humble man in a battered hat had no chance against the "changeable, charming, warm-hearted" President, who was not only one of the most glamorous figures, but the most careful and skilled politician of the century.

Roosevelt's only serious problem during the campaign was to convince the public that he would not lead the United States deliberately into war, and that he would not permit rearmament to wipe out the social and economic gains of the New Deal. He did both effectively. But if many people read isolationism into his promises to stay removed from the shooting, this was a matter of those being deceived who wanted to be deceived.

The image of a bold, heroic, morally superior, and neutral United States was an absurd one, as a series of Hearst paper cartoons tried to point out. It was an absurdity that both candidates had to pay lip service to, and Roosevelt did not feel he could attack it directly. But neither Roosevelt nor Willkie was prepared to sell the destiny of the nation short, just because people wanted him to do so.

Senator Carter Glass of Virginia said:

> ... A nation without spirit or an elevated soul is as bad as a derelict on the seas ... this country should not be content simply to eat and sleep and go to the movies. That would be a sorry contribution to modern civilization.

But in 1940 the United States showed no real signs of moral superiority over the fascist nations. Roosevelt faced a people who basically *wanted* only to eat and sleep and go to the movies and be left alone. He faced the same kind of electorate that in Great Britain, through the 1930's, had consistently refused to sacrifice for the future or destiny of the nation. As John F. Kennedy, the future President, wrote in his senior thesis at Harvard in 1940, in the years of decision English labor was sullenly unwilling to sacrifice anything for national defense, English business and industry determined not to finance rearmament, and the ruling circles determined to avoid anything unpopular.

One of the theoretical arguments of fascism, which had some appeal, was that totalitarianism avoided this kind of impasse. In the confused and bitter summer of 1940, more than one decent American, from Sunday schools to beer halls, said gloomily that the United States *needed* a dictator.

It was an era of some doubt about the efficiency of democracy as a form of social organization. This was natural because the democracies had so far made a poor showing under non-democratic pressure. There was not only not much optimism for the future, but a certain depression that the current war, even in America, would end the world as men knew it. All this led to ostrich-like attitudes. The image of the United States abroad was one of gloom, hesitancy, and non-commitment, but oddly coupled with a stubborn attitude of moral superiority that most foreigners found difficult to understand.

If Willkie was trying to run a campaign "above politics" the United States as a nation appeared to be trying to behave during a vast struggle for control of the world as if it were "above" power struggles.

But normally only politicians win elections, and only power wins power struggles.

In retrospect, the people of the United States, and certainly Franklin Roosevelt, its leader, confused cause and effect. The nation wanted a leader; the leader wanted a nation willing to follow before he led. Both were seeking a sense of high purpose to give them the morale for a long and difficult pull.

Roosevelt did preach high purpose, and hinted at high goals, but each time came back full circle to a promise of prosperity while all crusades were being waged.

But actually, in a seeming public apathy while the nation was eating well and attending movies, a vital reorganization had begun. A sense of purpose and firm action had come to Washington, if not in policy, certainly in procurement.

In 1939 the first "dollar-a-year men"—executives who worked for the government without salary—had appeared in Washington; Secretary Morgenthau had hired several at the Treasury. But it was not until the summer of 1940, when a huge defense budget was assured, that the influx of capable managerial talent began.

Many of the first key appointments went to the Departments of War and Navy, where new blood was badly needed. The world had changed, but most Washington agencies were still staffed with men who had come to the capital in 1933. They had been bright and eager then, ready to tear up and change the world. By 1940 too many of them were aging and tired.

The type of man Roosevelt had attracted to Washington to serve in government tended to be like F.D.R. himself—more a planner than a doer, more a theoretician than an executive. Roosevelt himself had never been a good executive in the traditional mold, certainly not a manager. Within his own Administration he left a series of overlapping jurisdictions, and hated to form any real chain of command. He himself was boss, and there was never any doubt of that. But all other agencies and executives of the Executive Branch were grouped around Roosevelt—there was rarely any linear command.

One reason for this situation was that F.D.R. enjoyed the jockeying—for power and position and his ear—and the jurisdictional squabbles this system inevitably produced. There were famous feuds within the Cabinet, some of which were well publicized. F.D.R. was perfectly content to let all these go on. Another reason there was no chain of command was that Roosevelt, who had the power to hire, hated to relinquish the power to fire, even in the middle echelons of government. No Cabinet officer, or Under- or Assistant Secretary, who did not have the actual power to fire anyone under him, could act as a true executive at all. Yet Roosevelt on more than one occasion prevented exactly this. He hated to delegate real authority, he liked to run things himself.

He was a master in the fields of political strategy, and he was a keen naval strategist and historian who could see with worried perception the issues at stake in the control of the Atlantic. But he was not familiar with the technical fields of industry and industrial production.

F.D.R. had never been a businessman, or a production executive, and actually such matters bored him. He loved to plan, and he more than not often knew a good plan when he saw it. He was known to speak favorably of certain issues— such as an economic reorganization of the United States in the 1930's, or Morgenthau's concept of an agricultural Germany later—that made his capable aides' hair stand on end. But usually Roosevelt could pick and choose, from all the programs, good or idiotic, that might be laid before him. However, with such instincts and tastes, F.D.R. always preferred advisors around him, rarely administrators. He never showed that he liked managers or executives, or the executive mind.

Yet even Roosevelt, by 1940, understood that American production—with the United States in the war or out of it— had become the key to the world's future. Britain was almost wholly dependent upon American heavy industry to provide it the tools of war; Britain alone could not outproduce Hitler's conquered continent. The Axis enjoyed an overwhelming preponderance of arms. Only the United States could change that balance. World War II, come what might, was going to be a production war.

What was needed, by July 1940, was a government organized to expedite production. Washington newspapers called for a breed of "new managers" to take over and win the production war. Fortunately, such a breed was available from American industry. These men arrived at a time when national defense forced incisive changes in the whole organization of government. This, in turn, would change the whole posture of the nation.

Roosevelt, whose most telling political blows had been denunciations of "economic royalists" and "intrenched greed" in the depression years, was now forced to extend a sweet reasonableness toward an American industrial machine he had never particularly liked, because it was indispensable for American world power. He had to seek out and conciliate business leaders, and above all, production men. He needed General Motors and Du Pont for the same reasons Hitler needed Krupp.

The New Deal denigration of industry and business as organized in America ended sharply in the swing toward armament. So long as armament continued, the pendulum was not likely to swing back again. Without industry there could be no effective armament. Politicians, in the White House or in Congress, could lay plans, plot national strategy, or strive for consensus, but they could not make guns.

Oddly enough, the very element of American society— business—that tended to be most opposed to Roosevelt's domestic programs was heavily inclined to favor his foreign policy. Every *Fortune* poll, which was heavily weighted with business and production leaders, showed that these groups were approximately twice as interventionist or world-minded as the nation as a whole. There were a number of reasons, in which education, regionalism, and culture played a part. No part of America was more identified, in its own mind, with Britain than the American Eastern upper industrial class. The Middle Atlantic and New England universities, which provided a disproportionate share of economic leaders, had long been pervasively anglophile and world-seeing.

The pulse center of American industry in the early 1940's was still New York. This was the financial and directional center, if not the actual place where the goods were made. And New York was the most interventionist—though not the most warlike—city in the country, just as Chicago was the most unenthusiastic about the war.

It was not only patriotism that was strong in all the upper economic classes, but a sense of concurrent purpose that brought acceptance from almost every man asked to serve in Washington.

By July, 1940, there were more than five hundred "dollar-a-year" men in the capital. Between then and April, 1941, more than seventy thousand were added to new war bureaus. Democracy, as a system, showed that its people possessed a bill of responsibilities along with their Bill of Rights.

What was begun, in 1940, was an American organizational and production miracle that had vast implications not just for the country, but for the world. Of all the nations in World War II, only America did not have to choose between guns and butter. It produced both.

None of this occurred without controversy, friction, and considerable criticism from the press. Some of Roosevelt's closest associates were never able to adjust their views to the times; others continued to distrust F.D.R.'s businessmen. When Roosevelt, who did not really like most big businessmen, had to turn to them for arms management, this forced some of his early New Deal associates down or out. In the end, good sense prevailed, however, and a sort of middle group assumed control.

The new "dollar-a-year" men were interested in production. Few of them held any theory about government or anything

116

else. When they managed business, they sought profits, logically, and not a theoretical "good" of the nation which could not be defined. Few of them cared for social gains, the theory of progressive taxation, or the status of the common man. They were concerned with making things for war, and getting them to the battlefields on time. In the end, their timetable conquered Hitler's.

The emerging group, as *The New York Times* remarked, looked more and more like a WHO'S WHO of Commerce and Industry as time went by. They set a pattern which was to last for many years; the key jobs in defense went to men who understood management and production.

The patriotism of these men who served under Knudsen and Hillman and Nelson in the early days has been well praised. Their capabilities, and results, could not be praised enough. A great deal of it was even taken for granted, as part of the normal American way.

There were continuing problems in organization, at first. Roosevelt was reluctant to appoint a real production czar, or give anyone outside of politics the powers Bernard Baruch had had in World War I. There was agitation in the press that this be done. But Donald M. Nelson, who eventually headed the Division of Purchases, Office of Production Management, understood that Baruch's enormous powers had never been really used in 1917-1918. Baruch had not needed them, and again in 1940-1941 the production chain of command in Washington found that the twin tools of patriotism and publicity were enough.

The old World War I powers were still on the United States statute books. The government could: 1. compel any producer to sell his output to the government; 2. make any manufacturer work for the government, and even reorganize, if required, to do so. To this a new power was added in 1940: the government was authorized to seize any plant and run it in the name of national defense. But these standby powers, with their enormous invasions of private property rights, were never really required. Phone calls usually did the job.

The original planning group for defense production in Washington was set up on May 28, 1940, as the National Defense Advisory Council, or N.D.A.C. The Council was headed by William Knudsen, head of General Motors, which began another American tradition. It took N.D.A.C. only twenty days to organize, which was incredible progress.

The Council shook down with a chain of command as follows: Donald M. Nelson, Executive Vice President of Sears, Roebuck, coordinator; Edward R. Stettinius, head of U.S. Steel, on raw materials; Sidney Hillman, chief of the Amalgamated Clothing Workers Union, labor; Chester Davis, agriculture; Ralph Budd, President of the Burlington lines, transportation. Leon Henderson, who was the one theoretician of the lot, watched prices.

The N.D.A.C. took only a hundred days to let more than ten billions in new war contracts. At a time when there was no precedent or procedure for this in recent memory, the progress was fantastic. All procurement contract logjams—legal delays, unsettled questions on taxes, profits, prices, labor, industrial reluctance, and sheer lack of knowledge of what to order—were broken almost by an effort of will. Six billion dollars in orders went out at one time, for rifles, planes, ships, and the new medium tanks of which the United States Army had none.

Expertize, experience, and equally important, liaison with their own kind and own world payed off. This liaison—this phone-call communication—got things done in a way existing government bureaus and Congressional committees could not. At the same time, veteran government civil servants, career men whose tenure went back to Hoover's or Wilson's time, such as William McReynolds, steered businessmen clear of the intricacies of Washington political and bureaucratic booby traps.

118

This new money, created by government credit and sent into the economy with rapid velocity, opened factories, piled up orders for materials and goods, and put men to work. It ended the Depression, which in spite of every other palliative, still lingered on—there were almost as many unemployed in 1939 as there had been in 1934.

This itself created new problems, long before N.D.A.C. was formalized into the Office of Production Management.

One was monopoly, with United States business linked together and cooperating, though on a national purpose, as never before. Giant industrial concerns, to expedite things, were making plans and deals and backroom agreements, which were suspect, if not always illegal, under the United States antitrust or collusion laws. When N.D.A.C. and its successor O.P.M. began to tie industry-wide deals together, trustbuster Thurman Arnold began to object at the White House.

Arnold was overruled. O.P.M. moves, no matter what kind of monopoly they seemed to create, were not to be prosecuted under the Sherman or Clayton Acts. Ironically, United States defense required some monopoly to avoid a duplication of effort, though the word itself remained anathema in Washington. The new monopolies—which were given a great thrust by the war—were called the products of "planning and priorities." Industry was, after all, plotting not against Arnold but against Hitler.

Under the impact of new credit money, prices began to rise. This was an inevitable facet of the industrial marketplace. The first moves to counteract this inflation were erratic, and even informal. Steel prices rose, then steadied, when the steel industry was threatened by the Administration with an anti-Big Steel publicity campaign. Sugar became scarce. Under his Presidential powers, F.D.R. raised the Cuban quota. This action not only made sugar more plentiful, it dropped the bottom out of the domestic price.

Raw copper prices moved upward, but when commodity

costs began to soar, Roosevelt halted them temporarily with public warnings. The President could not, however, completely arrest the pressures on prices.

F.D.R.'s public pronouncements about "holding the price line" in 1940 and 1941 always had an element of hypocrisy which was fully realized in government circles. In every emergency that put pressure on resources there was upward pressure on prices, which could not be held back except by the most stringent controls. One item could not be controlled without controlling virtually all items, and no price control could be effective without control of the source of supply. The President's actions, therefore, were more for public consumption than taken in real hope the economy could be kept free from inflation. Warnings put restraint upon industry, and also convinced the people who might be hurt that the President cared.

But for a Democratic—or, probably, any—Administration, coming out of a long depression, to deflate a rising boom was almost psychologically impossible. Any tightening of money, credit, or a substantial increase in taxes—all effective deflationary moves—were politically unpalatable. They created temporary unemployment in many areas. Inflation and employment tended to go hand in hand in America; they were too closely linked to permit the damping of one without some adverse effect on the other.

This fact was decisive, in price control, for an Administration whose principal political support came not from people holding cash assets or money but who worked for wages. Rising prices and depreciating money hurt—but full pay envelopes and increased orders were pleasant, too. Furthermore, the public and business would not willingly accept peacetime controls. The rising inflation was denounced from Washington, but, in effect, it was accepted.

N.D.A.C. did open an office for price control, called at first O.P.A.C.S., finally O.P.A. Leon Henderson, the administrator, tried to offset the effects of the extra government billions being dumped on the economy. He secured an agreement from chemical producers and from the wood-pulp industry not to raise prices through forward buying. But industries, which anticipated a continuing defense program, with continuing pressure on commodities, production facilities, prices, and labor, simply could not stop "buying forward." Inflationary or boom periods create their own psychology.

Voluntary agreements did not work well, but O.P.A., like virtually every eventual wartime bureau, was set up and primed a considerable interval before Pearl Harbor. Long before it was noticed by the public, Washington was effectively planning and organizing for actual war.

The question of war-production profits was a thorny one. While it was generally held that higher wages paid to workers in defense factories were good, there was a prevailing prejudice against manufacturers becoming rich at public expense. Industry was not eager to build new capacity—for which no peacetime need was foreseen—without a tax write-off. The Treasury, on the other hand, was not eager to let them finance a vast new building program out of war profits, with favorable write-offs, which meant that the government would be subsidizing private industry with public money. The depreciation and write-off question was compromised so that both sides could live with it and their consciences, but the question of "excess" profits and how they should be taxed remained.

The original idea in the Administration was that there should be no "excess profits" at all—which was interpreted to mean that no American industry should profit in any way from orders for defense or war production. Such orders were to be considered in "excess" of regular civilian production, and to one school of government theoreticians it seemed both sound and eminently patriotic not to allow anyone to profit from national defense. But appealing as the notion was to many people, it was obviously unworkable in practice. It was no way to secure wholehearted cooperation from United States industry, which was governed by the profit motive, and whose cooperation was imperative for any viable production program.

Defense orders, it soon became obvious, would completely engage the facilities of some plants, and these would be penalized severely—while less patriotic industrialists merely refused to handle government orders. Clearly industry had a right to a reasonable profit somewhere along the line. No one, for example, suggested that workers in defense plants should get no pay on Friday.

Yet this question held up Congressional action, and therefore actual defense production, for many weeks. A workable, but not entirely satisfactory, system was finally agreed upon between government and industry. There was to be a severe excess-profits tax—the tax based on profits exceeding earnings in "normal" years—but the 1940 compromise stated that there were to be no special taxes on any production once the defense needs were met.

In actual practice, then and later, during the war, most company records showed that defense production was never so profitable as regular civilian production. Many new industries grew up, merely to satisfy government needs, but in the older, established ones, a certain sourness toward government contracts lingered on.

With the Administration calling for both guns and butter (which had Henry Morgenthau of the Treasury and Marriner Eccles of the Federal Reserve System at odds) and F.D.R. promising to retain the forty-hour week, no sweat, no tears, and no profits, only a remarkable amount of good sense on the part of everyone kept the production miracle going.

Henry Morgenthau, who would never be given sufficient credit for his vision in seeing the coming war and preparing the United States Treasury to finance it, went to Congress with a number of important financial concepts for fiscal 1941:

1. Revenues should provide a reasonable proportion of the new defense expenditures, which meant raising taxes. Neither Morgenthau nor the President ever suggested that the defense effort should be pay-as-you-go; this kind of discipline was considered politically unfeasible.

2. A fair share of the burden should be spread over the entire public.

3. The tax structure should be planned to aid mobilization by reducing the amount of cash available to the private sector of the economy. This would keep commodities from being diverted to private consumption and dampen inflation.

In 1940 middle income Americans paid very little in taxes, and low income families paid none.

It was already anticipated that the eleven billion dollars authorized for 1940, and already spent, would be followed by an equal amount in 1941, and even more in 1942. By 1942 the Treasury was planning on being on a full mobilization or war footing. Withholding taxes—something new and revolutionary—went into the planning stage in early 1941.

None of this was immediately popular, yet it was not really vulnerable to attack. The same dominant public opinion that refused to face getting in the war still insisted on spending "everything necessary" to arm the country for defense. Defense was the most popular, and noncontroversial issue to come along in years.

To finance the defense program—it was carefully never called a "war program"—Morgenthau and his swarm of assistants proposed unprecedented taxes on the private sector. Ironically, while these new taxes were described as "severe and heavy" and the press concurred, they were lighter and lower than the American taxpayer would probably ever see again. As *Fortune* magazine and *The New York Times* put it, an economic revolution, based not on the New Deal but armaments, had begun. It would not and could not end until the

United States ended its newly aroused awareness toward the world.

The new taxes raised the corporate levy from 24 percent to 30 percent, with a 50 percent excess profits tax on anything over an arbitrary "normal year" base.

Typical Federal excises went to $.08 on cigarettes, $4 per gallon on liquor, $.025 on gasoline, and 5 percent on transportation.

Personal income taxes on an adjusted gross income (net income after deductions) of $10,000 for a couple with no children in 1941 were raised to a total of $528, with a tax of $1628 proposed for 1942. This was not a middle-, but a high-income bracket in the early 1940's.

The rich would not fare nearly so well: a hypothetical $5,000,000 income, of which there were none around, would pay almost $4,000,000 in Federal tax. But a couple with an income of $2500, which was an excellent middle-class salary in those years, paid only $11. This would later be lifted to $72.

The lower-income brackets, in years when $125 per month was an average worker's pay, were not to be asked to pay any Federal tax at all.

These taxes, of course, were raised subsequently. But the theory and practice of taxation for the war had been set by 1940-1941. The revenues asked by government did not, because the measures were halfway, strain excessive private purchasing power from the economy, because most "high velocity" or spendable money was in the lower brackets. Nor did they even begin to finance the cost of arms. The result was an eventual price inflation, and an enormously swollen national debt, which the Treasury handled and kept going with admittedly immense skill.

This debt management, and the adroit expansion of public credit to unheard-of sums, was one of the amazing phenomena of the economic revolution. It presaged a whole new era in American public finance, but it also created problems of inflation and money management that would still remain unsolved twenty-five years later, when the nation was to face similar defense production crises.

One salient fact of the new era was soon noticeable: while the government called upon citizenry to sacrifice and cut back and eschew profits, not one single government agency showed itself willing to retrench or sacrifice anything at all to the new state of national affairs. In 1940-1941 when the basic tax rate rose from 2.2 percent to 6.6 percent and lowered exemptions for individual citizens, every government agency in Washington asked for more, not less money. Some real distortions arose, because it now proved virtually impossible to curtail various Depression-years projects, in human terms. Farm prices began to rise steeply, but farm price supports required as much, or even more, money than before. The Depression finally sputtered out, by 1941, with the vast industrial production for defense—but federal relief was continued at the immense rate of one hundred million dollars per month. Rising employment seemed to have no effect on the public dole, except to increase it as prices rose. Here again a certain pattern was set, one that was to cause lasting social effects and severe strain in coming decades.

Cleverly, each government bureau seeking money now labeled its rising expenditures "for defense" or in the interests of national defense. Existing programs were quickly reclassified as "defense" programs, with keen psychological if little fiscal, sense. Money for the Federal Fish and Wildlife Service even carried a defense label. It was to be a lasting fad.

There was another factor to the defense revolution. Labor troubles had naturally been endemic all during the years of economic crisis—but in times of limited employment, when jobs were scarce, organized labor had not really been able to gain maximum benefit from the New Deal legislation favoring it. Just as armament production necessarily produced a fiscal, financial, and governmental revolution in American processes,

125

it created a sort of labor revolution, too. As most economists recognize, organized labor cannot exercise its full potential power except when business is good—customers are crying for orders—and the labor supply is relatively tight. But when these two factors of good business and tight labor are present, as in 1940-1941 and again in 1966-1967, labor leadership is able to flex its muscles, and with or without government sympathy, get almost anything it desires.

In 1941 a large number of major industries were still not unionized. Ford and Bethlehem Steel were prime examples None of them, however, were to survive rearmament without succumbing to unionism.

The nationwide rash of strikes that broke out in 1940 and intensified in 1941 was partly due to the age-old factors of supply and demand, and collective bargaining between employer and employee. Some were for logical things for the here and now, such as higher wages. But the strikes that began to cripple defense production were caused by another factor as well: a labor movement drive to enhance labor's overall position, and secure all gains, before peace set back the whole economy, and all heavy production. Almost everyone—economist and union man alike—believed a severe deflation would follow the war inflation, as it always had historically.

The union drive to end depression wages in 1940 was generally successful. There was no reason for it not to be; logic was on labor's side. Employers, with more orders than they could handle, and assured of profits, went along. Labor, like raw copper, was in sudden new demand, and the prices for both spiralled. But the strikes that began in late 1940 took a different, jurisdictional tone. Some were still for wages, from appetites whetted by early success. The worst ones, which stalled essential production in industries like motors and Big Steel, were instigated to consolidate union power.

The A.F.L. and C.I.O. staged bitter feuds for new unions in new plants, resulting in new work grinding to a halt. Immense pressures were put on industries, such as Ford, which still refused to recognize a national union. 1941 was to be a bad year for labor peace.

There was not, however, much evidence of something continually claimed by employers, and repeatedly charged in the press—that the organized Communist movement was responsible. The Communist line, until June 1941, was strongly against American rearmament or defense, but the Communist influence in certain unions aided, but was not the salient factor, behind the persistent strikes.

The labor drives were generally successful, although they inflamed public opinion almost to the flash point. Rearmament, not the New Deal, gave unionism its final weapon in the war for recognition. Pressures came on industry from both below and from N. D. A. C. in Washington; Knudsen asked his colleagues to yield here and there to break the logjam. The union position was solidified at last in all heavy industry; and with this new position, and with the new demands for defense production, a new revolution in the position of the skilled worker in America was underway. By 1944—when there was a general stabilization once again—the blue-collar worker would have generally surpassed the white-collar worker who was not unionized and whose services were not so obviously and strategically geared for war in almost every economic respect.

The problem of labor disputes was never entirely settled, of course. In a democracy, and in a society like America, they could not be, even during the war.

The sum of all the profound changes in industry, government, finance and labor, which changed society itself, was not quickly recognized in 1940. It was not to be fully recognized or admitted even after the coming war. One reason was that the fact that America had solved its economic cycle as Hitler had—by rearmament—was never really palatable with the groups most inclined to favor the actual social gains.

President Roosevelt, as the national leader, faced severe domestic problems in 1940-1941. These included getting tough with labor, sometimes demanded in the national interest when labor, in its own genuine interest, struck plants that could not be allowed to be struck. They included raising taxes to finance a vast defense. They included the ordaining of sacrifices for every segment of the economy and the public, including government itself. In all of these F.D.R. chose to steer a middle course. He argued and persuaded for American sacrifice, and he hinted it was necessary. He was very slow to demand it, or to implement it into law.

He tried to do nothing that might injure the nation or its historic interests, but he also tried to do nothing that could cost him liberal support.

There was extensive criticism of his budgets in the press, primarily because they failed to cut out non-defense expenditures.

Where is the sacrifice? trumpeted *The Washington Post.* The Republican *New York Herald Tribune* took the same line. Even *The New York Times* editorialized that Roosevelt's calls for spending and failure to mobilize the economy were "totally unimpressive."

The seven billion dollars earmarked for regular New Deal spending and relief measures stuck in all conservatives' throats. Schedules for the W.P.A.—make-work projects begun during the worst of the Depression—still called for one million six hundred thousand men to be on the rolls for 1941. One billion dollars was to be spent for work relief and poverty projects. F.D.R. resisted all pressures against these. His theory and practice was that, bad times or good, the government would have to employ a great many "otherwise unemployable" human beings, who not only had real needs but had volatile votes as well.

His chief critic in all these years—a generally unsuccessful critic—was Virginia's Senator Harry Byrd.

128

The great hope expressed in Washington was to have "only four million unemployed by the end of 1941."

That goal, of course, was met, though not in the precise way Washington planners envisioned. But the reduction of unemployment to about four million (in the 1940's a far greater numerical ratio than it would be later, due to the rising population) would not and could not solve the problem of specific areas of poverty in America, though no government bureau was willing to admit as much.

Through all this ferment of change, and historic process of altering the American industrial machine, Roosevelt felt he knew what he was doing as President. He felt it absolutely imperative that the standard of living of the poorer groups not be cut, war or no war, inflation or no inflation.

It had already become a fixed idea in Washington that price inflation was always preferable to a rise in unemployment, and with a growing federal debt, some inflation was actually beneficial to the government. In the Revolutionary War, the Continental Congress had, in effect, financed the whole war via a violent monetary inflation through the issuance of paper currency. No one advocated issuing "Continentals" again—but the depreciating paper of 1776 had the salutary effect of forcing the Revolutionary generation to bear the whole monetary cost of that war, and to erase the public debt at its end, through repudiation. Roosevelt's problem was two-fold: he had to finance defense without cutting into the standard of living of his voters, but at the same time devise sound means of maintaining the currency and credit, the destruction of which also almost ruined the fledgling American Confederation in the 1770's. In other words, F.D.R. had to be able to afford both a war against poverty at home, and a war against alien philosophy abroad.

The rapid buildup for American defense was expensive and overall, wasteful. Projects were started before contracts were even let, and red tape was cut with verbal orders. There was a certain amount of graft. There was much more confusion and sheer waste, inevitable in starting into motion a machine the almost unimaginable size of America's industrial plant.

The planning and coordination of defense production was a job beyond any one man's comprehension. No single individual could have solved it, and in the end, only an integrated, cooperating, skilled, and highly disciplined society—from Washington coordinator to Detroit industrialist to California aircraft worker—did. Because a practical and patriotic attitude was taken by all, America could also afford the initial waste. The strikes, shortages, confusion, indecision in Washington, and delay—all hysterically reported in the press—and the interminable carping in Congress, were always more apparent than real. Things got done.

Modern war had become peculiarly a production war. Production, as nation after nation found, was more decisive on the battlefield than former élan. Hindenburg, at the end of World War I, summed up American production and American producers in one phrase: *They understood war.* None of this was very romantic, or intellectual, or had much to do with world strategic planning or moral theory. The fact that American production by 1941 was the dominant factor in World War II, but was never really given its due by all the American people, was because businessmen and blue-collar workers make machines, but intellectuals and moralists and romantics write the books most men read.

The defense proposals and acts passed by government in 1940, 1941 and even later, never approached the severity and total mobilization of those of World War I—which were aborted by an early Armistice. The difference was that World War I was begun in an era of vast, popular emotional support. World War II was not. A defensive war was run under different rules from a popular crusade.

One newspaper summed up the world of 1940, as probably most Americans were beginning to see it: *Headaches, heartaches, bankruptcy, and a new, but probably not better world.*

130

9.

Buying Yesterday

Immunity from invasion can be accomplished within the price range of the taxpayers, by an expenditure not greater than the average cost of the army during the ten years preceding the depression. Major General J. Hagood, 1937.

An army or navy is a tool for the protection of misguided, inefficient, destructive Wall Street. Henry Ford.

America will not rearm. America talks in a loud voice but acts very slowly. Luigi Barzini, Italian Senator, 1940.

Our defenses must be invulnerable, our security absolute. President Roosevelt, May 16, 1940.

The new defense program . . . calls for new ways of military thinking, new developments in American war doctrine. Hanson Baldwin, 1940.

Dollars cannot buy yesterday. Admiral Harold R. Stark, Chief of Naval Operations, 1940.

Although it was not recognized or admitted to any great extent, American military doctrine in the 1930's showed a remarkable resemblance to British doctrine. Both were insular, isolationist, and defensive in nature, predicated upon a withdrawal from the actual power balance of the world. The British contem-

131

plated empire defense; the United States considered only hemisphere defense. Both strategies put reliance upon strong navies, and made the sea arm the primary means of defense. Both philosophies took into account geography and international law.

The British and United States navies were on a par, co-leaders in the world. Anglo-American naval power, in fact, was and was intended to be dominant. The British guarded the Atlantic, while the huge United States fleet was built for the specific task of overawing Japan. Neither power had a true "two-ocean" navy, however. Out of long cooperation, the British counted on United States naval units to guard the back door of the Pacific, while it had long ceased to occur to American planners, by the 1930's, that a British fleet would not always bar the eastern approaches to the hemisphere.

Both the British and United States army and air forces were denigrated by this defense doctrine. The army was assigned quite limited tasks: the guarding of installations, coast defense, and at most, responsibility for small expeditionary forces to make limited landings abroad. The air forces were permitted no strategic role at all. In Britain they were allowed the vital one of island air defense, for which the R.A.F. planned with superb success. The United States, mesmerized by its wide oceans, did not even go this far.

But by 1940 both defense doctrines were not only in crisis, they had been proven utterly fallible. Neither geography nor international law any longer provided adequate security. Strong navies were still needed, but balanced sea, land, and air forces were even more urgently required.

As one American planner said, eyeing the Luftwaffe's immense expansion: "Give Hitler the air bases, and he can conquer the world."

In 1940, the British saw their hoped-for deliverance by the French Army vanish and for the first time began to build land forces in earnest. In the same way, United States military strat-

132

egists suddenly had to stop relying on the notion that Britannia would always rule the Atlantic.

For the first time, both nations suddenly realized the immense importance of control of the air, not only over their homelands but over any future battlefield. The agony of France had proved the decisiveness of air power on the modern battleground.

All the democracies had fallen far behind in the quantitative and qualitative technics of war through the 1930's. Anglo-American-French military hegemony had actually disappeared by 1935; from this point on the Axis powers, even without the Soviet Union, were superior. Part of this falling behind was due to a mistaken world view and reliance upon an international law that did not exist, but much of it was also due to the fact that all three democratic states tried to hold down spending for defense.

French, American, and British strategists, in making their plans public, always stressed the importance of cost effectiveness, and were always constrained to argue that defense must be accomplished at the lowest possible expense. Thus a terrible inconsistency was built into all democratic war plans; in war, as in almost everything else, a nation gets exactly what it pays for. In the 1930's despite much theorizing, there were no short-cuts to adequate defense.

In contrast, all the totalitarian powers considered their expenditures in arms as investments, from which they expected to secure great gains. And all secured material success with this policy, even before they went to total war. Before 1935 France and England refused all revision to territories and treaties. As soon as Italy and Germany showed they were armed, the long Allied retreat and policy of appeasement began.

Between 1934 and 1938 the German state increased its military budgets 1400 percent. France increased its hardly a fraction of 1 percent. This petit-bourgeois, penny-pinching attitude of national investment cost France the greatest sum of all: defeat on the battlefield. Nothing could have been more expensive to France than that.

The American attitude was hardly any different from the French. The thing that saved America in the 1940's was not the oceans, but the shock of the Anglo-French experience. Three facts emerged in 1940 that changed the United States armed forces' entire stance:

1. Modern war required greater quantities of arms than any Allied planner had even dared estimate, let alone ask for. In 1939 France and Britain estimated the war could be fought with not more than two thousand warplanes, and French aircraft production was scheduled at only two hundred per month. By 1940 everyone knew the war was going to require many thousands of planes. The same inflation of estimate applied to guns, tanks, trucks, warships, and the whole paraphernalia of war.

2. The emergence of global strategy, on the part of the Axis, added new dimensions to the war. Axis troops fought in Africa, laid plans to conquer the Near East, and Japan was being brought into the alliance, which would extend the potential theater of war across the Pacific and Far East. Because of increased technology, which made light of vast distances, and a German leap from European to world power, the old, limited, insular pattern of defense was shown as inadequate. Britain was being forced to fight across the world, not just in Europe. It was seen that America might have to fight abroad, in South America or elsewhere.

3. The dynamic quality of Axis thinking—the continual, almost reflex expansion of German arms over land areas, together with the building of large air and sea armadas, plus the psychology to attack when ready—eroded the former democratic notions of passive defense. Economic warfare had always ranked high in Anglo-American thinking, with the feeling the Germans could be brought down by blockade and

economic sanctions. But the Germans showed no intention of letting themselves be worn down. They planned to overrun the world first.

It was these three major considerations that led the United States government to plan a hugely increased war machine in 1940. Significantly, though this rearmament and mobilization was always presented to the people as for the defense of the hemisphere, United States strategic planning was never so limited.

The Army did not plan and prepare ground forces to stand off a landing operation by the Axis—it began to prepare a large, mobile expeditionary force, for use anywhere in the world. For George Marshall, the Chief of Staff, and his close associates in the War Department, the further the final defense of America began from America's shores, the better.

Further, the newly created, virtually independent staff of the Army Air Corps did not consider seriously an R.A.F.-type defense network for North America. It began to put its faith, and its funds, in tactical aircraft to support expeditionary forces, and above all, into strategic bombers.

The Navy faced no such doctrinal crisis, except in the field of naval air power. The Navy needed expansion, and it got it —a 70 percent increase voted in 1940. The Navy had to consider defense of the Atlantic once the Battle of Britain began. The question of carriers or battleships caused much heat and smoke in naval and civilian circles—until it was finally seen that *air power over the sea was, in effect, naval* power, just as air power over land is land power, not some mythical realm of its own. The naval carrier replaced the naval battlewagon as the new ship of the line, but the battle was not won until carrier power found and sank the *Bismarck*.

The Navy, also, enlarged its vision to include the world. All of the American armed forces, in their planning staffs, recognized America's changed position in the world long before the public did, and their position was largely sold to

Roosevelt. Roosevelt concurred with the emerging staff views. He himself was a competent amateur naval historian; he readily grasped strategic concepts. He was aware that in the apparently coming Hitlerian world American security could only be assured by sound strategic positions and relationships of power. Significantly, his Congressional message of May 16, 1940 called for the first steps to assure that the United States would enjoy both superiority of arms and strategic position over the emerging Axis.

The arms could be designed by the military forces and built by American industry. But the strategic position that the United States manifestly had to hold was the British Isles. This had nothing whatever to do with the historic Anglo-American friendship. It was simply a matter of the fact that whatever power controlled the British Isles and blocked the North Sea and the Mediterranean at Gibraltar effectively blocked Hitler from dominating the Western Hemisphere. Regardless of what happened in Central Europe, or in the Middle East, so long as Hitler was barred from the British Isles he was restrained from actual control of the Atlantic.

This realization was by no means confined to the Cabinet or the American military staff. *"The most vital base of the Anglo-American sea power is the British Isles, on which the British fleet is based, and the critical region is the North Atlantic Ocean from Ireland to Dakar,"* Walter Lippmann wrote. He saw Britain as America's strategic frontier, although he was gloomy about the prospects of its defense. Roosevelt's government was in complete agreement with Lippmann's statement, although it tended to be more sanguine about the British holding on than Lippmann was in 1940. And on this concept was based almost all American defense strategy between May 1940 and December 1941—the time the newspapers had already started to call "the undeclared war."

There was, of course, the problem of an aggressive Japan, far across the Pacific. But Germany with most of the resources

136

of Europe to call upon, was already immeasurably stronger than an only partially industrialized Japan. Japan had a large fleet, but this was even in 1940 overmatched by the United States Navy. Therefore, the vital strategic interests of the United States lay in the Atlantic, no matter what Japan might do.

The United States had three possible strategic orientations to take. One was to withdraw and contemplate only the defense of its national territory. Another was to extend defense to the entire hemisphere. The final course was to wrap national security in a world view, and to accept defense of United States interests at the earliest point of engagement—even if this were ten thousand miles away.

In 1940, Roosevelt publicly rejected the first course; the public enthusiastically backed the second, though with some confused thinking about the manpower situation. The tradition of the Monroe Doctrine was strong, but a consistent policy of hemisphere defense was completely passive. It meant waiting, even in the face of a threat to security, until the hemisphere was attacked. It was only an expanded isolationism, and strategically made no sense. The Secretary of War argued in front of the House Foreign Affairs Committee that the defense of Great Britain was at least as important as a defense of Paraguay to the security of North America. Many of the gentlemen listening did not agree, but the Secretary's arguments showed that the Administration had already adopted the third course.

The rejection of this course emotionally by a majority of the American people, and its implementation—slowly and painfully, in the face of that opposition—marked what also became an undeclared war between the government and the public. When F.D.R., in what he considered America's interests, assigned current P-40 fighter plane production in 1940 to the British government and not to the United States Army Air Corps, he had to do so secretly.

The third strategy was, of course, one of expediency. It was also active; it did not stem from a territorial concept but a concept of meeting potential danger whenever and wherever it appeared, especially in the Atlantic. It naturally increased the chances of an *earlier* war; though to all the men who tried to implement it, it decreased the eventual American danger of defeat in that war.

This course was opposed by all those who opposed war for any reason; also those who could not think beyond the territorial conception of war. Some people rejected the idea of the United States' defending the British Isles or foreign territory with treasure and blood. They could not recognize the principle that by aiding Britain—even at the cost of war—the United States might be defending itself.

Territoriality had begun to have less and less meaning in the modern world. Technology, and the emergence of active "attack" totalitarian philosophies with a world view, had begun to make it obsolete.

Thus the changing military strategy for defense—and not an eagerness to mix in a great crusade against totalitarianism —changed the entire military posture of the United States, and altered its political posture as well. In 1940, while F.D.R. was not unaware of the logic of power relationships, it was not an "arrogant determination to use military power" or to involve the United States in an unwanted war, but the insistent and almost unanimous advice of his naval and military staffs that set the Administration down the path of extended involvement.

A rapidly changing and evolving military doctrine—which no longer accepted territorial isolation or passive defense as feasible—was transforming American world relationships as fast as it was changing the face of the American economy. The Roosevelt policy was thus a reaction policy, not one of initiative. The United States was more successful in the end than France or Britain, but not because its planners were any wiser. In fact, they made precisely the same mistakes. America, however, due to its geographic isolation, and the determination of the British nation, got two more years in which to digest the lessons of Poland, Norway, and France and, more important, to correct its recent errors.

Unfortunately, however, the same strategic blindness and war fear which pervaded America in the 1930's and early 1940's far outlasted World War II. A majority of the American public, apparently, never understood or agreed with the military and Cabinet views of advanced defense against *any* potentially hostile nation. Leaders changed, mistakes were forgotten, and lessons unlearned, only to have to be learned painfully once again.

Meanwhile, Navy Secretary Knox's words to Congress, before a rather hostile Senate Foreign Relations Committee, summed up the new national policy succinctly. He rejected any limitation as to the future location of a theater of war. The new zone of military operations, in the view of the government, should be whatever military expediency required. Knox testified:

> I am not going to shut the door when the vital interests of the United States are at stake. We will have to fight, no matter where, when our vital interests are affected. . . . When only fighting will preserve the United States, we will fight, no matter where it is.

Knox, along with Hull, Stimson, the military chiefs, and Franklin Roosevelt by 1940 believed the vital interests of the United States were at stake on the isle of Britain. They had positive as well as negative reasons for wanting an understanding with the British. The British were more highly mobilized and militarized than the United States. Britain in 1940-1941 had a more effective army and air force than the United States, and an industrial machine that was turning out more war goods. Their loss, in a future war, could not easily, if ever, be counterbalanced by increased American preparedness. In this light, the desire of the American military staffs for a unified Anglo-Saxon strategy was both urgent and understandable. The failure of military chiefs and the Cabinet to secure this was not one of strategy or conception, but a failure in selling their views to the American people.

The President faced a very real problem of having to commit United States forces in the Atlantic region, far away from American shores, without public support or even popular consent. It was a problem he preferred to let simmer while the military preparations went forth. So long as Britain held out, it would not become crucial or force him to tip his hand.

Meanwhile, the United States, always the first industrial and financial power, rose from about seventeenth to a position of something slightly less than parity with the Germans in the military world. It was another undeclared but bitterly waged battle between the timetables of F.D.R. and Adolf Hitler, not for power alone, but for the eventual control of the entire world.

Wars do not spring from armaments, but arms can fulfill political purposes. The United States political leadership first began to see this at the time of Munich. Henry Morgenthau, Harry Hopkins, and F.D.R. were all impressed as well as shocked by Hitler's adroit use of his Luftwaffe to secure his demands in 1938. Two days before the Munich pact was signed, the President met with the then Secretaries of Navy and War, Woodring and Edison, Louis Johnson, the Assistant Secretary of War, the Chief of Naval Operations, Admiral Stark, and Generals Marshall, Craig, and Arnold. Arnold was chief of the United States air arm. Harry Hopkins was at this meeting, and earlier, he had convinced the President about the necessity for power in the air, which at this time, even in the military, was a controversial question.

Discussing the political implications of air power, Roosevelt came out for more warplanes. He said bluntly that a new regiment of field artillery, or a new barracks to house the troops in Wyoming, or new tools in an ordnance depot would not scare Hitler "one goddam bit." He wanted planes. Airplanes were war machines that would influence Hitler's policies.

And so they might have, except that America did not have many of them.

Air Corps General Arnold briefed Roosevelt on the air situation in the world. Germany had an estimated 6,000 first line combat planes, 2,000 in reserve. France had 600, England about 2,200. Italy had 2,000—but of course, in Italy's case, planes themselves were not air power, and Arnold said so. Italian organization, discipline, and apparent will to fight was lacking; Italian warplanes were also inferior.

The United States Army Air Corps contained only 1,650 officers and 16,000 airmen. Its first-line planes numbered a few hundred, and almost all of these were obsolete. Thirteen B-17 bombers—all on order, or planned—were scheduled for delivery by the end of 1938.

Arnold hopefully transmitted to the President the estimates of his air staff for future United States defense: 7,500 planes. He did not really expect to get this many. The ground forces and the Navy expected equal consideration in any expansion, and pointedly said so. Arnold, pushing the Air Corps' darling —heavy bombers—would not have obtained them except that he had first gotten Hopkins' ear, and Harry Hopkins more than any man alive had Roosevelt's. F.D.R. approved Arnold's figure.

This request for only 7,500 planes was laughable in retrospect: between 1940-1945 the United States produced 229,-230 military aircraft. But in the atmosphere, and budgets, of 1938, it was phenomenal. And the decision to produce them, and the new B-17 Flying Fortress bombers, was to be decisive in the air war, in a way that civilians in the modern age found it difficult to understand. Seventy-five hundred combat aircraft, and a production capacity of 20,000 per year, were planned and agreed upon in September, 1938. This set things in motion, from retooling to pilot training, that were vitally important two years later.

The lead time for modern weapons in this era was very long. The first B-17 was tested (it failed) in October 1935. The time between a decision to produce aircraft, and their appearance in numbers in the skies, took years. The United States was to use no aircraft in World War II that were not already at least designed before the war began. If the United States had not started to rearm in 1940, it would have had no weapons to fight with in 1942; it would have first been prepared to take the offensive sometime in 1944-1945. If aircraft production had not been granted a green light as early as 1938, the battle for Hitler's air space would never have been won by 1944, and no Allied invasion could have been launched.

The same lead-time requirements applied to other weapons and weapons systems. The Garand or M-1 rifle, the basic infantry arm, was adopted in the mid-1930's, but did not go into production until World War II. The class of destroyer that formed the backbone of the Navy in 1941-1945 was one of the vintage of 1934. In 1938 and two years later the United States had no weapons on the ground with which to play a part in the international political arena, but fortunately it had them on the drawing boards, and even more fortunately, it had the two years in which to begin production.

The problems involved in going from a tiny, starved regular military establishment to one of the major war machines on earth were immense. To all foreign observers, it was incredible that they were solved at all. Most incredible was the fact that the Army, Navy, and Air Corps were able to plan coherently, and then to mesh their plans quickly with private industry without any real overall government control.

The military forces had to make up their minds what they needed, which in a time of explosively rapid weapon-and-doctrine change was not easy. Then they had to coordinate with industry the production of huge quantities. Mistakes were made, shortages developed, and bottlenecks appeared. These were all reported fully and sometimes hysterically in the press. But in each case—even the famous aluminum shortage—the trouble was amazingly short-lived.

The overall progress, beginning in 1940, was fantastic. Contracts totalling ten billion dollars were let in one hundred days, for guns, tanks, ships, and planes. This could not have happened if the military staffs of the United States had not been current with the world situation and fully prepared to move.

In the spring and summer of 1939, all arms programs still faced a rough reception in Congress and in the press. The Army, particularly, was hard put to defend new appropriations. Army witnesses in front of Congressional committees were asked sarcastically in the post-Munich period: "Will you tell this committee just what you mean by 'emergency?' " and "What is a 'sudden emergency?' Who is this new country we are supposed to be afraid of? Just who are we going to fight?"

Questions like these, which are quoted from the Congressional Record, were obviously beyond the purview of the military men to answer. Actually, the impetus should logically have been the other way around: Congress should have been asking the military what they were doing to meet the growing danger. In this era, and in fact all through and after the war, the nature of American civilian government continually forced military leaders to advance what were essentially political or geopolitical arguments, based on their own reading of the world scene. The dichotomy in outlook is perhaps best illustrated by one simple case: almost all American military planners saw Munich as a disastrous strategic defeat for the democracies—a view F.D.R. shared—while literally millions of civilians, politicians and otherwise, saw it as a sensible "negotiation."

The abuse of the military before Congress, seemingly based

on the notion that the staffs wanted a war, sharply changed once the Battle of France began. Now, the wind began to blow in another, tragicomic direction. The Navy, under questioning, was forced to admit that it was not equipped to control two oceans. The Army had to concede it could not effectively fight anyone, even Brazil, and the Air Corps was shown to exist primarily on drawing boards.

Some of the same civilian leaders who had systematically starved the military forces with ridiculous budgets, while bullying generals and admirals into keeping quiet about their misgivings, now went into a frenzy because cost effectiveness and the bottom dollar had not created a force equal to the "sudden" emergency.

In Congress, in the press, and among the general public there was considerable carping and anger toward a democratic military leadership that had allowed itself to fall behind the Nazi war machine. This was a classic case of a democracy berating its public servants for not doing the very things public policy had not permitted them to do.

The fact that the United States made few military mistakes in this crucial period was largely due to the brilliance of General George C. Marshall. Few men did more, and few men ever earned or deserved more respect.

Marshall was not a statesman or a politician, but a soldier in a state where the military was always subordinate, and accepted its subordination. Marshall did make some mistakes in his life, most of which were in that twilight zone between military doctrine and world policy; but these were not really his mistakes. Marshall made military recommendations based purely on the military, not geopolitical, situation—and if his civilian superiors accepted these, or acted upon them, later creating political difficulties for the United States, the fault was basically theirs.

But Marshall as Chief of Staff of the Army, which included the air forces, refused to be panicked in his approach to de-

144

fense. He bore all criticism, even ridiculous carping, with measured calm. He did not let the Army be influenced either by sudden public fads or passions, or by its own internal pressure groups. He abetted the building of air power, and gave the airman the independence within the Army structure that modern doctrine demanded, and which in Britain and Germany had already resulted in separate air arms. He organized armored forces against the opposition of the traditional—and sentimentally powerful—cavalry arm. But he did not neglect the infantry. Marshall planned a beautifully balanced force of armor, infantry, and air, and his courage, intellect, and character made this force come true.

He removed the unfit and the inevitable deadwood accumulated in a long period of peace. He promoted younger officers for merit, denying the seniority that had become a fetish in the services. He recognized that war was now three-dimensional—land, sea, and air—and made or acquiesced in new and eminently sensible joint commands, in which a naval officer might command all forces in a predominantly sea area, or an airman might control all ground forces in a theater where air action played the predominant role. This doctrine of joint and unified commands was revolutionary. Some mistakes, however, were made, as in Hawaii, where an old and inherently messy command situation was never clarified.

Marshall became Chief of Staff in the fall of 1939, when Roosevelt jumped him over dozens of officers of senior rank. But even with F.D.R.'s support Marshall and the services between 1939 and 1940 had one almost insurmountable problem. This centered in the men who ran the War and Navy Departments—the nerve centers of national defense.

Nothing was so indicative of the denigration of the American military in the 1930's as the type of man appointed to the defense secretariat. The Secretary of War was a constitutional Cabinet post, but in 1933 it was the one Roosevelt and the nation felt least important. F.D.R. took much more pains and care in appointing the Postmaster General.

Harry Hines Woodring was a supporter of Moral Rearmament, which enjoyed a big vogue in the thirties. A Kansan, and isolationist by bent, he was appointed Assistant Secretary of War in F.D.R.'s first Administration. In 1936 he became Secretary of War.

Louis Johnson, a West Virginian lawyer with political ambitions, was appointed Woodring's number-two man in 1937. Johnson, whether he was promised anything or not, came in believing he would soon get Woodring's job.

What soon developed was a lasting feud. Woodring and Johnson despised each other. They refused even to speak to each other except when necessary. Both men were bald, spectacled, and looked alike. But Woodring was rather meek and mild, Johnson florid and rather loud. Harry Woodring, unable to exert himself, unable even to fire Johnson without F.D.R.'s consent, sank into a sort of apathy. Johnson began to make the day-to-day decisions for the War Department, and that was a disaster of another sort.

In 1938 Johnson stopped the new Boeing B-17's—which all tests both before and during the war proved were the best heavy bombers of their time, and far better than anything either the British or the Germans made—from going into production. Johnson, overruling the entire Air Staff, opted in favor of cheaper planes.

Louis Johnson had no real understanding of modern war or the modern world situation, then or later. He did not and could not correlate military policy with international events or political policy. He thought he understood the mood of the American public. His major concern, then and later—he was finally to become Secretary of Defense just before Korea—was to save the people money. His first question, when presented with a new design, was not, is this the best, but is there anything we can get cheaper that might do the job?

146

The Air Corps' Major General Maxwell Andrews violently disagreed with Johnson's decision on the B-17 Flying Fortress. He pleaded for a long-range bomber, not the lighter, medium-range aircraft Johnson preferred because of lesser cost. He was overruled, and for questioning civilian management, put back to the rank of colonel. It must be said that the public neither understood nor much cared about the issues, and generally agreed with the civilian brass.

This kind of situation created an enormously unhealthy climate in all the services. The Air Corps' Arnold, and the Army's Marshall, found the secretariat of War a complete bottleneck. They could get nothing done. By 1939, Johnson and Woodring were engaged in a violent jurisdictional squabble over who would do what and where in the War Department, and they divided the Department into two camps. The military officers had no place in this fight, and could not even find a sympathetic ear to listen to their worries about the real war abroad.

One side effect was that no one ran the War Department, and Henry Morgenthau, the Secretary of the Treasury, very nearly took it over. Morgenthau was one of the activists in the Cabinet, who saw and planned for the war long before most officials saw it was coming. He organized the Treasury, at a crucial time, to finance national defense. He did a number of things, all for the good of the nation, which he was never fully given credit for and for which he was maligned at the time. A deep and fervent hater of the Nazis, he tried to organize the world in economic warfare against them, and with some success.

But Morgenthau was aware of his British counterpart, Lord Beaverbrook's authority over all British aircraft production, and took this arrangement too much to heart.

The problems and management of defense were almost all concerned with the production of war matériel in 1939-1940. The War Department's civilian posts, essentially, were production coordination jobs. The Treasury, naturally, with its control of money, was much involved—and because much of the work was new and there was as yet no sound defense production doctrine—actually more than forty government bureaus got in the act. The Secretary of War should have fought off this encroachment, but he was too busy battling in his own halls with Louis Johnson. Morgenthau, one of the strongest men in government, almost usurped both Woodring's and Johnson's jobs.

Morgenthau did accomplish some things that probably would not have been done otherwise. But not being directly concerned with defense, Morgenthau's focus and main concerns were wrong. His primary worry was that the Allies be supplied, lest they lose, and the needs of the burgeoning American services came last. One result of this plan of action was that he got into a feud with the Air Corps which redounded to no one's credit.

At a time when Arnold and his staff were battling for every penny and every inch of tight plant space, Morgenthau secured a Treasury ruling that all money going into plant expansion for *aircraft to be shipped overseas* was subject to a tax write-off. The same did not apply to expansion for United States home defense, or for production for the United States Army. This naturally encouraged civilian producers—who had close and good relations with the services—to take British orders first. There was no planning, no program, and no chain of command, that could set up priorities. In the Air Corps' eyes, Morgenthau planned to give all its beautiful new planes away —which was a very accurate assumption.

Service officers went to Woodring, but neither he nor Johnson were any help. Morgenthau stood higher in the pecking order around F.D.R., and in the "janissary atmosphere" Roosevelt had encouraged, the man who stood closest was most likely to prevail.

Ironically, in spite of the often-proclaimed German efficiency, almost the same situation obtained in Nazi Germany. The Nazi government boasted a series of wonderfully efficient and obedient bureaus for production, and a skilled industry eager to listen and obey—but production and design decisions were not planned.

Hitler retained overall control. The man who saw him last —whether it was about airplanes this month, submarines or tanks the next—very often came away with the authorization to have his way. German offices and bureaus of war, production, navy, and air force were frequently at complete odds, and the infighting was severe. But when one man ran such a vast shop, in effect no one ran it.

In this sense the vaunted "Führer principle" or the idea that a dictatorship could get things done was false. Dictatorship could make vast policy decisions far easier than democracy. But in day-to-day matters, because no one except the dictator possessed real power, production and management sank into the same morass that had surrounded the brilliant court circles at Versailles. Bureaus feuded and sought the great one's ear.

In Washington, this situation was soon corrected. Afterward, there was never any doubt of the efficiency of free men working in a common cause compared to slavish bureaucrats. Deep in the war, it was Washington that made almost every right defense decision, and Germany—from too few submarines to the restriction on fighter planes—that made them wrong.

One episode of the Army-Treasury feud is highly revealing.

The security regulations of the United States excluded foreigners from access to certain secret knowledge or defense premises. But the French Air Ministry at one point wanted to look at Douglas' new top secret A-20 bomber. When Army officers and Douglas executives refused the French request, the French took it to their friend at court, Secretary Morgenthau.

Morgenthau went to Woodring, who took Morgenthau's

word that F.D.R. "approved." Woodring then issued an order verbally to the Chief of Staff of the Air Corps, General Arnold, to clear the French commission for "100 percent cooperation." Arnold immediately referred to the legal restrictions, and was told to forget them. He did, and signed an order allowing the French to see the bomber.

But if this was the way things were done in Washington, with a verbal hint that the "boss approved," things could become very messy in the field.

The Douglas A-20 bomber crashed in a test flight. Ten civilians were injured by the falling wreckage, and there was considerable property damage. The story hit the Associated Press wires, which also reported that one of the injured men in the plane was a M. Chmedelin of the French Ministry for Air.

The Senate Military Affairs Committee—which did not acknowledge F.D.R. as boss—summoned General Arnold for questioning.

Isolationist Senator Bennet Clark of Missouri raked Arnold with queries as to why the French were flying the bomber when it was against the standing regulations. Arnold, brought up to tell the truth like any soldier, had to say that Secretary Morgenthau had ordered Woodring to do it.

The Senate wanted to know if the Secretary of the Treasury was running the Air Corps. Arnold had to admit that it looked that way.

Morgenthau, however, much wiser to Washington ways, cut back sharply when he was put on the stand: *"Arnold signed the order."*

Later Roosevelt called Arnold in and roasted him. He told Arnold that there had to be full cooperation with friendly nations, even regarding the sale of recent secret equipment, which was a sensible policy. But F.D.R. was most upset over the fact that War Department witnesses were not "on their guard" in front of Congressional committees. He was "unhappy" with the way Arnold and others were answering questions. They were telling the truth, even when it was damaging.

He then informed Arnold that if bureau chiefs couldn't put Congress off, he would find some who could, and those "who couldn't play ball would be sent to Guam" or some suitable place.

General Arnold got the point, but it was a year before he was back in F.D.R.'s good graces, or was again given a personal interview or allowed to attend a social meeting with the President.

Arnold had to go to men like Harry Hopkins to state the services' case. Hopkins fortunately had both keen good judgment and the President's ear. He helped Arnold and Marshall and other military chiefs immensely in this time, although like Morgenthau, he held no defense post or office.

Meanwhile, the several internecine feuds went on. Roosevelt, who was by no means unaware of the situation, by some quirk of nature found them amusing. But by 1940 the troubles in the War Department had become a Washington, if not a national, scandal. The day Hitler invaded France the whole thing abruptly ceased to be a joke.

F.D.R. realized, perhaps with some reluctance, that the military departments had to have strong men, and men who could run their own shops. They demanded expertize in a time of crisis, not political savvy.

Two prominent Americans who had wholeheartedly adopted the new doctrine of activist defense were Frank Knox and Henry Stimson. Both were Republicans. Knox had even been Alfred Landon's running mate in the disastrous 1936 Republican campaign. He had come up the hard way: grocery clerk, sign painter, soldier in France and at San Juan Hill with Teddy Roosevelt. He had become a colonel, and at the age of sixty-six he was a nationally known publisher.

Stimson was a different breed: Yale, exclusive clubs, Harvard Law School, colonel of artillery in 1918. He had been

Secretary of War under President Taft, Secretary of State under Hoover. Like Knox, he opposed almost all of Franklin Roosevelt's domestic spending programs. He was seventy-two.

But both men belonged to an old, and by now almost forgotten Republican group of internationalists, who had come up with Theodore Roosevelt. When the mainspring, and principal political power of the Republican Party had switched toward the Middle West, the old Republican Large Policy—the idea that America should take a "large" part in world affairs, had withered. Almost forgotten until their letter writing and editorials resurrected them, these two old men belonged to the generation of Charles Evans Hughes, Elihu Root, Theodore Roosevelt, and John Hay—men who had been abreast of their times, and who had acted in the broader interest.

Opposed to F.D.R.'s domestic politics, Knox and Stimson loyally supported his outlook overseas. Both took a public line long before their appointment: for conscription, for sending all munitions and arms to England, and even the use of the United States Navy to convoy the shipments if needed.

This was a belligerent, almost inflammatory line in early 1940. It bothered many people, both Republicans and Democrats, who could no longer combine internationalism with Republicanism, particularly since that Party had sunk slowly into a hardening isolationist attitude, partly natural, partly because of hatred of F.D.R.

Roosevelt, in early 1940 and even much later, had never taken so firm an interventionalist line. He was still paying public lip service—at least by silence on certain things—to isolationist sentiment. He did make coherent arguments for the new defense doctrine, before Congress and in fireside chats, but his discussions tended to be intellectual and passed over many people's heads. All that came through was the often-expressed hatred for the dictators, and the idea that he would still maintain the peace. Men like Knox and Stimson, making public statements, were actually carrying the ball for F.D.R.

152

With a certain stroke of genius, F.D.R. abruptly appointed Knox and Stimson as the Secretaries of Navy and War. Both were capable men, both able propagandists, both eye to eye with the Administration on foreign affairs. Even better, their appointment did two things: it threw a certain confusion into Republican ranks, and it showed, or should have shown, the public that this was not a partisan war. Hopefully, there was no Democrat or Republican label on American Defense.

Most of the men in Washington and elsewhere who saw, and forged the emerging doctrines, wore Party labels lightly, if they had any at all. Many were military men who had never voted. Here, a pattern for the future was also set. It would create a certain dichotomy in American cabinets which split on domestic concerns but agreed on national affairs. It was a uniquely American solution, but enormously effective in most respects.

Woodring was requested to resign. He sent back an angry note to F.D.R. the text of which was not revealed. Another job, in government, was planned for Louis Johnson.

The appointments took both the country and the Senate, which had to confirm them, by surprise. The isolationist or peace bloc was stunned when the Senate clerk read off the names of Knox and Stimson for confirmation.

Democrat Rush Holt of West Virginia muttered, "Treasonous," under his breath. Several Senators who read *The New York Times* yelled, "Warmongers!" The term "hawk" had not yet come into vogue.

In the Cabinet, both men turned quickly and naturally down the lines they had proclaimed as private citizens. Both were, and remained, considerably ahead of Roosevelt; if he was cautious, they were belligerent and privately made no bones about it.

Within a few weeks, the whole complexion of the defense departments changed. The holdovers from the peacetime 1930's were eased out. New blood came in, reading like a

WHO'S WHO of the future: James Forrestal as Under Secretary of the Navy. Robert P. Patterson as Under Secretary of War. John J. McCloy as Assistant Secretary of War. Robert A. Lovett as Assistant Secretary of War for Air. They were bankers, lawyers, and businessmen, but they generally had one thing in common. They had a world, not just a national, view, and they all agreed with the changing concept of United States security.

Their geographic origin and business background were significant. They tended to be international bankers, or lawyers or businessmen with overseas interests. They were not the kind of production engineer or salesman whose eye was always on the domestic scene, or the type of farm boy raised in Kansas, Missouri, or Minnesota who thought that the interests of the House of Morgan and the interests of the American nation as a whole did not, and could never coincide.

The fact that protection of an American world investment had some bearing on the United States entry in Europe in 1917 was almost unbearable emotionally to many Americans from the Midwest. But the men who most easily saw and adopted the new world stance—McCloy, Forrestal, Stimson, and Patterson—were men who understood America's true position in the political and commercial world.

The new secretariats worked well with both William Knudsen's production boards and the professional military services. The world was changed almost overnight for the military officers; they had chiefs who understood their principles and agreed with their concepts of a pragmatic defense. The new chiefs, like the military, were more geared to events than to what the public happened to believe. With industry, Washington bureaus, and the armed services finally meshed in common purpose, the American production miracle could proceed.

There was no longer any argument about the fact that the United States would have to retain control of the Atlantic. Senator Clark might want no navy, but too many otherwise isolationists, like David Walsh of Massachusetts, lived too near the sea. They demanded a two-ocean navy for the first time in American history. The United States Navy of June, 1940 consisted of 15 battleships, 6 aircraft carriers, 37 cruisers divided between light and heavy, 237 destroyers, 102 submarines, and 1,300 combat naval aircraft. This was considered more than enough to control Japan.

The new Navy, programmed for a 70 percent augmentation, was designed to contain Hitler, too. The funds voted and contracts let in July, 1940, provided for 35 battleships (including new 45,000 tonners), 20 carriers, 88 cruisers, 378 destroyers, 180 submarines, and 15,000 planes. This was the greatest shipbuilding program in world history. The first vessels were to start coming off the ways in 1942, and all were to be at sea in 1944.

The air forces were programmed for 35,000 planes, exclusive of naval aircraft. Twelve thousand, with ground support and trained crews, were to be ready to strike by April, 1942.

The Army was programmed for a mobile strike force of some 1,400,000 men, with adequate reserves and all accompanying hardware. In fact, the orders for military equipment were deliberately raised beyond those foreseen for the standing forces. This Army, Assistant Secretary Patterson proposed, must be prepared to fight by the spring of 1942. It would number between thirty and fifty full divisions.

In addition, the United States was to supply the British with ships, tanks, and aircraft—at least 14,000 planes and 3,000 tanks by 1942.

The United States was thus planning to be ready to fight at least a defensive war by the spring of 1942. There was widespread sentiment inside the Cabinet, not made public, that by 1942 the United States would be so engaged.

Late in 1940 the German forces totalled approximately 8 armored divisions, 214 first-line infantry divisions with almost 100 more in reserve. The German air force contained

40,000 planes, while German industry built between 2,000-3,000 more each month. The total Axis navy was smaller than the total American—but immensely larger than anything the United States could muster in the Atlantic without British aid.

The United States in 1940 had two years to try to accomplish what the German state had done in eight.

10.

Festung America

I have done this because I believe my country is in mortal danger.
Charles A. Lindbergh.

Germany has no interests on the American continent. German
Foreign Office, 1940.

The time will come for the United States to withstand our weapons.
Adolf Hitler.

The urgent question of destroyers for Britain was allowed to
simmer the whole summer of 1940, while the battle of the
Atlantic gradually became the crucial theater of the war.
Winston Churchill said later that the control of the seas against
the German submarine menace was the only problem that
really worried him. The R.A.F. was holding its own over
Britain. But in the Atlantic, the lifeline to America over which
both British arms and food were carried, British ships were
being sunk at an alarming rate.

Ironically, both the British and Germans had underrated
submarine warfare between the wars. In 1917, the Imperial
German policy of "unrestricted submarine warfare" had almost brought Britain to its knees before the United States
entered the war, and the convoy system was devised. But by

1918, the convoy system of guarding ships, and British anti-submarine measures, were 99.08 percent effective. They were so effective that British naval planners tended to downgrade the U-Boat menace after the war.

Several things were overlooked. In 1918 the Royal Navy manned an immense fleet of 495 destroyers, and it was buttressed by an additional 100 United States, 92 French, and 67 Italian escort vessels. The World War I submarines were a new instrument of war, not perfected, and they ran slower than merchant vessels. Also, and crucial to the 1917-1918 campaign, German naval forces were bottled up behind the North Sea. The British blockade and the use of thousands of naval mines in these waters made it almost impossible for German U-boat commanders to reach the open sea late in the war.

The Germans, always land-minded, took these factors too much to heart. Hitler spent lavishly on the Luftwaffe and *panzerarmees* and starved the undersea arm almost to impotency. The German Navy began the war in September, 1939 with only 56 submarines, of which 43 were operational. By late 1940, the number the Germans could put to sea was only around 25.

But two factors changed immensely from 1917. One was the German strategical situation: when France fell, the German Navy had bases with easy access to the Atlantic. U-boats could range the open seas from Greenland to the Antarctic, because the World War II submarine was faster, heavier, and more deadly than its prototype of 1917. Submarines could hit British merchant vessels anywhere across many thousands of ocean miles, greatly increasing the need for escort ships.

But the British had spent no money on antisubmarine warfare in the years preceding 1939. Training, doctrine, and technology had not advanced. Worst of all, the number of destroyers—the best escort vessel—had dwindled from almost 500 in 1918 to a total of 192. And the British Navy, unlike World War I, now stood utterly alone.

With his limited resources, German Admiral Dönitz of the submarine command began a protracted war of attrition at sea. Except for the fatal errors of German bureaucracy, the German Navy might have won the war. Dönitz' U-boats eventually sank 3,000 Allied ships, killed 30,000 Allied seamen, and sent uncounted tons of supplies and equipment to the bottom. He almost starved out the British, and he gave Churchill and the American Cabinet many sleepless nights.

The British developed new means of antisubmarine warfare: new escort vessels, detection devices, better depth charges. But these came later in the war. They also began a frantic shipbuilding campaign, but by the summer of 1940, in the vital destroyer class, they had suffered a net loss of 23.

The Germans kept sinking British ships faster than they could be built. They sent a large part of the American matériel just now coming off assembly lines to the bottom of the Atlantic before it could be used.

The London Naval Treaty of 1930 had a clause that "submarines should not sink or render incapable of navigation a merchant vessel without having first placed passengers, crew, and ships' papers in a place of safety." This restriction was, of course, ridiculous, and no combatant between 1939-1945 observed it. The United States was to use unrestricted submarine warfare against the islands of Japan with immense effect. But characteristically, the Germans, who had signed the London Naval Treaty, were the first to violate it. The naval war in the Atlantic was brutal, savage, and finally decisive, with no holds barred on either side.

When Roosevelt and the Cabinet had embarked on a double course of action in May 1940—rearmament and aid to Britain short of war—the desperate condition of British control of the Atlantic made these two objectives conflict. Public sentiment in the United States was now overwhelmingly for a two-ocean navy, to hold the Atlantic in case the British failed. It was not in favor of the transfer of American military equipment abroad. Yet as Churchill explained vividly, if American aid "short of war" did not reach its destination, it was aid thrown down a rathole indeed. He needed 50 destroyers, on loan or by transfer. These 50 additional ships would still give the British less than 300 escort vessels of all kinds, but they would reduce the pressure on the Royal Navy from desperate to merely acute.

The transfer posed a genuine dilemma for F.D.R. He wanted to give the destroyers to the British. The 50 in question were a World War I model, though built in the 1920's. They had become "overage" by United States naval standards after sixteen years; all were scheduled for replacement by 1934 models in the building program now underway. The old four-stackers were inadequately gunned by current standards; they were of no practical use in the Pacific against Japan. But they were eminently suitable for convoy work by the British.

The United States Navy, unlike the Air Corps on the matter of release of new planes, had no objection to letting them go. But serious legal and political obstacles stood in the President's way.

None of the isolationist and peace sentiment in the country would support such a move. This seemed an act of war. It was no part of cash and carry, because Churchill did not propose to buy the destroyers; Britain was already almost out of foreign exchange. The peace and chauvinist sentiment, together, was dominant, and Roosevelt's feelers to the Congress convinced him that Congress would not act on a legal bill to transfer the destroyers to England. At best, it would act only after prolonged and acrimonious debate.

The splinter "Century Group" of the Committee to Defend America by Aiding the Allies eventually provided the government with the answer. The Century Group, which included men like Dean Acheson and military analyst George F. Eliot, was already calling for open war, but it put its legal minds to work on the problem, first, of getting Churchill his destroyers.

Acheson wrote a series of "briefs" showing that the transfer could be made lawfully under the President's Constitutional powers.

The final solution was brilliant, both legally and politically. Isolationist sentiment, opposing military aid to Britain was vociferous for building up American defense. Some isolationist senators had already suggested that the United States take over British territories and bases in the Atlantic and Caribbean "in its own defense." The Century Group proposed to Roosevelt that the destroyers be exchanged for the transfer, use, or lease of British territory or bases in the Western Hemisphere, the value of which the public would easily understand. Second, the transfer could be made by the President, completely without the approval of Congress, by using the powers "inherent" in his role as Commander-in-Chief of the armed forces.

The British would get something they needed desperately in exchange for bases they did not need, while the United States Navy and air forces would get strategic sites of great value in any coming battle of the Atlantic. Roosevelt liked the idea, especially the bypass of Congress.

The matter was taken under secret discussion with the British government, and under quiet study by Attorney General Robert Jackson and Under Secretary of State Sumner Welles to determine its legality. These studies leaked out, but Roosevelt refused to comment when asked by the press if such a deal was in the works.

The Attorney General found the power to make the transfer "implicit" in the Commander in Chief's Constitutional powers. F.D.R., who had extended the domestic powers of the Presidency both by precedent and law, now extended them even more by executive action. He did this for a specific purpose, for an end he believed vital at the time. But he set a precedent that would remain—and be used again and again, so long as the United States remained involved in the active world.

All of Roosevelt's extensions of executive power were in

pursuit of some specific goal, not in pursuit of power for its own sake, as some of his critics feared. But certain inherent dangers in the extension of executive power remained. It did not matter for what reason Presidential power increased in the long run, because it did not again easily retract.

During these years Wendell Willkie, the nominal head of the Republican Party, approved each executive action Roosevelt took. But he argued that F.D.R. should not have avoided the will of Congress in the destroyer deal, and he specifically stated that each "emergency power" extended during the crisis should be handed back or abrogated immediately after the crisis had passed. But this was not Roosevelt's way; it was his nature to want to hold on jealously to everything he got. And every strong President who followed him would feel exactly the same way.

The Administration avoided Congress on the destroyer deal for three basic reasons: 1. to secure quick action; 2. to avoid damaging debate, which might further divide the nation, and 3. to make sure the deal was consummated at all.

Since no money was involved, Congress did not have any hold over the President. Here something of crucial importance for the future was discovered: if the President acted, the Congress and the public, presented with an accomplished fact, had no means of counteracting him. They could approve or disapprove—but they could not set the act aside. A formal repudiation of a President whose Party controlled Congress was also unthinkable. In 1940, F.D.R.'s executive action was audacious. Later, such acts would be routine. Roosevelt, for example, in 1940-1941 would never have dared to commit troops in the same way he committed aid to the Allies.

There was inherent damage to republican democracy in this Presidential role. But the whole problem of the twentieth century was that mass democracy was not geared to play a big power role. It had not been effective in America, France, or Great Britain since 1918. This ineffectiveness, this insistence upon debating and compromising foreign-policy issues, and this tendency to put domestic issues ahead of problems overseas, where the real danger lay, had brought the whole survival of modern democracy into question.

If the response to fascist attack had continued through the 1940's in the same halfhearted, bewildered manner it had been conducted in the 1930's, Western democracy must have perished. As it was, it had to make some compromises with the *Führer Prinzip:* by 1940, Churchill, not Parliament, guided Britain, and Roosevelt, not the Congress, had assumed the moral and symbolic leadership of the United States.

Public outcry against the destroyer-bases deal did not develop. The quickness of the act took the isolationists by surprise. Also, the link between warships and bases in the Western Hemisphere confused the isolationists; acquiring these bases was a major isolationist, Fortress America, goal.

The deal that Hull and Lothian signed on September 2, 1940, was simple: bases in Bermuda and Newfoundland, which enjoyed self-rule within the Commonwealth, were presented to the United States as a "gift" for ninety-nine years. Six other bases, in the Bahamas, Jamaica, St. Lucia, Antigua, and British Guiana, were leased, rent-free, for the same period in exchange for 50 destroyers. The first news of the transaction did not come from London or Washington, but leaked out of Bermuda, where the House of Assembly met in secret session and approved the deal.

The exchange not only gave the United States Navy and air forces important bases on the approaches to the hemisphere. It took the United States measurably closer to the European war. This was not the act of a neutral power, or a power that took no interest in the outcome of the war. *"It wants no abnormal quickness of wit to see the implication,"* the British *New Statesman and Nation* editorialized with satisfaction.

Certain Americans saw the implications, too, and did not like them. Two days after the destroyer deal was signed, the largest, most important, and most effective anti-war organization in the United States was formed. This was the Committee to Defend America First.

Many Americans believed that "isolationism" as experienced and practiced in the 1920's and 1930's was something traditionally American, or stemmed from George Washington's Farewell Address, in which he warned of entangling alliances. Nothing could be further from the truth. This kind of isolationism was purely a twentieth-century growth.

Most evidence shows that the Founding Fathers had a clear and cold notion of where the United States fitted into the greater world. Eighteenth-century Americans were not distant either in mind or geography from the Old World. They had been under European rule for generations. They were maritime in geography; the dominant elements of the new nation were strung out along the eastern seaboard; and a general consciousness of European origin was yet strong. America was an "island" nation, but not yet a continent. In the eighteenth century the United States looked outward, across the Atlantic and to the Caribbean. The United States was by no means self-sufficient before it became an industrial power. From its very beginnings it was aware that events in Europe, the power center of the world, vitally affected it from day to day.

The power realities of world politics were understood in government. Thus Benjamin Franklin went to Paris, to dance with an autocratic court to make an alliance to secure American freedom; Washington could and did insist upon restoration of commercial relations with Great Britain before the echoes of a bitter war had died; and Thomas Jefferson, in a time of general hostility to the British Crown, could and did write, *"We must marry the British fleet and the British nation."*

The United States, to protect its independence, played off Louis XVI against the British Parliament in 1777, and later, Parliament against Napoleon. Monroe, with his eye on America's destiny, could work out a pragmatic alliance with Can-

164

ning's British navy in 1823. There was no rejection of, but a cool and wary willingness to defend America's interest in the cynical and power-ridden politics of the world.

The Founding Fathers of the United States did not expect world approval for themselves, their politics, or their nation —and got none. But they had no notion of withdrawing from that world; nothing in their eyes could have been more dangerous.

United States policy in the early years of the Republic took three main lines. All were finite and in search of specific goals. The first goal was to dominate the North American continent, and later the Caribbean, in the interest of American security. The problem was to keep the Old World—where the power was—at bay. No thinking American felt secure if any European power could extend its influence in the hemisphere. The British acquiesced; the Mexicans were beaten in a war; smaller countries, once Spain had been driven out, were overawed. *The United States assumed a self-appointed role of hemisphere defense, and to a certain extent, forced its predominance and that role upon the hemisphere.* In the beginning, the United States was audacious. Later, the role was taken for granted.

This was at heart defensive; American weakness was understood. Washington warned against foreign alliances that could get the United States in European wars, where the country stood to gain nothing but could be badly mauled. In effect, from Monroe's time the United States had an alliance with Great Britain, never signed. The United States was almost a complete beneficiary: it need not get in Britain's wars, but Britain protected America's front door. The United States need keep a worried eye on Europe only if Britain failed, and during the nineteenth century Britain was the dominant power in the world.

The British were content with this; they had renounced all territorial ambitions in the New World after 1815. The important commercial relationship with the United States stood, and it was in the British interest to help keep all other powers out. Britain, by 1815, had assumed the "island" geopolitical stance in its classic sense: it did not seek hegemony over its neighbors and trading partners, but it was concerned that no other power did so.

It was a role that the United States, as Lord Lothian foresaw, would some day itself have to assume.

A second line of American policy in the early days was to keep a firm eye on hostile developments anywhere in the world, and if possible, frustrate them. Monroe's doctrine was in response to the Holy Alliance's threats. Lincoln and Johnson moved against Napoleon III in 1865 for precisely the same reasons. The purchase of Alaska was as much defensive as ambitious, and so was the march from sea to shining sea. The men on the trail were in search of land, wealth, or the big sky—but the men in Washington who aided and abetted the move West by every hook and crook, like Andrew Jackson, had an eye on a far larger canvas. They saw, even if they did not always talk, destiny.

The third line of American policy was the protection of American private commercial enterprise wherever it chose to go. The United States flag was defended on the high seas by an audacious navy acting on Presidential order, now against Barbary pirates, now against Malays or Chinese. A vigorous consular force was sent abroad, to gain by cajolery, negotiation, and not only bribery but sometimes a threat of force, certain things American enterprise desired.

In this period the United States materially assisted the Royal Navy in wiping piracy from the seas, and more than one Latin-American historian feels that United States diplomatic activity and interest—and real influence—was greater in South America then than at any other time.

By 1900 the United States dominated its hemisphere, and was thus, at the time, geographically secure. The United States had taken its place, with France and Britain, as one of the three major commercial nations. Its private interests, in London and Peking, as well as Havana, seemed completely safe.

Here, there seemed to be a certain loss of finite purpose. The United States was now a great power, and through its immense success, a status-quo-minded great power. But the nation collectively was much like a man who has at last achieved great wealth and position but has no real idea what to do with them. The United States entered the twentieth century without ambitions against anyone, but also with an unfortunate lack of international goals. The old ones were all achieved—or seemed to be; the new outlook took on an incoherent, fuzzy outline. The United States now professed to stand for "international morality," "peace," and "justice."

But these things were not finite; they could not even be defined by any broad consensus. No Administration nor diplomatic service in history, not even that of the United States, could achieve something this incoherent. International politics was played for control of commerce and resources, for borders and provinces. It was always colored by fear, hatred, injustice, and force. It was after 1900 that the United States foreign service and American diplomacy tended to become laughing stocks, not only in the world, but at home, too. The home front, however, never realized what the trouble was. Americans sent their diplomats around the world, talking morality and good cheer to men who were prepared to slit each other's throats for something each felt he had to have—and the United States never had anything constructive to say or do about that. In fact, almost as soon as Americans understood that other peoples were prepared to fight for something, they washed their hands of the whole mess.

The same people who had fought Great Britain twice for independence, Mexico for the Southwest, and Spain for world power, now assumed that the act of war had different dimensions.

The United States went to war with Imperial Germany in 1917 for almost exactly the same reasons President Jefferson went to war against the Barbary pirates. But Americans did not accept this fact at all; they lost touch with reality. They refused to accept the positive limitations on the act of war. By war, the United States could prevent a German hegemony of Europe, which would be detrimental to American long-term interests. But by war, the United States could not "end all wars" or make "the world safe for democracy."

The United States was the real victor in World War I. It gained its political goals at a very small cost in blood, increased its industrial capacity, and even gained gold and treasure at the expense of Europe. But the American people had entered that war, seeking a permanent peace in the world without ever realizing that this was not a reasonable goal.

When it became evident that World War I was not the last, and that the nations of the world were inherently no different in 1919 than they had been in 1914, one result was widespread national disillusionment. This centered in liberal circles, whose members consciously rejected the notion that it had been moral for America to fight for its commercial and political status quo. But it also pervaded the whole population. Not understanding what war was all about, the American public became utterly distrustful of the act of war, for any reason except to resist overt attack.

There was still a minority that argued that the United States had a "peculiar mission" to advance peace and justice. But the new majority, after 1918, preferred to break all moral and political ties with an obviously "immoral" world. Behind the oceans, and the comfortable, if not admitted, power of the British fleet, this seemed feasible. A strong navy was maintained, for the sole purpose of overawing Japan. The result of this was that by 1930 the United States not only had no enduring ties with any nation or power structure but also collectively had no idea at all just where it stood or belonged in the hierarchy of world powers.

This was very different from the noninvolvement in Europe on the part of the early Republic. Then the United States had been too small to count in the power structure of Europe —but through an understanding with Britain was able to discount any possible European attack in the crucial years. American statesmen were always very much aware of that power structure, however, and wherever possible, particularly in the hemisphere, sought to increase the United States' own power.

The withdrawal of the world's leading commercial and industrial power from that world was entirely another matter. It was a psychological failure of the first order. At the same time Americans argued there *was* an international morality and law they argued just as vehemently that there was, or ought to be, no power structure. They refused any responsibility for both. The result was inevitable: a jungle world. But it was a jungle world where Americans did not even realize the attacks of the denizens sooner or later had to be directed at them. America, fully as much as France or the British Empire, represented the modern, democratic, capitalist, industrially and financially superior world that certain "have-not" powers were psychologically determined to overthrow.

Americans were urging sixty-three nations to sign a pledge to war no more in 1929, when Hitler was writing that no order which would not defend itself by force could last. *"God has not permitted some nations to take the world by force, then defend this robbery with moralizing theory,"* Hitler snarled; and he was absolutely right.

However and by whatever means the Western world arrived at its superiority, it could not be forever defended by theory alone. But faced with a jungle world they themselves helped perpetuate, Franklin Roosevelt and Cordell Hull combined for long years in only preaching at it, not doing anything about it. Gradually, these men, and most of the men in government on

169

the executive level, learned painfully that the United States did fit into the modern world and that if Hitler continued to be opposed only with moralizing theory they would soon be preaching into the muzzles of his firing squads.

By September 1940, Roosevelt's Administration, Stimson, Knox, Hull, Morgenthau, Ickes, and hundreds of others, stood almost where Jefferson and Monroe stood many years before, and suddenly saw things with the same clarity.

But there were millions of others who did not. One of the most important, and the man who bothered Franklin Roosevelt the most, was Charles Augustus Lindbergh. More than any other man, he expressed the new isolationism of America; and he became its intellectual and emotional, if not its moral spokesman. When a small group of wealthy and influential men founded America First in 1940, they looked to Lindbergh, a national hero who had been leading his own fight, in his own way, long before.

Lindbergh was born in Minnesota, the son of a Swedish-American Congressman who voted from his heart and mind against entry in World War I. On his son's birthday in 1917, Congressman Lindbergh wrote: *"The world has gone mad."* He died without being otherwise persuaded. In some ways young Lindbergh's whole mind and heart were early formed; in some ways he was to be no more responsible for his actions than later Americans such as Bettina Aptheker and Staughton Lynd, who inherited a mental outlook as well as genes. In America, it is an illusion that fathers do not pass on ideas to the sons.

At the age of twenty-five, Charles, Jr., was the first man to fly the Atlantic Ocean. That year, 1927, he became one of the foremost heroes of America, and the world.

Everywhere he went, from cowpatch airfields to New York and Paris, women mobbed him. He was stolid, good-looking, quiet, reserved. He married well. He earned money. He was made a colonel in the United States Army Air Corps reserve.

170

The kidnap-murder of his son in the early 1930's was a world-wide sensation. Deeply hurt, and by his nature angry both at the scandalous press interference in his private life and government interference in his business relations with aircraft companies, Lindbergh moved to England.

He came to be regarded, not quite fairly, as both a military and an aviation expert. In 1936, the Air Corps asked him to inspect and evaluate the emerging Luftwaffe, using his position as international hero; the United States military and air attachés in Germany had never been able to make the faintest dent in Nazi security. Lindbergh did so. For their own purposes, the Germans opened all doors to him; they honored him and feted him and also showed him things about their air force no one else had ever seen.

Lindbergh was both impressed and sold a certain bill of goods. From that time on, he considered the Luftwaffe invulnerable, which it was not. But he also came back and said it was superior to anything in the West, which was true, though not popular.

Lindbergh gave the War Department and the United States Embassy in England detailed, accurate reports on everything he had seen. As General Arnold, who always respected Lindbergh the man, if not Lindbergh the political and military analyst, said, the reports were of great help. They told the Air Corps much—but they had a side effect, which was to frighten United States Ambassador Kennedy and other Americans and Englishmen as well.

Lindbergh moved in good social and governmental circles in England. His views, and chilling descriptions, of the Luftwaffe did much to bring about the atmosphere of Munich in Great Britain's ruling set. His sincerity could not be questioned, but neither was his expertize.

In 1939, Lindbergh and his family returned to the United States. As a reservist, the War Department requested his services as a technical consultant. Here, again, as the only American who had ever seen the Luftwaffe up close, or knew its leaders, he rendered certain valuable service. But Lindbergh returned from a warring Europe profoundly depressed. He was obsessed with the fear that once again the United States would go to war, and to no more avail than in 1917. He had seen Europe swept by fascism, deathly fearful of Bolshevism. He was not for any of these things. He was against them all, and to a certain extent, the very world that fostered them.

Dining with conservative radio commentator Fulton Lewis, Jr., Lindbergh expressed some of his views. Lewis, who had certain fears of F.D.R.'s interests overseas, invited him to speak on radio. Later, when the war began, Lindbergh agreed. He was subject to his own beliefs, and also to some very bad advice, from a number of men who hated Franklin Roosevelt.

As a national figure, and a national hero, Lindbergh was perhaps the only man in America who could command an air audience halfway as large as F.D.R. He went on the air from Washington, on all three national networks, from the Carlton Hotel. His speech was simple, direct, and blunt, like the man. It expressed the core of American isolationism—the patriotic, not the deluded or selfish core—and it created a small national explosion.

It sliced into the cautious pro-Allied sentiments of Roosevelt's own fireside chat of September 3, 1939, and it unquestionably set back the mood of resigned, not eager, interventionism. Lindbergh gave, or seemed to give, alternatives. He said:

> In times of great emergency, men of the same belief must gather together for mutual counsel and action. If they fail to do this, all they stand for will be lost.

He had set himself up as a rallying point.

> Let us not delude ourselves. If we enter in the quarrels of Europe during war, we must stay in them in time of peace as well. It is madness to send our soldiers to be killed as we did

172

in the last war if we turn the course of peace over to the greed, the fear, and the intrigue of European nations.

He rejected the notion, being suggested by the Administration, that the war was a defense of Western Civilization. He branded it as essentially internecine:

> . . . age-old struggles within our family of nations—a quarrel arising from the errors of the last war.
>
> The treaty of Versailles either had to be revised as time passed, or England and France . . . had to keep Germany weak by force. Neither policy was followed . . . as a result, another war has begun . . . a war which may even lead to the end of our Western civilization.

Everything he said to this point was perfectly true. But Lindbergh, unlike F.D.R., drew different conclusions.

> We must be as impersonal as a surgeon with his knife.

The American attitude, Lindbergh believed, should be one of saying a pox on both houses. Then he stated what was, in England and France and America during the 1930's, the hard intellectual argument against war with Hitler:

> If we enter the fighting for democracy abroad we may end by losing it at home.
>
> We must not be misguided by this foreign propaganda to the effect that our frontiers lie in Europe . . . the ocean is a formidable barrier, even for modern aircraft.

A major point of the speech was the denial of all foreign responsibility or connection. Lindbergh considered America a world apart. He wrote off both the Nazis *and* their victims. He acknowledged European origins, but stated the American destiny was to take a different course:

> The German genius for science and organization, the British genius for government and commerce, the French genius for living and understanding of life—they must not

go down here as well as on the other side. Here in America they can be blended to form the greatest genius of all.

He proclaimed this moral and intellectual isolationism feasible, if the United States armed, because of distance and the oceans.

This speech drew battle lines. In a very real sense, it threw Lindbergh up into opposition to the Administration, even before the Administration had officially or publicly adopted the new, active concept of defense. Certain officers and officials of the War Department had known what he was going to say and tried to dissuade him from doing it. The speech, and the prominence it was given, angered President Roosevelt.

Lindbergh probably never realized he was actually attacking the last world war, and America's entry into it. He was looking backward. He did not have a good grasp of the past; he could see all the errors of the popular passions of 1918 that led to the stupendous errors at Versailles. He was reliving 1919—and if the technology of 1919 had still held, his course, whatever its morality, might have been possible.

Lindbergh was a superb flyer, a good mechanic, and an honest patriot. He had no perception of the historic meaning of the pragmatic British alliance, of the importance of the British fleet. He was enormously insular, and in his way, intensely moral: he was willing to die for peace, but not for a peace, which after millions were dead, would not reform the world. He understood aircraft—but not the psychology that made men build warplanes. *The world has gone mad....*

Millions of Americans, with no better perception, agreed with him. His words touched most of those who did not like Germany, but were afraid Germany would win, and therefore wanted to remain uninvolved. These people could not see the historic consequences of a German victory. All those with a latent or active anti-foreign bias, those who were disillusioned with the power politics world, and those who were pacifist at heart—and these were millions—took comfort in his "expertize." Above all, his words struck a responsive chord in those industrialists who feared the social consequences of a new war. Among these men, on both sides of the Atlantic, Lindbergh had become a new kind of hero.

But the speech raised hackles among a large body of American intellectuals. These people, who included Dorothy Thompson, Walter Lippmann, Heywood Broun, and others, were not warlike at the time. But they had a profound hatred of Hitler and his world revolution. Lindbergh's equal condemnation of Europeans, Nazis and anti-Nazis alike, in their eyes almost tarred him with the Nazi brush. Fascist notions were read into his speech. Lindbergh was described in columns as "militaristic." He was called "Herr von Lindbergh." He most bothered those writers and others who were anti-Nazi, pro-British, but had not yet made the leap to the side of American militarism and preparedness.

The great rearmament program of 1940 was in line with Lindbergh's and his supporters' ideas, and for some months the scope of the program silenced their outcries, but America's increasing cooperation with the British, and the destroyer deal, brought their sentiments out again in full force.

The America First Committee was the idea of a Yale law student, R. Douglas Stuart, Jr., a son of the first vice president of Quaker Oats. The Committee's gray eminence was General Robert A. Wood, board chairman of Sears, Roebuck & Co. Its immediate heavy contributors and financial backers included a blue-ribbon group of conservative businessmen: Edward Ryerson, Jr., steel magnate; Sterling Morton, of Morton Salt; William H. Regnery, Western Shade Cloth Company; and Robert Young, railway genius. Two of its principal Congressional spokesmen were Hamilton Fish and Senator Burton Wheeler. Its writer was Kathleen Norris. Its hero was Charles A. Lindbergh.

Its principal atmosphere was gloom.

Stuart announced four broad policy objectives of the Committee:

1. To create impregnable American defenses.
2. To keep any foreign power, or coalition of powers, from successfully attacking a prepared United States.
3. To preserve American democracy by keeping out of a European war.
4. To stop "aid short of war" which weakened national defense and at the same time threatened to involve the United States on Britain's side.

Behind these objectives were several assumptions:

1. Germany would dominate Europe, and should be allowed to do so.
2. England or the Commonwealth could make a deal with Hitler, and thus continue without American intervention.
3. Behind three thousand miles of ocean, the United States could hold its own in Hitler's New Order world.
4. Entry into a foreign war would make Roosevelt a dictator, and bring socialism or other dangerous economic or social change.

The stance of the America First Committee was thus—though it seemed belligerent and brash to some—defensive and passive, and its main concern was not with what would happen abroad, but in preventing undesirable events at home. Literally thousands of top business leaders across America agreed. Like Joseph Kennedy, who since coming back from England had preached gloom and doom, these were men who still retained what can only be called a Munich-mind.

Most of them did not see their intellectual and emotional link with the Englishmen who had masterminded Munich, or who had thought they could live off the coasts of Hitler's Europe. By an accident of history, the same kind of men who

176

formed America First had been in control of British affairs at the very moment Hitler chose to drive for power.

In the 1930's Britain was not ruled either by socialists or aristocrats, but by a combination of industrial and economic power that was blind to the structure of the modern world. As both Dr. Samuel Johnson and Henry Cabot Lodge the elder, a good Republican, remarked, some breeds of businessmen are not, by training, outlook, or inclination, fitted to understand or manage public affairs. World politics transcend such things as profit or loss or even efficient management: they require, from century to century, a keen sense of drift and destiny, of human tragedy, and above all, the grasp of transcendental goals.

Churchill and Roosevelt smelled Hitler out; Chamberlain could not. It is almost impossible to imagine Franklin Roosevelt, Winston Churchill, or John F. Kennedy, the son of Joseph, springing from the business role. It is no denigration of the superb talents of Herbert Hoover or Neville Chamberlain —to state that they were managers and businessmen with no knowledge of a tribal leader's job.

British industrialists in the 1930's were as impervious to the notion of a fascist world revolution as their counterparts in the America First organization were to be in the 1940's. The problem was that there was not one, but *two* world revolutions brewing during the decade. Since 1917, all Westerners had become aware of Russian Communism, which openly avowed the destruction of virtually everything Western Christian civilization stood for. Russia, wracked by bloody revolution, had been more or less contained behind its frontiers by French and British diplomacy in the 1920's; Russia was not apparently an imminent threat as a great national power. But the Russian ideology had spread like a great underground stain through Europe. In the years of desperate economic crisis during the international depression, Marxism enjoyed a certain vogue. The Western ruling groups, who could not solve their critical

177

economic problems, and who were aware of the restlessness of their unemployed, had an understandable fear of all the things Communism promised the poor. Actually, they magnified this danger; it was more psychological than real—but the psychology affected Western and above all, British policy.

Most current political thought in Great Britain in the 1930's (shared in France) held that a new war, or even the burdens of an armament program that pinched living standards further, would create an imminent danger of a Marxist revolt by the Western masses. Actually, the more typical response in relatively advanced nations to the economic crisis was fascist, not Communist, totalitarianism. Fascist tyranny, coupled with national power as in Germany, was more *immediately* dangerous to democracies like France and Britain than world Communism. But tragically, many Britons in high places seemed to see Nazism as a sort of antidote to Communism.

In his first years, Hitler was even praised because he destroyed the German Communists. The very real hatred of the Soviet Union's ideology, which was peculiarly strong in the British Establishment, or decision-making circles in the 1930's, consistently blinded these men to the dangers of a powerful, nationalistic Germany.

Unable to risk either rearmament or a possible conflict with a rising Germany, British ruling thought hopefully seized on the notion that Nazism could be an effective counterpoise to Russian Marxism. Hitler could serve a useful purpose by barring Communism from the West, and even more hopefully, destroy both himself, and Russian power, in an eventual war in the East.

This idea became fashionable at the very time when any effective British diplomacy required that Britain seek a diplomatic rapprochement with the U.S.S.R. aimed at encircling Germany. This would not have been unusual: in 1914, Britain and Czarist Russia were allied against a common danger, although their systems of government were utterly different and there was a definite and historic hostility between the two powers.

The British could not bring themselves to wage this kind of diplomacy, however, because the personal antipathy of British statesmen to the Communists ruling Russia was too immense. Chamberlain, for one, positively detested Soviet Russia and all its works. He feared it more than Germany. Until 1938, at least, he still held some hopes that Mr. Hitler might yet prove to be a gentleman. The focus on the Red revolution threatening the West, to the exclusion of the more dangerous Brown revolution, was almost fatal.

For the record, the U.S.S.R. several times tried to make a pragmatic *war alliance* with the West in the 1930's, but was treated with both suspicion and contempt.

In another fashion, the British rulers of the 1930's were quite unlike the men of the previous centuries. They were surprisingly insular and blind; they looked inward, to the British economy, not outward to the structure of the world. The dominant men, such as Sir Samuel Hoare, Sir Arthur Balfour, Sir John Simon, and Chamberlain himself, were not British aristocrats but quite provincial British businessmen. Their instinct was to think that the historic fears, hatreds, emotions, and ultra-rational drives of nations and peoples could be managed the same way capable and sensible men managed a business. Men like Churchill or Eden or Duff-Cooper, who said otherwise, irritated them. They remained convinced to the end that somehow a deal could be fashioned with Mr. Hitler. Chamberlain's cabinet, and United States Ambassador Joseph Kennedy, who approved of Munich, were as utterly ignorant of the ultra-rational psychology of power relationships as Charles Lindbergh.

It was true that the pacifist nature of Britons during the 1930's, and the national reluctance to spend for arms during a depression, influenced Chamberlain's course. But no real attempt was made to lead the people to an acceptance of a harsh destiny because no leader saw that destiny.

In the 1930's the one great stabilizing power in the world was Britain, but by 1938 it had obviously failed in this role. When France fell and Britain was pushed back to the wall, the center of gravity of the Western world moved westward. Yet, as late as 1941 a prominent American banker, who was to leave his children millions, stated plaintively: "What the hell can you do with a fellow like Hitler, who just won't make a deal?"

This man was a member of America First and as blind to the truth of America's eventual destiny as the British Establishment had been to its own.

America First, the spiritual counterpart of British isolationism, was as willing to let Britain go by the board as Chamberlain had been to make Czechoslovakia the price of "peace." The committee's psychology, rarely articulated, was that a deal, even a bad deal, was infinitely better than a world war and all the disruptions and changes in American life and society America Firsters believed such a war would bring.

With the United States government moving rapidly toward an acceptance of an Atlantic strategy and an Atlantic war, if necessary, America First put an enormous stumbling block in its way. Its advertisements—full-page in many papers—its great rallies in Madison Square Garden, New York, and in Chicago, strengthened antiwar opinion, and caused interventionists such as the Century Group a deep despair.

Many Americans saw that public opinion, liking Roosevelt but agreeing more with Lindbergh than the President on war, was tying the President's hands. They were desperately afraid of more "too little, too late," and they wanted to proceed with greater speed. They had come to pin all their hopes on Roosevelt, and there was a great fear in intellectual circles in late 1940, even after the destroyer deal, that he would fail to lead.

But F.D.R. who had been described as "changeable, warmhearted, charming and sometimes gullible" could be something quite different when he had made up his mind, or he was crossed. He could be "hard, stubborn, resourceful, and relentless," too. F.D.R. had no intention of letting either the public or America First destroy his national policy.

The best both could do was to delay Roosevelt, and in some things to drive him underground.

11.

Liberalism, Lunacy, and Lend-Lease

Look, the morning is approaching . . .
The day of East Asia is coming.
Happily the swastika and the red, white and green banner
Fly in the wind. It will become spring.

> Saburo Kurusu, Japanese Ambassador to Berlin, 1940.

This war is the climax of all political failure.

> Charles A. Lindbergh.

The fact is that the people have not yet made up their minds that
we are at war . . . they have not yet buckled down to the deter-
mination to fight this war through; for they have got into their
heads that we are going to get out of this fix by strategy. That's
the word—strategy! Abraham Lincoln, 1862.

On September 27, 1940 Germany, Italy, and Japan did the government of the United States a great favor: they formalized a developing geopolitical situation and a vague threat into the Tripartite Pact, which could only be aimed at isolationist America.

The Pact contained only 419 words in English, which ironically enough was the only language in which Germans and Japanese could communicate. It stated, simply, that if the United States joined Great Britain in an Atlantic war, Japan would attack in the Pacific. If the United States attacked

Japan in the Pacific, Germany and Italy were to strike in the West. The purpose was obvious: to bully the United States into continued neutrality, and to make it back away from the European war, and finally, if necessary, to force it to fight a two-front war. The Germans hoped the Japanese threat would take American attention from the Atlantic. This did not happen, however, and the principal reason was that Washington was hostile to, but not very much afraid of the Japanese. The United States Pacific fleet still had the Japanese outnumbered and outgunned.

The Japanese were almost at the point of striking against the Dutch and British possessions in East Asia. They needed them economically; above all else, Japan needed Indonesian oil. But Japanese strategists realized that the United States probably would not stand by if Japan moved south. For their part in the Tripartite Pact, they hoped Germany would engage both the British and United States in the West, and thus open Japan's opportunity to Asian conquest.

This was strategy and a war of nerves on the grand scale—but it only solidified thinking in Washington. It did not divert Washington from its increasing attitude of intervention, because Roosevelt's Cabinet made an immediate assumption that the Atlantic interests were most vital, and the Japanese threat less dangerous than the German. The only immediate effect this had for the Japanese was to make Washington not only more hostile, but more firm in its anti-Japanese stands. Japan took over French Indo-China in 1940 by applying pressure on the Vichy government. Washington condemned this, placed an embargo on shipments of iron and steel to Japan, and warned Tokyo that it would accept no further territorial revision in the East.

The sale of oil to the Japanese navy by Anglo-American oil companies, however, was not stopped. The British government was afraid that such a move would make the Japanese attack British interests in the East, and the dominant view in F.D.R.'s

Cabinet agreed. Washington was prepared to resist Japanese pressure in the Pacific, which would take the form of naval action, and surprisingly, almost the entire public concurred. The isolationist or peace bloc senators did not oppose getting tough with the Japanese—Wheeler and Vandenberg, for example, were proponents of the policy. But they did oppose any kind of land war in defense of European colonies. Taft of Ohio said bluntly that no American parent was ready to have sons die for some place with an unpronounceable name in Indo-China.

Roosevelt and Hull permitted the Japanese occupation of Indo-China to proceed. They even agreed tacitly—though they obviously did not reveal this to either the Japanese or Americans—to stand aside in case the Japanese invaded Thailand. But Roosevelt firmly drew the line of American intent at the Dutch East Indies or British Malaya. His notes to the Japanese government left that regime under no illusions that either area could be occupied short of conflict with the United States.

In October 1940, the State Department advised all American nationals living in the Far East to return home.

Hitler and Mussolini met at the Brenner Pass on the Austro-Italian border on October 4. A few days later, Italy invaded Greece. The attack was unprovoked, and for no other purpose than an expansion of the new Italian Empire Mussolini still dreamed of creating. But in the mountains of northern Greece and Albania this campaign bogged down. The Italians, both in Europe and in North Africa against the British forces in Libya, began to have real troubles in realizing their dictator's great schemes.

The British Navy kept control of the Mediterranean in spite of the large Italian fleet. The Italian army failed to perform creditably, either against the British or the Greeks, which caused English, American, and German observers considerable amusement.

In New York, *Help Greece Now* posters joined the long sad

184

procession of signs begging for help for Finland and bundles for Britain. Considerable money was raised, although aid for Greece never achieved the popularity and almost blue-ribbon social status the committees to assist Britain had reached. A high proportion of the Social Register by 1940 was engaged in British war relief, especially in cities on the eastern seaboard.

Cordell Hull, of course, condemned the Axis attack on Greece, using terms and phrases that had been used before.

During 1940 and 1941 the feeling that the British were actually losing the war continued to grow in America. They were holding, but they were on the defensive everywhere. The air battle over Britain remained in doubt; few observers saw that the crisis had passed in 1940. The German armies still posed a terrible invasion threat. The British were doing well against Italy in the Mediterranean, and by stripping island defenses they were continuing to hold Suez and Africa. But this very defense of the Near and Middle East against Italo-German pressure disturbed many of Roosevelt's staff.

Naturally, Americans saw the North Atlantic and the British Isles as the theater of greatest interest to their own security. They preferred that the British make a decision to hold here, and to let the imperial lifeline go, if reinforcing Africa meant taking risks at home. Churchill, however, continued to risk sending American aid and scarce British arms to North Africa in preference to building up home isle defenses. For one reason, the R.A.F.'s success gave him confidence the Germans could not successfully invade England. But the main reason —which, ironically, Americans failed to discern—was that areas such as Malta and Egypt had much the same relation to Britain's eventual security as Britain had to North America.

Churchill, more than once, was forced to convince F.D.R. of this. The arguments, utterly logical, did not completely dispel American pessimism.

The overall gloom was shared by many influential Americans. One of the most prominent was Ambassador Joseph Kennedy. Kennedy was one of those rightly impressed by the German might in the late 1930's, but his lack of confidence in the British and French during the "sitzkrieg" or phony war became profound. Once prominently considered a possibility to replace Roosevelt as the Democratic nominee in 1940, Kennedy confounded many people by coming out very early for a third term for F.D.R. Although Kennedy, an economic conservative, had completely soured on F.D.R.'s domestic policies, he considered Roosevelt's promises to keep the United States out of war genuine, and therefore felt the President was indispensable. Kennedy had come to believe that Germany would certainly win, that the British contribution was at best worthless, and that a war with a powerful Germany would be futile and destructive to America, perhaps even fostering a domestic Communism. He reiterated these views in several public places, dismaying not only the British, but Roosevelt.

Kennedy acknowledged Churchill's toughness, but once told Churchill that he was the only tough Briton left. He did not believe that Churchill could galvanize a people who so obviously were reluctant to fight through the summer of 1940.

These views soon brought Kennedy into complete conflict with the Administration. Kennedy was aware that F.D.R. was determined to aid Britain, and by aiding Britain, increase enormously the risk of eventual war. Further, his very open lack of confidence in the British war effort made it impossible for him to continue to represent F.D.R. at the Court of St. James, since the British, with whom he had been popular prior to the war, now considered him pro-German, or at the best, anti-British. Returning to the United States, Kennedy became an avowed isolationist.

In response to a reporter's question if the British could be considered to be fighting for democracy, Kennedy labeled this "bunk." He said the British were fighting for their own survival. While on narrow terms, this was absolutely true, state-

186

ments like these damaged the President's efforts to build moral and emotional support for his strategic policy of aiding Great Britain.

By late 1940, a certain form of "schizophrenia"—as *The New York Times* described it—had settled on the American mood. The Gallup polls regularly revealed that approximately 60 percent of all Americans acknowledged that Britain was fighting for American interests, at least by proxy, and favored increased aid. But at the same time, less than 13 percent—an increase of only about 6 percentage points since June, 1940—said they were willing to go to war with Germany now.

This schizophrenia was to last another year with very little change. American opinion, group to group, and region to region, had solidified. Certain patterns—some antithetical, some paradoxical—had become clear.

Although certain sections of the press, especially "The Three Furies"—the New York *Daily News, Washington Times-Herald,* and *Chicago Tribune*—were almost hysterically opposed to any further intervention in the war, a majority of the United States press supported aid for Britain. There was even considerable cautious sentiment for war—as being "inevitable."

This was a great change from the fall of 1939, but of course, it was part of the press's job to analyze and digest as well as disseminate the news. The press was one of the first American institutions to have its doubts about continued isolation. It was overwhelmingly critical of the Administration, now, for not doing more.

But the press did not have, then or before, dominant influence over American opinion. Eighty percent of the press, for example, had opposed Roosevelt for reelection and editorialized against his domestic policies for eight years, completely without political effect.

Important—but not greatly influential—intellectuals formed committees and discussed strategy to get the American public to face the fact that it was, or should be, in the war. These included Rupert Hughes, Edna Ferber, John Farrar, Herbert Agar, and Walter Millis. They were fought by other writers such as Albert Payson Terhune, Kathleen Norris, Norman Thomas, and Dr. Charles Morrison, editor of *Christian Century*.

Wealthy and important industrialists such as Henry Ford, Sterling Morton, General Robert Wood, and Lessing Rosenwald, paid for isolationist ads and propaganda. Other powerful men, such as Joseph Kennedy, continued to preach a certain gloom and doom: America could not afford a commitment against Germany to defend the world.

Lindbergh drew large crowds, arguing that involvement in war would only defeat the cause of American democracy by bringing an American dictatorship at home.

Walter Lippmann suffered from a slightly different type of schizophrenia: his hatred and understanding of Hitler warred against his deep fear of United States commitment in tasks beyond American power.

While interventionism influenced more intellectuals and a higher percentage of the social elite, isolationism seemingly was more active in financial support of the cause. Verne Marshall, editor of the Iowa *Cedar Rapids Gazette* was able to pay forty-one thousand dollars for full-page ads in sixty newspapers across the country denouncing the war, and to repeat with seventy-nine.

There were frequent attempts to smear the antiwar or isolationist groups with the Nazi brush, especially in intellectual circles. However, Dr. Leon Milton Birkhead's assertion that there were fifteen to twenty million pro-Nazis in the United States never came close to the truth. Isolationism was not pro-fascist sentiment. The best estimates of the time were that never more than 1 percent of Americans favored Germany or Italy to win the war.

Antiwar or isolationist feeling did, however, assist the Axis powers, whose policy was to win in Europe before the United States, with its immense production potential, became involved. Further, the idea of a stalemated or negotiated peace had become the isolationists' principal argument. Lindbergh's assertion that the European war was "internecine" or really a European "civil war"—without moral implications for America—was strongly pushed. Because the isolationists did not think the game of fighting Hitler was worth the candle, and would be ruinous to America, their greatest hope was that a stalemate could be achieved, with "no victory" for either side. Neither antagonist, however, showed any inclination to heed this kind of American advice.

Senators Tydings of Maryland, Vandenberg of Michigan, McCarran of Nevada, Holt of West Virginia, Johnson of Colorado, and Wheeler of Montana—a mix of Democrats and Republicans that stretched across the liberal-conservative spectrum—led a Congressional group that made public statements that President Roosevelt could negotiate a "just peace" if he would only make an effort.

The President was accused of not trying to seek an end to the war, but only of trying to involve the United States in it. Wheeler himself went further than the others, as acknowledged leader of the Senate peace bloc: "F.D.R. is going to plow under every fourth American boy."

This kind of statement turned F.D.R., who by now really did not believe that the United States would be able to stay out of the shooting forever, almost white with fury. He called the accusation "dastardly," and reiterated he did not *want* to go to war, or send American troops overseas. But he saw the United States' options narrowing rapidly.

While the President repeated he did not desire war and had no notions of sending an expeditionary force to Europe, the militant secretaries of the Navy and War, Knox and Stimson, made speeches and public statements denouncing the Neutrality Act and arguing for American naval intervention in the Battle of the Atlantic. As Cabinet members, they could not have done this without the President's approval. When Frank Knox was quoted in the press as saying that "the only hope for peace for the United States was the defeat of Germany," F.D.R. did not refute him.

Knox and Stimson, however, represented a small minority of opinion, although it was powerful opinion strongly entrenched in the government. Knox and Stimson were domestic conservatives. There was very little "liberal" about them, just as the new, vigorous breed of executives in the sub-Cabinet posts—McCloy, Forrestal, Patterson, and Lovett—were not liberals in the intellectual or political sense.

These men did not generally approve the direction of internal politics in the 1930's—but their main interest was in foreign policy.

Such men could be found among Democrats and Republicans. Regardless of which political party they came from, they were an intellectual progression from the old American "Large Policy" that had been developed in the late years of the nineteenth century. The "Large Policy" had been so named because it meant taking a large view of the world and accepted a large American place in that world.

Both Theodore Roosevelt and Woodrow Wilson were devotees of the "Large" view, and the Large Policy had been the dominant American policy for several decades. Neither Wilson nor Theodore Roosevelt, for example, had been afraid to implement American intervention, either diplomatic or military, when American interests seemed to call for it. Roosevelt helped negotiate peace between Russia and Japan in 1905, and saw to it that the Panama Canal was built. Wilson entered the European War in 1917 and created the League of Nations; he also intervened in Mexico, Santo Domingo, and Haiti. The Large policy was much older than twentieth-century isolationism, which was almost wholly a reaction from the bitterness of disillusionment with World War I.

190

The men who ran the Large Policy considered world order, American interests, and American security inseparable, and like Knox and Stimson in 1940, they had held that there were no "territorial limits" to either American security or interests. The concept, then and later, was of course strategically sound. But it had run into disfavor with much liberal opinion, because it was deemed to have an imperialist tinge. Actually, American liberals had come to a belief in intervention short of war only because of the image of Hitler. Liberal opinion, after World War I, had rejected the inevitability of power politics and above all, United States involvement in it. It had been instrumental in keeping the United States disarmed. It had changed only when presented with Nazi viciousness.

Liberals came reluctantly to the conclusion that Hitler could not be lived with and that he had to be destroyed, by force if necessary. But this view tended to see Hitler as a monster, and not a perfectly natural manifestation of his times. They did not come to any conclusion that the psychology of power relationships upon which Hitler played was eternal. Thus most active liberal opinion now urging the destruction of Nazism enthusiastically supported aid to Britain and F.D.R.'s moves toward intervention, but without accepting the emerging doctrine of American defense. They were prepared to accept armaments and world involvement, but only for the specific, one-time goal of restoring peace. In Large Policy terms, then, the most rabid liberal interventionists of 1940-1941 were fundamentally and psychologically isolationist.

Hitler forced them to revise their policy, but not their outlook. They had not come over to the idea of a necessary defense of the status quo in the United States interest. With Hitler gone, they would not be convinced of a new interventionalism unless convinced of a new monster, or a new *immediate* danger.

One of the phenomena of the 1930's was that the isolationism, originally fostered by liberals disgusted with the aftermath of 1918, gradually became the belief of economic or business conservatives. The principal reasons for this were a fear of the economic consequences of rearmament or war, both of which could bring social change. This group did not like Hitler either, but held to the last the illusion that Hitler was preferable to Bolshevism, and somehow thought there could be a choice. This last idea Hitler himself carefully cultivated. But this group was more nationalist-minded than the liberals, and had less fear of the *ideas* of war or rearmament, only their consequences.

Almost, but not quite, merging with the economic conservatives such as Kennedy, Wood, and Ryerson, were the American constitutionalists. These had a real fear of F.D.R.'s assuming un-American, dictatorial powers.

For a decade, the industrial societies had been generally unsuccessful in controlling their economic cycle, and this had fostered dictatorship abroad. In every nation governmental powers had been increased in the effort to control the economic swings. Nineteenth-century economic and constitutional liberalism, or laissez-faire, was almost dead. While F.D.R. was still firmly bound by United States law and was nowhere near being a Caesar, he had still become the most powerful President in peacetime history. Traditionalists instinctively understood that foreign involvement or war would increase Presidential powers, and this they feared. A great number of Americans who understood, and agreed with, the new doctrine of a worldwide defense could not support it enthusiastically because it seemed to strengthen the President. They did not believe that new powers granted would soon, if ever, be returned.

The dilemma here was that the Congress, or the courts, simply could not implement any kind of effective policy abroad, and if the United States did become involved, time and circumstance demanded that the President have almost a free hand.

Actually, in the early 1940's all three groups—liberals, economic conservatives, and constitutionalists—hoping to maintain the equality of the three branches of government were fighting a losing battle. The technology and strategy of defense, which narrowed the world and caught the United States up in it, was to be dominant over ideology or what the American people wanted. An American government could no more escape the logic of power relationships than could the Roman Republic situated among hostile City States in Italy centuries before Christ, nor the British government of the eighteenth and nineteenth centuries. If the United States became insular, like the Britain of the 1930's it could only do so at its extreme peril.

In 1940-1941, however, the only consensus on defense was the sentiment the Gallup poll regularly revealed: more than 90 percent ready to fight if America were attacked at home, only about 10 percent prepared to go to war or accept an active power role for any other reason.

There were interesting breakdowns, socially, educationally, ethnically, and regionally, within this broad pattern. These were also consistently shown by the polls-in-depth, which also indicated the inconsistencies in the convictions held by all human beings: no American was completely motivated or influenced by one idea or emotion alone.

Ethnically, Jews and Negroes were most opposed to Hitler. This was an obvious response to the racial attitudes and practices of Nazism. But these two groups were not the ones most prepared to fight.

White Protestant Anglo-Saxon Americans in the South and on the eastern seaboard were most disposed to aid the British Empire. But white Southerners were much readier to fight. The Northeast was highly in favor of granting aid, but not inclined to war. The white South was six times as ready as the nation as a whole to accept combat with fascism.

The Sons of Italy, and Italian-Americans generally, Scandinavian and German-American groups, tended to be genuinely neutral. They were neither pro-British nor pro-German. Ethnic groups from areas which had been overrun by Hitler were violently anti-German, with the exception of Scandinavians, who were influenced by two factors. They had assimilated to the point of losing ethnic consciousness, and regionally were in the most isolationist or neutral area—the Middle West.

The Pacific coast, in these years, was belligerent toward Japan, but not much interested in events in Europe.

Irish-Americans showed an almost schizophrenic tendency: they were still antagonistic toward the British Empire and Winston Churchill, but somewhat belligerent toward Hitler, too.

New York City was most interventionist in spirit, but not the most warlike. Chicago was the most isolationist city. Texas was by far the most belligerent state. It led all others in the percentage of volunteers for the armed forces, and there was widespread disgust that the United States had not already got in the war. The Texas mood was not anglophile, but intensely nationalistic.

No isolationist rally was ever held in Georgia. Almost without exception every Southern Democratic congressman and senator was in favor of increased intervention, and some were prepared to vote for war.

Farmers and rural people, generally, were less afraid of war than city dwellers. The very poor were also more prepared to fight than the American rich, who felt they had more to lose. The college generation was not as sanguine about defense as the older population. Its mood tended to apathy, escapism, and worry about the draft.

Veterans and patriotic organizations, such as the American Legion, had switched from original isolationism to near-belligerency. But the basis of this was again nationalism, not an appreciation of new strategy. All nationalistic sentiment, from Texas to Virginia, and from the American Legion to the Daughters of the American Revolution, enthusiastically supported armament and increased national defense. This mood bordered on, and could quickly become, antagonism and belligerency against any foreign nation that defied the United States. Nationalist opinion began with Fortress America, but in 1941 was tending to go one step further.

There was evidence, however, that the most pro-intervention groups frightened more people than they convinced. A large part of the clergy, of all denominations, was torn between an active dislike of totalitarianism and an even greater hatred of war. The outright pacifists, who agreed to fight only if American soil were attacked, made little noise, but were much more numerous than most Americans thought. Serious estimates in 1941 set these at 20 to 25 percent of the population, with higher percentages among women.

One of the peculiar phenomena of the period—and one that annoyed and greatly damaged originally respectable isolationist groups and organizations—was the rush of extremists of all stripes, from ultra-right to Communists, to join movements such as America First.

The Communist line opposed American intervention; Communists tried to infiltrate the executive ranks of America First, but with little success. The extreme Right did much better, and its infiltration was one of the things that most discredited Wheeler's and Lindbergh's efforts for a sincere debate.

America First did avoid connection with the German-American Bund, but other pro-Germans, like George Sylvester Viereck, actually organized some local branches of the organization without America First's national leadership being aware of it. Nazi propaganda was specially prepared for America First, and sometimes unwittingly used. And the leaders of America First did make one immense mistake, by accepting support and membership from home-grown American fascist groups. William Dudley Pelley's Silver Shirts, the Ku Klux Klan, and Father Coughlin's Christian Front began to show up for America First rallies, or in some areas even run them. The damage to the Committee's image was profound.

The men of America First and 80 percent of the American people were in agreement on staying out of the war. But America First expected and was prepared to accept a Nazi victory, then make a deal to live in a Nazi-dominated world. Ironically, the men who founded America First were deeply afraid of American totalitarianism, and never realized that they were unwittingly fostering it.

In time, the Silver Shirts and other assorted hoodlums did drive some original America Firsters out of the organization.

In all parts of the nation, polls stated that the wealthier and better educated were more in favor of increased aid to Britain than the nation as a whole. Gallup's poll of the men and women who were listed in *Who's Who in America* showed a startling fact: these people, of generally high intellectual attainment, were almost 50 percent in favor of immediate war. They included several times as many belligerents as the ordinary population.

But in spite of all the noise and arguments, the mass rallies for and against intervention, the basic dichotomy in the American mind was clear. A majority wanted aid to Britain; a greater majority refused to accept a foreign war. The first allowed the Administration to proceed, the second made its pace painfully slow and hesitant. Any commitments to the British that went beyond material aid or goods had to be kept quiet, and underground.

In December 1940, Secretary Morgenthau informed the President that the British were almost out of cash. Foreign assets and gold had been liquidated steadily since 1939. There was no more money to negotiate new cash-and-carry contracts for arms. Also, American industry would run out of current orders in April 1941, unless some means of granting credit to the British government were found.

Secretaries Knox, Stimson, and Chief of Staff Marshall were

in complete accord that Britain could not continue to resist German invasion without material American aid. When Morgenthau proposed that the Administration lend the British money to buy arms, Stimson said, "Lend, hell. We are buying security, not lending."

The Administration determined to place a bill before Congress authorizing the President to "lend, lease, or sell" war goods, and to appropriate money for it, to an initial amount of seven billion dollars. Since money was involved there was no way around Congress; the bill would have to be debated. There was very little concern that the bill would be defeated in the prevailing sentiment to aid Britain, but it would be delayed.

There was also going to have to be another national defense appropriation, raising the amount spent to twenty-six billion dollars in two years. These were unprecedented sums, but there was again no question that the money would be voted.

To ease the way for Lend-Lease, and to try to arouse the nation from its continued apathy toward the events in Europe, the President scheduled his fifteenth fireside chat. This was made from the White House in December.

Roosevelt said:

> Never before since Jamestown and Plymouth Rock has our American civilization been in such danger.

He named the enemy: the Tripartite Axis. He stated that if the United States were to block the Axis' drive for ultimate world control, it would unite in ultimate action against America.

He clearly detailed the Administration view of the German program: to conquer all Europe, then to use the skills and resources of Europe for world domination. He did not state categorically that the United States could keep out of war, but he did deny that the Administration wanted or intended to go to war, or that he had any intention of sending an American expeditionary force abroad. His words had been carefully tailored, to urge the United States into greater awareness and action, but not to face the public with a policy or action from which it would recoil.

He did say that the course of aid to Britain offered "the least risk" and the "greatest hope" of staying out. He tried to torpedo the persistent hope for a negotiated peace. He was not against one—but the United States had no "right or reason" to expect one, or even "to encourage talk of peace until the aggressor nations . . . abandoned all thought of dominating or conquering the world."

He tried to explain Atlantic strategy:

> If Great Britain goes down . . . all of us . . . would be living at the point of a gun . . . to survive in such a world, we would have to convert ourselves permanently into a militaristic power. . . .
> At one point between Africa and Brazil the distance is less than from Washington to Denver.

He stated that the notion that the Axis had no reason or desire to attack the United States was:

> . . . the same dangerous, wishful thinking which destroyed so many conquered peoples. The vast resources and wealth of this hemisphere constitute the most tempting loot in all the world.

He denied the idea that the Axis could be appeased.

> No man can tame a tiger into a kitten by stroking it. There can be no appeasement with ruthlessness. A nation can have peace with the Nazis only at the price of total surrender.

He referred to the background of totalitarianism, "the concentration camp and the servants of God in chains." He said the proposed "new order" was an unholy alliance to dominate and enslave the human race.

He then stated bluntly that Great Britain should get more guns, planes, ships, and tanks. He asked for a great effort and a "great sacrifice" but no sacrifice, however, of any American social goal.

> I would ask no one to defend a democracy which in turn would not defend everyone in the nation against want and privation.

He cautioned labor and management against strikes, and urged:

> We must be the great arsenal of democracy.

Finally, he stated that on his latest and best information, the Axis could not win.

Immediate reaction was overwhelmingly favorable. Seventy-one percent of the public said they agreed with F.D.R., and 54 percent—though many with reservations—were in favor of Lend-Lease now.

The "arsenal of democracy" concept, not connected to any proposed expeditionary force or shooting war, had great appeal.

Columnist Raymond Clapper described the speech as calling for "war one degree removed from direct hostilities."

Lindbergh tried to refute F.D.R. by saying that a stalemated peace, without victory for either side, was still possible.

In presenting the Lend-Lease bill, H. R. 1776 as it was aptly numbered, to Congress, the Administration made the clearest and boldest delineation and explanation of the new Atlantic doctrine yet stated:

On January 9, 1941 Secretary Knox testified:

> I . . . believe that a victorious Germany would move over to this hemisphere as soon as she could accumulate the strength to do so, and certainly very soon, unless we now take steps to check her career of reckless aggression.

Secretary Hull stated on January 15:

> Were Britain defeated, and were she to lose command of the seas, Germany could easily cross the Atlantic—especially the South Atlantic—unless we were ready and able to do what Britain is doing now. Were the Atlantic to fall under German control, the Atlantic would offer little or no assurance of security.

Knox, on January 17, went into greater detail.

> If you will glance at the map, you will readily observe that there are but three exits into the Atlantic in Europe: the channels of the North Sea (north of the British Isles), the English Channel itself, and the Straits of Gibraltar. Our entire western world has been safe from attack from Europe because the British fleet has always stood sentinel at these three exits into the ocean, and the British for many years have accepted, and assisted us in the maintenance of the Monroe Doctrine. That has sufficed to make the Atlantic barrier secure.

Knox and Stimson again and again advanced the concept of modern defense strategy that the United States staff had evolved: in an age of airpower and rapid communications, no decent strategy could allow itself to be hampered by territorial restraints. *No enemy could be allowed to occupy the most important strategic positions, even if they seemed to lie outside American boundaries of responsibility.* Lines of defense could not be rigidly drawn, like a Maginot Line, across the ground, or even across national boundaries. Strategy must take into account, in each case, the possible necessity of advancing the lines of final defense.

Stimson was not in favor of holding the hemisphere and waiting for attack.

> If our military experts are forced to place the defense line farther out, I am inclined to say that they are dead right.

War had to begin where the enemy was, or when he reached a position from which he could hurt you, Secretary Knox continued the thesis. He ruled out no area of the globe as a possible area of United States interest, and rejected the idea that Europe was in a different part of the world.

These were all cogent arguments for entrance into the war at that time. They were understood as such by the few thoughtful observers. But the Administration called for no other action except increased aid under Lend-Lease. This disturbed many analysts, who either did not understand, or refused to accept, the President's policy of not pushing the United States faster than public opinion traveled.

Dr. Charles C. Morrison of the *Christian Century* had hit a sore point when he wrote:

> Such a war will not be America's war. It will be the President's war. America has never fought a President's war.

Franklin Roosevelt, the greatest consensus President in American history, had no desire for the United States to fight a President's war. The people did not yet accept or understand the concept of advanced defense. Like certain animals, they were wedded emotionally to territoriality and the defense only of their own little plot of earth. They did not accept the fact that Britain was of such immense strategic importance to the United States—because it contained hostile power behind the ocean—that it could not be allowed to go down.

If Roosevelt pushed the United States too far, if he got it into a shooting war by his own initiative or seemed likely to, certain of his political advisers had informed him that a "peace party" might easily win the Congress in 1942. If he followed the logical extensions of his own Administration's policy, it meant advancing the zone of American defense to Europe, and joining the British in the battle of the Atlantic.

This meant moving American ships or planes or troops into a war zone and opening fire on a potentially dangerous enemy before Americans themselves were attacked or fired on. Roosevelt was extremely dubious of the political effects. He would take an unenthusiastic and divided country into a dangerous war; he did not think he could risk it, although this was exactly what Frank Knox, Henry Stimson, and several hundred far-seeing strategists were urging.

The Lend-Lease bill was debated until March 1941. Predictably the isolationist and peace bloc senators opposed it: Clark of Missouri argued that it was a war bill, and both he and Wheeler complained that "war would bring the United States dictatorship." But the arguments were not strong, and they gained no support. The opposition Republicans were split and refused to oppose the bill as a bloc. An attempt to attach a rider to the bill curtailing the President's power as Commander in Chief to send military forces overseas was beaten off.

The bill passed overwhelmingly in the end, under an almost unanimous press attack for quicker action. The Congress' deliberation—part of the normal democratic process—was condemned universally, and this condemnation in many influential quarters strengthened the President's hand.

The bill appropriated seven billion dollars and gave F.D.R. greater peacetime powers of commitment than any President had ever had. He was empowered to have made, sell, buy, transfer, or give, any "defense article." The definition of "defense article" was in effect left to him. It was a blank check to commit American goods and arms abroad.

The President was also permitted to give or exchange any defense information with other powers at his option. Its terms allowed the government to have British ships repaired in American yards, and to have the British fleet refitted and refueled at the American taxpayers' expense.

The bill was rushed to F.D.R. after passage, and he signed it within minutes. The vital flow of equipment to the British Isles was not interrupted by a day.

The reaction in the country was generally favorable. Most people thought it was a reasonable step to "keep the United

States out of war," because the bill had been so described. It seemed a safe way of hurting Hitler.

The British were overjoyed. United States flags were hoisted in London, and Churchill described H. R. 1776 as a "new Magna Charta" to a Parliament. Several uniformed American military officers sitting in the galleries of the House were applauded. Jan Christian Smuts said shrewdly, "Hitler has at last brought America into the war."

In Australia, crowds sang *The Star-Spangled Banner,* making up most of the words.

The German government tried to minimize the bill, but Virginia Gayda, the Italian analyst wrote darkly: *"Soon Japan will say her word."*

Meanwhile, equally important, but highly secret strategy meetings were going on.

12.

Deals Beneath the Table

There will be revolution in this country if the Administration gets us into this damnable war. Senator Burton K. Wheeler, Montana, 1941.

I am unalterably opposed to convoys. Convoys mean shooting and shooting means war. Congressman Robert A. Taft, speaking for a bloc of fifty Representatives, 1941.

We of the United States can no more evade shouldering our responsibility than a boy of eighteen can avoid becoming a man by wearing short pants. The word "isolation" means short pants for a grown-up United States. Vice President Henry A. Wallace to the Foreign Policy Association, April, 1941.

The people are too goddam dumb to understand. Harry Hopkins, 1941.

A Gallup poll taken in late 1939 showed that 13.6 percent of all Americans believed everything their government told them; 35.3 percent believed most of it; and 32.7 percent believed "some of it." Only about 2 percent of the population had no confidence at all, and this percentage corresponded closely to the small segment of Americans who wished for, or were biased in favor of, an Axis victory.

In retrospect, the records show that the government was

remarkably open in its treatment of the news. There was some misrepresentation by Administration witnesses, both publicly and in front of Congressional sessions. This followed two seemingly divergent, but actually complementing patterns. F.D.R. and other spokesmen tended to minimize the seriousness of the British position and to attack any notion that the British were losing the war. General Marshall and other military experts at the same time did exaggerate German military production, and particularly overemphasized German shipbuilding capacity and the number of German aircraft disposed for action. While Admirals Raeder and Dönitz were able to convince Hitler to build more submarines, the German Navy remained low on the Nazi priority list. This reduced the immediate danger to America.

At the same time when Marshall testified that the Luftwaffe had 18,000 tactical warplanes in action, and 18,000 in reserve, British intelligence estimated the German air forces at about 19,000 effective aircraft, which were in turn widely dispersed. However, it was true that potential German-dominated European naval capacity was greater than that of the United States, and current German aircraft production in early 1941 still exceeded American production by far—2,500 planes per month to 1,200 United States in March, 1941, or more than twice as many. But the British were making as many warplanes as Nazi Germany.

It was to ensure not only Anglo-American parity, but a comfortable Anglo-American superiority in vital air power that led the American staff, with the best of intentions, to use pessimistic figures. And the British, despite a vast shipbuilding program, were not winning the Battle of the Atlantic. The tonnages being sunk by Dönitz' submarine campaign were frighteningly high.

In the spring of 1941 the Admiralty stopped issuing weekly loss reports. The official reason was to prevent important information from accruing to the Germans, but the major reason was that, privately, the British government was afraid for morale on both sides of the Atlantic.

Churchill was aware, and told Washington, that Britain could not get through the year 1942 without a vast American shipbuilding program if the present losses continued. The United States would have to supply Britain not only with thousands of planes to maintain air superiority, it would have to furnish under Lend-Lease, hundreds of new freighters, too.

The use of American shipyards by the British Navy, authorized in March, helped the British naval effort immensely. The battleships *Warspite, Malaya, Resolution,* and *Rodney* were repaired and refitted at United States naval yards; the carriers *Illustrious* and *Formidable,* and the cruisers *Liverpool, Orion, Dido,* and *Delhi,* battered by German air action in the Atlantic and Mediterranean, were brought back to combat readiness. Literally scores of lesser Royal Navy ships, destroyers and frigates, were serviced at American ports and yards.

But this was not enough. Too many ships were going down. Churchill advised Washington that it was urgently necessary that the United States Navy assume convoy duty in conjunction with the British in the Atlantic.

The Administration was highly in favor of the idea. Both Hull and Knox said that "aid to Britain must reach its destination or we shall be beaten."

Thus the battle for Lend-Lease opened up a new front. Aid to Britain was indeed being carelessly dissipated if the German Navy was to be allowed to sink it before arrival. By March 1941, prominent American newspapers such as *The New York Times* had begun to treat convoying of British ships and goods by the United States Navy as "the big question."

Wendell Willkie, who had no powers, real or implied, as the titular head of the Republican Party, but who was beginning to speak for more Republican sentiment in 1941 than he had in 1940 when he backed F.D.R.'s foreign policy, said that the United States now had two alternatives. It could become a vast military power in isolation, without allies—since militarily the Latin American republics did not count—with a resultant erosion of freedom under the stress of mobilization, and with the probability of war in the end. Or the United States could face the facts of international dependence, *with or without war, as necessary.* He stated the United States must do anything necessary to keep the British Empire—its last remaining friend—in operation. He spoke with greater clarity on the subject than the President—but Willkie, as a private citizen, had neither the prestige nor the power and responsibility of Roosevelt. Nor could he suffer any consequences.

The spring of 1941 seemed to be even more disastrous than the grim summer of 1940. The battle of the Atlantic went into crisis. British shipping losses reached an admitted four hundred thousand tons per month, and at this time Germany stood very close to knocking Britain out of the war. The small German Navy was accomplishing more than the vaunted Luftwaffe. But the shipping crisis, which worried Churchill more than any other aspect of the war, did not make so deep an impression on the democratic world as the less strategic but far more spectacular German conquests in the Balkans.

Hitler moved eastward, and into Africa. German units were ordered to Libya, in North Africa, and these disciplined veterans soon halted what had become a series of British routs of the hapless Italian army. Other German units penetrated Syria, and Germans instigated a revolt in Iraq, aimed at driving out British influence and opening up the entire Middle East to German conquest.

In March 1941, Hitler placed impossible demands on the Yugoslav government, which was still neutral and now one of the last surviving independent sovereignties in Europe. Yugoslavia was asked to allow German occupation, and to permit free passage of German troops southward. The government, seeing no chance of defeating Hitler, signed such an agreement —only to be overthrown by a clique of patriotic army officers led by General Dušan Simović. Simović, a graduate of the French military academy at St. Cyr, showed great courage in defying the Germans, and he had unusual popular support. But German panzer divisions invaded, and overran the smaller, and only partially mobilized Balkan state in a matter of days. Yugoslavia was taken over.

Bulgaria, which had a pro-Slav population but was ruled by a pro-Axis government in Sofia, chose not to resist and joined the German drive. Romania, in which a fascistic regime had also come to power, had already taken the same course. Now, only tiny Greece, deeply involved in a bloody conflict with Mussolini's Italians in Albania, stood in the way of German conquest between the Atlantic Ocean and the Soviet border.

German troops poured through Bulgaria, down into Thracian Greece. The bulk of the Greek army was far to the west, where it had been thoroughly drubbing an Italian army immensely superior in everything except morale. Through 1940 and early 1941, the Greeks' defense of their homeland equalled anything the ancient Greeks had done against the power of Xerxes' Persia. But Greek courage, like Serbian courage, could not prevail against the combination of the Nazis' massed infantry, stinging air power, and overpowering panzers.

In the first few days after Germany declared war and invaded the country, Greek troops piled German corpses high on the Salonika front battlefield. Emotional Greek crowds flocked the streets of Athens, shouting, "Down with Germany!" They marched to the British and American legations, and sent up rousing cheers for both Roosevelt and Churchill.

Churchill responded. Greece had been something of a British protectorate, and the British had promised the Greeks aid in case of a German war. Churchill was desperately short of effective ground forces, with trouble breaking out all over the Middle East, but he ordered a three-division expeditionary force into Greece, made up of men from Great Britain, Australia, and New Zealand. He was criticized for taking this risk both in the United States and at home. He was, however, determined to match Greek courage with British honor.

The Germans, operating on a plan arranged down to the last detail, were not stopped. They took losses, but ground forward steadily. The flower of the Greek Army remained on the Italian front, with only tenuous communications with the Greek forces fighting the Germans in the east. The Greek forces finally broke, though they continued to resist with courage and in good order. By the fourth day of the invasion, German troops were in Salonika.

On April 15, 1941, British sources admitted that Greek and British forces were in retreat. Although Greece was now split by a German wedge, a new line was erected running from the Gulf of Salonika to the Adriatic Sea. But this new line was pierced by German armor; Greek valor and Greek bayonets could not prevail against tanks and aircraft. On April 19, exulting German mountain battalions hoisted a Nazi battle flag atop Mount Olympus.

The Greek strong man, Metaxas, had died. His successor, Premier Korizes, committed suicide in a fit of depression over the sufferings of his country. King George II, who was himself of German ancestry, assumed control of the government and the army and worked heroically to stem the tide. But within three days, the Greek armies in the eastern part of Greece were forced to surrender to the Axis generals, Jodl and Ferrero. King George declared the capital transferred to the island of Crete, and fought on.

The British expeditionary force now absorbed the brunt of the German onslaught. Standing with remnants of the Greek armies, the British took up a defensive position at Thermopylae, where twenty-five hundred years earlier Leonidas of Sparta had died defending Greece with his three hundred Spartans.

The Germans attacked the stubborn Anglo-Greek troops with waves of infantry and bombers. The attack failed. Then, the German generals brought up massed heavy artillery, a weapon the Persians had not enjoyed. On April 24, the pass fell, and the British had no choice except to fight their way back to the sea. It was a Greek Dunkirk.

But it was again another moral victory. The British emerged in good order, inflicting heavy losses on the Germans; the Royal Navy was able to evacuate 48,000 of the 60,000 British troops landed in Greece. On Mount Gerania and Mount Cithaeron, immediately north of Athens, Australian and English troops held off battering panzers for many crucial hours. But when the last British soldier had been embarked in Piraeus, Greek resistance, on a formal basis, collapsed. German motorcyclists roared into Athens, meeting a stoic calm on the part of the citizens. The fourteenth national state had fallen to Nazi power.

There was one last act. A Greek soldier was ordered to lower the blue-and-white Greek colors from the Acropolis. When he had done so, he wrapped the flag around his body and stepped off the edge of the Acropolis parapet, falling silently to his death three hundred feet below.

But the battle went on in Crete. Fifteen thousand Greek soldiers and the British expeditionary force fought again, holding out for twelve days. They were overwhelmed by thousands of Germans landed on the island by assorted German vessels, and a final blow was the airborne assault by 10,000 picked paratroopers. Again the British evacuated, and only the Greek government and a few thousand Greek soldiers were able to make their way to Egypt.

The Germans and Italians took full control in Greece, and ruled the country with extreme cruelty, committing many acts of modern barbarism. Thousands of hostages were murdered, populations deported, and towns razed during the next five years.

The resistance in Greece, and especially on Crete, however, fatally delayed the German plans for Syria and Iraq. Because of this delay, British forces were able to move into Iraq and crush the pro-Axis revolt and to occupy Syria, denying it to German ambition. Strategically, the conquest of Greece and Crete was of very little value to Hitler; it meant only another hostile people to hold down.

Churchill had never expected the Anglo-Greek forces to win. He had merely been showing that Britain, even in extremity, tried to keep her word. He was also thinking far ahead to the future. But the success of German arms had an immediate, bad effect on Allied morale. The Greek campaign seemed to indicate that the British and their allies could not match the German juggernaut in land battle. The example of Crete seemed to make the existence of any island in Allied hands, even Britain itself, precarious in the face of the Luftwaffe. From the English Channel to the Dardanelles, Hitler now ruled supreme, over an empire vaster than even Napoleon had conquered.

The brilliant three-week blitzkrieg in the Balkans added new luster to German arms, even while it further besmirched German honor. Now, many Americans began to regard the Wehrmacht with something approaching awe. With one victory after another coming in record time—against the best Allied predictions—influential American media such as *Time* magazine and *The New York Times* editorialized that the German war machine was apparently unbeatable.

Adolf Hitler, the modern conqueror, was assuming the proportions of an evil genius. The hour of fascist totalitarianism seemed to have struck. Everywhere, the democratic effort was always too little and too late. Hitler, always moving first, had become invincible. He had conquered all Europe except Russia and Spain, and he had a working agreement with both totalitarian nations. His legions threatened Suez and the entire Middle East. India, which had eluded Napoleon, seemed suddenly within his reach.

The United States officially condemned the conquests of

Yugoslavia and Greece, but took no belligerent action whatever. There was a certain amount of strain in F.D.R.'s Cabinet this spring: the question was even put to the President, do we fight or stand by?

These were weeks during which Roosevelt began to show visible signs of fatigue. His face was drawn and gray with worry. He was only fifty-nine years old, but his responsibilities already had begun to kill him slowly.

More blows came, on top of the German successes in the Balkans. The Japanese government and the U.S.S.R. signed a five-year nonaggression pact, which was immediately interpreted as freeing the Japanese to move against the United States and British in Asia. The Soviet government, increasingly uneasy over Hitler's triumphs close to its frontiers, was merely trying to protect its rear in Siberia; but as American newspapers now openly speculated, the pact would permit Japan to launch an attack on the Netherlands East Indies, the major source of its oil, without Soviet interference. Disturbed, F.D.R. ordered the Pacific Fleet to hold maneuvers—a war-of-nerves gambit he hoped would give the Japanese pause.

The public position of the President in the face of all this democratic disaster seemed to be one of hesitation. Unfortunately, he created much doubt about his own intentions among many of his most loyal supporters. Defeatism became rampant in Democratic circles; the political areas of the government were infected with gloom. Many men were prepared to follow F.D.R. anywhere he led them, but his failure to act, and the effect this seemed to have on the nation, got some men to worrying in public over the "morale" of the country. As always, the gloom was much more real in Washington than in the nation at large. The majority of Americans were going back to work, throwing off the Depression, and not very much concerned with what was happening far away.

And this was precisely F.D.R.'s problem. He told his intimates that he could not act—the people wouldn't let him act.

They were not sufficiently convinced of any ultimate danger to America. But there was more to it than that. The President did not wish to provoke the Japanese, thus adding to the world-wide conflict. He and his advisers could see no immediate way of committing American power, such as it was, effectively against the Nazi juggernaut. It seemed judicious, therefore, to proceed slowly; to let events take place, while the United States hastened to rearm.

The policy, considering all the factors involved—especially United States military weakness—was strategically sound. But it inevitably confused the public, and created greater divisions among them, such as always occurred in an absence of clear-cut Presidential moral leadership. In effect, F.D.R. allowed America First and the isolationist movement to enjoy an enormous resurgence because, while he was making definite undercover moves toward thrusting the United States into the Atlantic war, he publicly stated he was opposed both to the idea of convoying and any entry into the shooting war.

Presidential hesitation and the crushing German military victories added up to a turn of public opinion back toward isolationism. On April 1, 1941, the Gallup poll showed fully 79 percent of the people opposed to sending of American troops overseas, for any reason.

In this consensus, isolationism, defeatism, pacificism, and the small subversive elements, both Communist and fascist, all combined. Senator Wheeler began to have more calls for speeches around the nation than he could fill. In Chicago, at a mass isolationist rally, Winston Churchill's name was repeatedly booed. At one point, Lindbergh, detailing the facts of Britain's slow losing of the war, seemed embarrassed at the number of Americans who cheered. Lindbergh was not anti-British, anymore than he was pro-German. He was simply an American who felt that nothing overseas was, or ever would be, worth fighting for. The only thing he held against Winston Churchill was that by continuing to fight, Churchill and Britain were slowly dragging the United States of America toward war.

But this reaction pushed Lindbergh and Wheeler into rasher statements, and a more hysterical attack on war. Lindbergh and America First moved into the hostile territory of Manhattan, to hold an immense rally of "that silent majority of Americans who have no newspaper, or newsreel, or radio station at their command" but who hated war. Lindbergh was increasingly unhappy with the majority of all news media, and the men and women who worked for them. The media, unlike the public, day by day became more convinced the United States could not stay out, and even less convinced it should.

Lindbergh openly accused Franklin Roosevelt of plotting a war the American people did not want. He had lost the liberal opinion everywhere by now, and he was unpopular in the South. But he seemed to hold the Middle West, and he found strange allies everywhere. One was a sizeable group of Irish-Americans, who seemed to take a weird joy in British woes.

Many of these men and women, patriotic Americans in all respects, hated the English for past wrongs against Ireland, and the "suave, monied, Anglophile East" for fancied wrongs against themselves. Lawrence Dennis, Kathleen Norris, Jafsie Condon, Senator David Ignatius Walsh, and John T. Flynn were all articulate members of America First, not because they were subversives or Hitlerites, but because they hated more the people who were in favor of intervention.

Lindbergh continued his strident argument:

1. The United States was unprepared for war.
2. The United States could not beat Germany in battle.
3. England was losing.
4. All of this made a "negotiated peace"—not further intervention—a practical necessity.
5. Further, America had an "independent destiny," that it

214

could only fulfill by never sending another expeditionary force abroad.

But step by step, as the world fell to Hitler, Lindbergh was being forced to deny all moral considerations. As each nation was attacked and overrun by rampant totalitarianism, he was forced to write it off. America, with its independent destiny, was no one's keeper, and Lindbergh wanted it to be no one's friend. Having eschewed morality or the idea of any world order in which the United States had a place, he had to fall back on purely defeatist, military arguments: Germany was going to win, anyway. Lindbergh felt it was more moral to surrender than to fight.

And these arguments, as a number of prominent leaders pointed out, were hollow: the United States was potentially far stronger than Nazi Germany, although Germany had more divisions on the ground.

What really was at stake was whether America was to take an active, or a passive role in world affairs.

The President, utterly opposed to a passive role, fought back. He stated at a press interview that the notion that the totalitarian countries would win was held only by a minority. With some asperity, he repeated "this was a dumb view," and he was "sorry that some who held it were in such high places that they could publicize it."

Inevitably, the question came up as to why Lindbergh, who was a reserve colonel, had not been called up with the rest of the Reserve and National Guard, in the draft calls and mobilization of the year before. Here Roosevelt hesitated for a moment. Finally he said that during the Civil War many aliens, all liberty-loving people, had fought on each side, but at the same time both sides had failed to call native-born Americans to the colors. These were "the Vallandighams."

The analogy was not exactly accurate, nor was F.D.R.'s history perfect. Vallandigham had been an Ohio Congressman in 1862 who had strenuously opposed President Lincoln's

215

prosecution of the Civil War. Vallandigham was not pro-South, but he did not believe the Union should be preserved by force; he was in favor of an international negotiated settlement of the secession question, and he advised Union soldiers to desert or not to fight in Lincoln's war.

He was arrested and tried by a military tribunal for sedition, and sentenced to prison. This caused a great uproar and criticism of Lincoln in the name of American liberty and free speech. Lincoln commuted the sentence to banishment. Vallandigham was sent South, where he wasn't wanted, either, and eventually took refuge in Canada.

Lindbergh, when he read this statement in the press, took it as a slur upon his patriotism. He resigned his colonel's commission, and his letter of resignation was immediately accepted. When war came, and Lindbergh asked to serve, he was to be curtly refused, at the President's order. F.D.R. never forgave Lindbergh for his opposition. When Lindbergh, flying as a civilian volunteer test pilot in the Pacific, shot down two Japanese fighter planes, this act of courage was never officially recognized.

There was a vindictive streak in Roosevelt, that at times seemed odd in so great and normally warmhearted a man. He rarely forgave anyone who had embarrassed him. General Hugh Johnson, an old foe from New Deal days, who joined the isolationists and wrote against the President's foreign policy, was not tendered a renewal of his commission when it expired, although the War Department found him fit to serve and recommended that he do so.

Some of F.D.R.'s close advisers asked him not to do this, saying it looked like personal spite. Mayor Kelly of Chicago, one of F.D.R.'s political chiefs, told him Lindbergh should have been silenced by calling him to active duty; as a believer in Fortress America he would have been bound to serve, and in uniform he could not have attacked the Administration. Taking people's commissions away only built up public sympathy

216

for them, Kelly said—the real enemies were men like Senator Wheeler, who was allowed to talk unscathed. But in this, as in most matters, the President's will prevailed. And F.D.R. had a keen sense of good politics, too. Attacking one senator, or the whole isolationist group in bitter terms, cutting them down, would have been taken by the Senate as a slur on all. The Congress was like that.

Kelly also told the President something that in retrospect seemed much more valid. He advised that F.D.R.'s attempts at convincing the American public on the issues of the war were all wrong. He thought the war-peace debate should be handled like a political campaign—in other words, the President's personal desires should be sold, in simple language, not presented like a great strategic study. Roosevelt talked about maps, and distances, and active or passive strategies, and about distant countries wanting to dominate the world. Kelly said bluntly "this kind of double-talk was fine for the intelligentsia" but it confused the ordinary individual.

Kelly thought the President should take the stump, say what was right or what was wrong for the country, and ask the country to follow him, and at the same time try to convince each segment of the population that the other guy was really going to bear the burden.

A number of people had already noted that whenever the President took a strong stand, or a real crisis brewed up, the public—even that part which didn't normally agree with him —tended to stand behind him. Kelly's advice was an odd mix of political brilliance and political cynicism, but it was not F.D.R.'s way.

He continued, in response to direct questions by the press, to state that he was against "convoying" and against sending Americans overseas. He promised that he would never send an American force abroad unless the United States were attacked, which was a contradiction of what the Secretaries of Navy and War were arguing publicly.

This hesitancy, contradiction, and doubt about real policy, as it seeped to the public, provoked a disgusted reaction from columnist Walter Lippmann:

> In this tremendous time the American people must look to the President for leadership. They are not getting leadership from the President. They are not being treated as they deserve to be treated and as they have a right to be treated. They are not being treated as men and women but as if they were inquisitive children. They are not being dealt with seriously, truthfully, responsibly, and nobly. They are being dealt with cleverly, indirectly, even condescendingly and nervously. They are asked to put their trust in the President, which indeed they must, for he is the President: but in return they must have his trust and they must have his confidence and they must have his guidance.
>
> Only the President, because he is the Chief Executive, is in a position to know all the facts. . . . Therefore, the President alone can lead the country . . . the policy of the Government must rest on the support of the nation. But the nation must first be informed, and always it must be dealt with squarely.
>
> There is not the slightest reason to doubt that the American people will in the future as they have in the past do whatever they are convinced they must do to preserve their independence, their liberties and their honor. . . .
>
> This people is made of better stuff—is more ready to face the truth, more ready to rise to the occasion—than the President implies by his cleverness and his maneuvers and his devices and his casual comment on great issues. . . .
>
> This is not the way to make democracy work and prove itself in the greatest test to which it has ever been subjected. To fail to inform the people, waiting for them to lead him, is not democracy but demagogy. To act as if the people had to be manipulated is to deny the very virtues on which rests the hope of democracy, it is to think that free men will shrink from the truth and flinch in their duty. . . .

For better or for worse, however, the President seemed to be reading the polls and not Mr. Lippmann. In fact, Lippmann might have been comforted, but at the same time even more outraged, had he known that by this time Roosevelt was proceeding steadily, though with deliberate secrecy, down an appointed course of doing what he thought the nation had to do.

At the beginning of 1941 Roosevelt sent Harry Hopkins to England. He had two purposes: one, to see through the eyes of the man he most trusted how the British were doing in the war; two, to give a secret, personal message to Winston Churchill—the embattled British leader who was at this time having his worst hour.

The defeatism in the government, and even among the American military staff was pervasive and endemic all through 1941. Admiral Ghormley had believed and reported "the British would not soon be beaten" in the summer of 1940, and this was the best many American military leaders ever granted the British. Ever since then, especially in the Atlantic, the British had slowly proceeded to lose the war.

They held command of the air over Britain, and their aircraft production, bolstered by United States shipments, had almost reached parity with the Germans. But the Germans were ten times as powerful on the ground of Europe; the British could defend their own cities from air attack only with great loss and exhaustion; and they could not yet effectively strike back at Germany. Worst of all, and crucial, the submarine menace could not seemingly be checked. Churchill did not conceal its seriousness at any time from Washington, though he did not advertise it to the British people.

The American chiefs of staff, placing British-German strength and past performance on the chart, were understandably not sanguine. For that matter, neither was Churchill: he never really tried to conceal the fact that he felt American entry was necessary for Britain to win the war.

But the President trusted Hopkins' opinion in most things

more than that of all of his other advisers combined, and history records that a series of joint F.D.R.-Hopkins decisions set the pattern for all of World War II.

Hopkins was always one of the most detested and underrated men in American government. In fact, his only real friend in high places was F.D.R. The reasons were complex. He was the son of an Iowa harness maker, an intellectual from humble origins. He was by nature a vehement partisan of every underdog, and he took up Roosevelt's New Deal with an almost bitter passion. He administered the Works Progress Administration and influenced many decisions affecting the poorer classes, and drew the hatred of all who hated or distrusted W.P.A. He was normally and naturally anathema to conservatives, and the feeling went both ways. But more than that, Hopkins had certain handicaps of a personal nature. He was frail, rarely in good health, homely, and he could be sour and blunt with all and sundry. He was more often disagreeable than not, with a keen, sardonic humor that could make men hate him easily.

But Hopkins had a rare, personal dynamism which invariably reached and impressed men in the possession of real power. He was nervous, but he was also hair-trigger quick. He was jealous of his intimacy with men in power, and let no one else crowd in if he could help it—but he did things that kept him at the right hand of power. He was never to be a popular, or even a well-known figure in American history. But in the 1940's he was the one American who most impressed F.D.R., Winston Churchill, and Joseph Stalin.

In the spring of 1940 he moved into the White House to be at Roosevelt's side. His position itself gave F.D.R. trouble: finally, he was appointed as Secretary of the War Cabinet, a post which constitutionally did not exist, and therefore did not require his confirmation by a hostile Senate. Here he had no salary, and no powers, except the immense power of influence over F.D.R.'s opinion. Several papers printed that he was in effect, though never in title, the Assistant President of the United States—a post which Vice President Wallace never held.

He earned these powers, and enormous and crushing duties, with his constrained passion, and his quick, incisive intellect. When things came up in Cabinet meetings or great issues were in question, Hopkins would let the conversation, or advice, travel in its usual dubious circles for only a little while. Then came his thin, irritating voice: "Mr. President, this is the point." He would then lay the point, whatever it was, painfully bare on the table, and ask the man in the decision chair: "Are we going to face it or not?"

Weaker men disliked him intensely for it; men like Roosevelt, Churchill, and Stalin appreciated him. He had one other qualification for the favorite's role. He had no personal ambitions, and he was loyal to his powerful friend.

Hopkins, by 1941, had only one real aim in life: the defeat, ruin, and physical death of Adolf Hitler, to the exclusion of all else. It was a burning conviction. He carried it to every conference table, at home and abroad. He had decided that Hitler must go, and it was a view he would do as much as anyone in the world, on political levels, to make prevail.

In January 1941, Harry Hopkins had lunch with Winston Churchill in London. It was one of the most significant "summit meetings" of the war. Hopkins fixed the Prime Minister with his keen eyes and said:

> The President is determined that we shall win the war together. *Make no mistake about it. He has sent me here to tell you that at all costs and by all means he will carry you through, no matter what happens to him.* . . . there is nothing he will not do so far as he has human power. . . .

He wanted Churchill to understand and make no mistake, no matter what Roosevelt was saying for public consumption. This began a long period of personal messages and, finally, personal meetings and friendship between Churchill and F.D.R. This special relationship, in 1941, was incongruous, because it was between the leader of a neutral nation, and one fighting a desperate war, who talked strategy that the one prayed for, and the other was hard put to implement.

Hopkins stayed with Churchill ten days. He was shown everything, without restraint. He attended the most secret war cabinet meetings, saw every secret British document. He flew back across the Atlantic and talked with the President until 2:00 A.M. the night he returned. They talked of many things, but the one point Hopkins put across with burning conviction was that the British would not fold.

And something else, of equal significance, had been arranged. The British military staffs now flew across the Atlantic for secret talks in Washington. No American except on the highest political and military levels knew this was happening. It was never revealed until a Congressional probe of Pearl Harbor in 1946 unearthed the information. The secret staff discussions were held between January 29-March 27, 1941, almost a year before the United States entered World War II.

The strategy meetings were officially called "United States-British Staff Conversations." The sticky question of the United States' being neutral was scrupulously avoided. The tone of the talks was set by the opening statement: *The broad strategic objectives of the Associated Powers will be the defeat of Germany and her Allies.* Britain and the United States were not allies, but "associated powers," each proceeding in its own way on a common mission. The British were warned not to discuss how and when the United States would enter the war officially; this was an embarrassing question to the American staff and one Roosevelt himself couldn't answer.

The whole problem of how the United States would get in the war was avoided. Discussion followed two lines: 1. actions the United States and Great Britain would take "following"

222

American entry in the war; 2. actions the United States would take to assist the British cause "short of war."

In the first, the broad strategy of Anglo-American cooperation during World War II was argued and firmed. *Here, between January and March 1941, not later, the grand strategy with which the United States armed forces were to wage the war was set.*

Fundamental differences between the American and British view were quickly apparent. The British, with great reluctance after Dunkirk, had finally begun to build an army—but they only contemplated a ground force of forty divisions, enough to defend the British beaches with superior air and naval power, and to hold the Middle East. For the rest of it, British planners no longer held to "economic warfare" as a means of bringing Hitler down, but they preferred to try the job through "air and naval" action.

Flanders Fields in World War I, and more recently, Dunkirk and Greece, had wiped out all British desire to mix it up with the Germans on the continent of Europe. The British staff, representing the British government, was not willing to assume the burden of casualties involved in a final test of strength with the Wehrmacht.

The view was thus emotional and wishful thinking, and not based on either military realities or logic. The American staff understood the historic British distaste for mass ground warfare in Europe—but asked the British to come up with a plan that did not involve some kind of mysterious German "collapse." The British had none—which was to give their strategy a fundamental weakness, and make it subservient to the American throughout the war.

The Americans said bluntly the Anglo-British forces could blockade or fly over Germany forever and never win the war. The official United States strategy called for sustained strategic bombardment of Germany from the British Isles to damage or destroy the German war potential, followed by mass landings

223

on the continent and a final invasion of the German heartland. A passage of the American plan read:

> We must prepare to fight Germany by actually coming to grips with her and defeating her ground forces and definitely breaking her will to fight.

The United States view, of course, was exactly right. Germany could not have been beaten by strategic bombardment as it was later mounted from England. There had to be a mass engagement, that would destroy the Wehrmacht and bleed German industry and manpower white and destroy the German will to resist. Bombing never did this. In fact, throughout the war it apparently increased the German will to fight as much as the blitz-hardened Britons. But with great good fortune for the Anglo-Saxon powers, the great bloodletting was to take place in the east, on the Russian front.

D-Day was thus an American idea, planning for which began in 1941.

Despite the differences of opinion, and the fact that the United States was still not in the war, two great decisions came from the conferences.

The first was that Germany, as the greater danger, should have priority of effort in the war.

In 1941, Japan was at war only with China, but even if it joined its Axis allies, it was discounted as a major danger. Japanese industry was weak; Japanese plane production was a fraction of the German. This decision was again correct. Japanese aircraft production in World War II never much exceeded two hundred in its greatest month.

Not only the immense German war machine, but the German potential influenced the decision to defeat the Nazis first. There was a real fear of German science, and new German breakthroughs as startling as the aircraft and armor that had destroyed France. The staff could not know that Hitler had frozen German scientific development in weaponry to concentrate on production of existing models, and that these fatal decisions would delay two German discoveries that might have won the war: the jet plane and the missile. But the mere employment of those weapons, too little and too late now on the German side, proved the staff's fears and assumptions eminently correct.

Concentrating on Germany, then, the strategy called for continued collaboration in planning and the blockade of Europe, with the United States assuming the main role in the Atlantic, steps to knock Italy out of the war, and the use of the British Isles as a vast staging area for a D-Day assault on Hitler's Fortress Europe.

The other decision—which would have been much more startling to the American public had it known about this—was the role of the United States "short of war." *The United States staff, with F.D.R.'s concurrence, agreed to assume convoy of all transatlantic shipping when the United States Atlantic Fleet was ready.* When the staff talks began, there was no United States Atlantic Fleet. But the Headquarters was activated in February, 1941, and new ships were now rolling off the ways. The British wanted American convoy assistance as quickly as possible.

But there were problems to American convoying that went beyond the fact that, under the Neutrality Act of 1939, this was still against the law of the land. The Neutrality Act forbade any United States warship or merchantman to enter the war zone—but a greater handicap was that the United States Navy was not ready for this kind of action. The United States Navy, heavy in firepower and battleships, was far behind the times in antisubmarine warfare, as far behind as the British had been in 1939. It needed bases, which were not yet developed in the Atlantic. Its ships were not yet even fitted with radar or the new British antisubmarine detection devices.

Here the British were willing to help. They offered valuable advice and the latest equipment, tested in battle. Even the most

225

highly classified information and discoveries were given over. But equipment and advice could not take the place of actual experience at sea, and it would be some months before the United States Atlantic Fleet would be ready to move.

For the time being, it would merely begin to "extend its patrols." If these patrols sighted any German or Italian vessel, they would not engage—but immediately relay the information to all British ships at sea.

The bases needed for convoy action on the North Atlantic run were being rushed to completion in Newfoundland, and naval air stations were being planned in Greenland.

Two other things could be done to assist the British navy. One was to have United States flag ships take over and carry all British cargo in the Pacific, thus releasing ships and tonnage for the Atlantic run. The other was that the United States Navy could convoy British ships from United States harbors north to Halifax, where the British convoys and escort vessels joined.

None of these, of course, were the acts of a neutral.

Admirals Raeder and Dönitz of the German Navy were highly disturbed. They advised striking at the United States forces in the Atlantic now, giving them no more time to strengthen and deploy. But Hitler, who was now planning new campaigns on land, and who still hoped to have won the war before the United States gave Britain effective aid, adamantly said no.

From this time on, the American and British armed forces were in close communication. The position of both American and British officers was awkward. The British had to observe a circumspect reticence about American efforts. The United States Navy, on the lowest as well as highest levels, had to implement each new action almost clandestinely.

During this spring the President publicly took the position that *he was against convoys because they meant shooting,* but stated the Navy had the right to "patrol" the seven seas. And he said the United States "safety belt" now reached one thousand miles into the Atlantic, and that the United States naval forces were "cooperating" with the British.

In April 1941, public feeling on the convoy question was shown by the Gallup poll to be entirely negative. By May, after the crashing events of the German spring in Europe, still only 41 percent approved. Roosevelt continued to deal, as Walter Lippmann had written with anguish, "cleverly and indirectly" and not to tackle a problem head-on until he had public support.

But now, both behind the scenes and in the public eye, the President had begun to move. He had already opened United States shipyards to British warships as well as freighters. On April 11, he cabled Churchill: the United States would extend its security zone to "about West Longitude 26°—a significant extension eastward toward the battle zone. He asked the British Admiralty to notify the United States Navy in "great secrecy" of its own convoy movements *so that our patrol units can seek out any ships or planes of aggressor nations operating west of the new line."*

Further, Roosevelt cabled the following statement to Churchill, to try to explain policies vis-à-vis the American public:

> It is not certain that I would make a specific announcement. *I may decide to issue the necessary naval operative orders and let time bring out the existence of the new patrol area.*

It was under this policy, and these conditions—unannounced military orders—that America entered the North Atlantic war.

Churchill transmitted this cable to the Admiralty "with a deep sense of relief." There had been much talk, and much planning. This was action. The British Navy, as its historian Roskill later wrote, arrived at its own "belief and relief" shortly afterward when the first shots fired by American warships made the American part in the Atlantic "real."

Other steps were made public. The meaning and progression

of each was clear. If the public did not understand, it was entirely because the public did not want to understand.

In February, Italy requested that United States consular offices in Palermo and Naples be closed. Ostensibly, this was done because "British bombing had made these ports hazardous for Americans." The real reason was to prevent American attachés from transmitting Italian naval intelligence to the British Admiralty, which was being done. The United States retaliated by closing Italian consulates in Detroit and New York.

On April 7, F.D.R. ordered all German and Italian ships stranded in United States ports seized to "prevent their sabotage." Danish ships were also seized, but this was called "protective custody." Secretary Morgenthau, whose Coast Guard ran up the United States flag on the seized vessels justified the action under Section I, Title II of the Espionage Act of 1917, which authorized the government to take over any foreign ship to prevent "injury to any United States harbor or waters."

Twenty-eight Italian, 2 German, and 36 Danish ships were taken. Most of the Italian freighters had already been damaged or sabotaged by the time the United States colors were run up. Washington passed the word to Latin America that it would look with favor on any similar action to the south. Various Latin American countries seized another 21 Axis ships. But Argentina and Chile refused to cooperate, and some 40 Axis-flag ships remained in American harbors.

The extension of the United States patrol area in the Atlantic became common gossip in informed circles in Washington. There was renewed discussion of the possibility of war. Germany ordered its own nationals in the United States to come home via Spain.

F.D.R. transferred ten 250-foot, 1,979-ton Coast Guard cutters—old rumrunner chasers—to the British Navy by executive action.

He opened up the Red Sea to American freighters, by

declaring Egypt was neutral and not in the war zone, which was technically but hardly substantially correct. This meant United States ships could ferry war equipment directly to the hard-pressed British in North Africa. This occurred as Rommel, the Desert Fox, arrived in Libya and promptly pushed the British back into Egypt.

Next, F.D.R. requested seize-and-pay authority from Congress in order to take over certain other foreign ships, such as Belgian, Dutch, Romanian. He had not needed approval for the seizure of Axis ships, since there had never been any intention of reimbursement there.

An agreement was negotiated with the Danish Minister in Washington for the building of United States bases in Greenland. This official ignored all orders coming from the German-dominated government in Copenhagen, cooperating fully in the granting of bases and in the seizure of Danish ships. This act put the United States Navy and Air Force within three miles of the German's own declared "war zone."

Also, Greenland was important for meteorological purposes. The weather descending toward the British Isles and Western Approaches formed there, and the Germans had been using Greenland as a weather station. A terse Washington announcement stated that these Germans had "been cleaned out."

Meanwhile, Roosevelt himself dodged all questions, pointedly asked by the press, as to just how far the "United States neutrality patrol" extended into the Atlantic. There was, in fact, some confusion in the government itself. United States-Canadian Joint Defense Commissioner Fiorello LaGuardia, a civilian, said, one thousand miles. Chief of Naval Operations, Admiral Stark—who should know—said bluntly, two thousand miles. The President brushed off the question. He said estimates were meaningless: *he would send patrols as far as United States security required, including the combat zone.*

A large bloc of Congressmen, headed by Robert A. Taft of Ohio, unleashed a considerable uproar over this. A private poll of the Senate showed forty-five senators in favor of the United States convoying halfway across the Atlantic—but a solid forty also opposed.

The *Bismarck* incident, in which a powerful German battleship slipped out into the North Atlantic, sank the British battle cruiser *Hood* in a spectacular battle near Greenland, and then was crippled by carrier planes and finished off by naval gunfire as it tried to reach France, drew public attention to the nearing war. Roosevelt took advantage of it to dramatize his stands: "It would be suicide to wait until they are in our front yard." This was, of course, what Knox and Stimson had been saying for almost a year, with F.D.R.'s tacit approval.

Again in May, the S. S. *Robin Moor,* a United States freighter, was sunk by a submarine in the South Atlantic, outside of the war zone. The Germans claimed the ship carried munitions, which was denied. The sinking was carried out with a courtesy highly unusual in this war: the crew was warned and allowed to abandon ship. No one was hurt, but the incident again drew attention, and roused American anger. The United States flag had been attacked on the high seas.

These incidents, and the emotions aroused by them, let Roosevelt make several other long-considered moves. Secretary Hull ordered all German consulates closed, and all German agencies, such as the Transocean News Service, to get out of the country by July. Morgenthau froze all Axis assets inside the United States. But here the take was very small: the Axis had been forewarned, and almost all German, Italian, and Japanese money had already flown. Morgenthau himself had warned them by declaring a boycott on firms doing business with the Axis, such as the Swiss, and by sending investigators from the Treasury searching through banks.

On June 7, Washington agreed to train eight thousand British pilots per year for the R.A.F. in American flying schools. This move was accepted quietly, but it angered some officers of the Army Air Force (USAAF) who were having troubles training pilots, too.

Exports to Japan from the Philippine Islands were ordered halted. Here again, the order came late; the Japanese had already bought everything for sale.

Roosevelt finally declared a National Emergency on May 27, 1941. The gunfire in the Atlantic had startled the public in a way the fall of France and the conquest of the Balkans never had, and there was general approval of the act. This declaration did two things: it increased the President's executive emergency powers, and it was a further jolt to awaken the nation to his course.

In making it, Roosevelt stated that a Nazi victory would be disastrous to the United States, and that the United States would meet the menace.

He did not specify just what further action was to be taken. But in June, the polls showed that for the first time a slim majority—52 percent—believed the United States should begin convoying now, and a three-quarters majority said to convoy if it appeared Britain would lose the war without it.

But now the axis of the war again swung far away. The United States press reported heavy German troop movements eastward. The air bombardment of Great Britain had ceased. German divisions entered Finland, with Finnish approval. The Romanian army, German-dominated, mobilized for war. *The New York Times* reported at least "130 German divisions" on the Nazi-Soviet border.

World War II was entering its decisive phase.

13.

Hobson's Choice

Onward Marxist armies, mainly infidel.
Smite the hordes of Wotan, ram the gates of Hell!
Onward Christian soldiers, armed for total war
Crescent moon and sickle going on before.

From the *New Statesman and Nation,* Summer, 1941.

Now we find ourselves promising aid to Stalin and his militant Communist conspiracy against the democratic ideals of the world ... if we go further and join the war and we win, then we have won for Stalin the grip of Communism on Russia, and more opportunity for it to extend in the world. ... It makes the whole argument of our joining the war to bring the four freedoms to mankind a Gargantuan jest. ... Herbert Hoover, July, 1941.

The United States and Great Britain do not now assume that there will never be any more war again. Winston Churchill, 1941.

The Soviet-Nazi Nonaggression Pact of 1939 tended strongly to blind most observers in the West to the fact that Hitler did not, in 1941, yet have military hegemony of the Eurasian continent. The pact was pure expediency on both sides, and showed a willingness to put aside an ideological quarrel and an historical Slav-Teuton conflict in the immediate interest of paramount strategical needs. It produced the paradoxical situation of Germany in control of the Atlantic coast of Europe

232

and pressing down to Africa, while Soviet power took over age-old centers of German influence in the Baltic.

By all historic logic Germany was a pistol pointed eastward, and the Russians never thought otherwise. Soviet policy makers had regarded a war against the Third Reich as inevitable from the middle thirties. The Soviet policy was never guided by ideology—though ideology was the factor that kept the U.S.S.R. alienated and hostile, mutually, with most of the world.

In the period between 1919-1933 the U.S.S.R. considered the Western powers a greater danger and sought to cultivate Germany. But Stalin and his policy men understood the real nature of Hitler quicker than their counterparts in the West.

The Soviet Union—not for "democracy," as Soviet propaganda proclaimed, but in its own interest—was the only nation in the world consistently to oppose the German rise to power. The U.S.S.R. approached the League; it sought to make an armed alliance with France. Soviet Russian policy abroad was guided by considerations of strategy, and almost nothing else. Domestically, the U.S.S.R. concentrated upon industrialization, militarization, and the erection of an economic empire. Soviet industry increased six times under Stalin, and the production of steel went up 300 percent, though the living standards of the people fell.

This produced great horror in the West—but the people of the democracies and Joseph Stalin had their eyes on different things. The comfort of the public ranked very low in the Soviet value system; the security of Soviet power came first. The rate of Soviet militarization—which was reported fully, but generally discounted—kept pace with Nazi Germany's in the 1930's, and after 1939 accelerated. Stalin increased Soviet military budgets forty times after Hitler came to power.

By 1939 the great paradox of the Soviet Union was that it consisted of a desperately poor people who lived inside a tremendously developed productive economy and a very powerful state. But this was not a greater paradox than the United States presented. Americans were immensely rich in world terms, fantastically productive, and yet exerted no real power at all.

The Soviet Union showed another marked characteristic. Highly militarized and armed, even by European standards, it did not seek war, as Germany did. But, unlike the governments and peoples of the democracies, the U.S.S.R. exhibited no apparent fear of war at all. The U.S.S.R. risked war a number of times in the thirties, when France and Britain, with paramount interests at stake, would not.

The Soviet Foreign Minister, Maxim Litvinov, who was married to an Englishwoman and who was more Western-minded than the average Communist official, staked his whole career on trying to erect a military alliance with the Western powers aimed at Hitler. Litvinov never proposed friendship, or a stoppage of the "class war"—what he did ask for was joint Allied-Soviet action to oppose each German threat by force of arms. Most of these attempts at diplomacy by the U.S.S.R. were never understood or known by the Western publics.

When Hitler abrogated Versailles and started to rearm the Reich, Litvinov promised to back the French government militarily if it sent Hitler an ultimatum. Again, when the Nazis marched into the Rhineland, the U.S.S.R. offered to take joint action with France, if the French were willing to fire on the German troops. Litvinov pleaded for a firm opposition to the Nazi annexation of Austria in 1938, and at Munich, once again, the Soviet Union showed itself ready to go to war—not for the Allies, but against Hitler—if France and Britain took a firm stand over Czechoslovakia. Ironically, in each of these cases the French ministers who hated Communism, the Soviet Union, and all it stood for, received more support and sympathy from Litvinov and Stalin than they ever got from the British.

234

Litvinov, who had Stalin's blessing in every action, called his policy one of "indivisible peace." The Russian effort was to secure some kind of firm agreement with the Western powers that in the event of aggression by the fascist revisionists—which threatened both democrats and Communists—all would go to war. History tends to indicate that this kind of common front, had it come about, might have completely stopped German aggression before it scored its early, vital successes.

German generals were terrified of the French reaction when they marched into the Rhineland, and even Hitler had issued orders that the German forces were to retreat precipitously if they were opposed. But Hitler, gambling, understood the fatal weakness of the democracies better than his generals.

The great problem, in Western eyes, with Litvinov's policy of "indivisible peace" was that peace could only be maintained by accepting the risk of war—and any risk of war was one no Western politician in the 1930's dared take. Based on the emotional hatred for the U.S.S.R., there was also much wishful thinking that Hitler and Stalin must eventually go to war, and in such a war the West might see both its enemies disappear without risk to itself. Both this hatred and this hope—and the underlying cowardice toward conflict that paralyzed effective political action—Hitler understood quite well, and he used these fears and hopes with great adroitness.

Russia was willing to risk war with Hitler all through the 1930's—but not alone. On the other hand, the Western powers were not willing to risk any kind of conflict at all.

Again, in Spain, the U.S.S.R. showed it would take certain war risks. Russia aided the Spanish Republican regime when the fascist powers, Germany and Italy, sent immense assistance to Franco. All of the democracies opposed Franco, but none would accept a risk of intervention.

Finally, just before the Allied sellout at Munich, the Russians held top secret talks with the Allies. The Soviets urged that secret staff conferences be held, in which future war plans against Hitler would be jointly devised—the exact same kind of staff conferences the United States and Britain later held in 1941. The Allies rejected the offer. Then, in the summer of 1939, when no realist any longer expected to avoid a shooting war, Stalin demanded that the Allies—who now made their first stumbling attempts at getting military cooperation from Russia—produce a war plan against Germany with teeth.

Stalin and Litvinov made it abundantly clear, *as late as August 1939,* that the U.S.S.R. was fully prepared to join the French and British in a major war to destroy Hitler. But Stalin demanded one solid guarantee: that if the war began, the Allies would not stand by in the West while he bore the major burden. The Soviet demands were for: 1. a British expeditionary force at least equal to the millions of men Britain sent to France in World War I; 2. solemn guarantees that France would not take a defensive stance behind the Maginot Line, but would take the offensive with an invasion across the Rhine.

In retrospect, this was the only possible strategy that could have defeated Germany. It would have naturally benefited the U.S.S.R., and probably left it in command of East Europe—but it could have stopped Hitler short of the holocaust, and the terrible destruction of Western power that eventually came about. Besides, Russia ended up in control of East Europe in any event.

The Allies failed to act in the final crisis. Chamberlain and Daladier still could not bring themselves to forego the hope that Hitler and Stalin might yet fight each other alone. Equally important, neither Allied power had a war plan. Britain had no intention of sending millions of men to the continent; France was determined never again to suffer a Verdun. When France finally made the U.S.S.R. an offer of alliance, on August 21, 1939, this offer totally lacked any guarantee of real military assistance. If Stalin had taken it, he undoubtedly would have got about as much aid as Poland eventually got—none.

Stalin was nothing if not a realist. Realizing that Hitler was

236

going to precipitate the Polish war, he also faced the fact that the Western powers were not going to mount any serious war effort in the West. If Russia came in on the Polish side, he would take the full force of the German fury—while Messrs. Chamberlain and Daladier smugly observed that it served him right. Stalin had no interest in saving Poland. On the contrary, Russia coveted a large portion of Polish territory in the East. On the Allied terms, a war with Hitler served no Soviet interest. With the supple Communist pragmatism, which lacked all morality as seen in the West, and was never understood in the West, Stalin prepared to switch sides.

Litvinov, whose efforts had failed miserably, was fired from his post. Molotov, his successor, described himself as a "thoroughly disillusioned man." His Soviet-Nazi Nonaggression pact was a cynical act, but in all fairness it hardly exceeded the cynicism of the Western leaders, whose furtive hopes were now completely dashed. By the pact, Russia seemingly bought time, freedom from German attack, and a large chunk of Poland. If the agreement also erased the German General Staff's overriding fear of a two-front war, and erased Poland, that was none of the U.S.S.R.'s concern.

Stalin and Molotov, however, for all their expediency, made a gross error. They overestimated Allied power fully as much as men in the United States at the time. They anticipated that Germany and the Allies would now wage a long war of attrition in the West, much like 1914-1918, after which the U.S.S.R. would emerge as the dominant world power. They did not anticipate the German blitz, or the brilliant military triumphs that by May 1941, placed an immensely more powerful Germany on the Russian border—a Germany with no effective enemies remaining in the West. Suddenly, there were only two scorpions left in the European bottle, and Molotov's almost servile groveling to Hitler was to be of no avail.

The fundamental interests of the two powers clashed; there was not enough room for German ambitions and Soviet security in one Eastern Europe. Most knowledgeable observers saw this, but many people were misled by the deliberate damping of the ideological and propaganda war by both Nazis and Communists. Because the Communist line took a pro-Nazi tone in the West, many Westerners believed the rapprochement real. These were the people who seldom understood that for both totalitarian powers ideology and propaganda were tools, to be manipulated in the current interest.

The Soviet Union, during the détente, had seized strategic areas such as the Baltic states without Nazi permission. The Nazis had retaliated with a march through Hungary, Yugoslavia, and Bulgaria, all of which had been neutral. There was no buffer left. Stalin's politics were power politics, though never the politics of prestige. He was not prepared to start a war with Germany, but he was not ready to back down, either.

But the only German diplomacy left by 1941 was the diplomacy of arms. Hitler had subordinated everything to the "supreme law of success in war." And he seemed to be fatally overcome by his own dynamism. The German timetable called for the conquest of both Russia and Britain. He was unable to reach Britain. He altered his timetable and sent the Wehrmacht marching east.

When the German armies crashed across the Soviet frontier in June, 1941, Propaganda Minister Goebbels read Hitler's message to the German people over the air:

> Germans! National Socialists! The hour has struck. I can at last speak frankly . . .

He gave his reasons for the attack.

1. The treaty with the U.S.S.R. had always been expediency, to avoid a two-front war.
2. A victory over England was not in sight; the air war was not won, due to American aid to Churchill.
3. The U.S.S.R. had grabbed too much: part of Poland,

the Baltic states, Bessarabia, Bucovina. It had encouraged the Yugoslavs to defy the Reich.

4. Russia could be overcome in four to six weeks.

5. Germany needed Russian oil, wheat, ores, but especially oil, to form a base to overwhelm England.

Then Hitler raised what had always been foremost in his mind, the specter of Bolshevism. He described this campaign as a crusade of Christian civilization against pagan Communism.

High Nazis actually believed this would unite all Europe behind them. Even as late as 1939 this might have worked; France and Britain would certainly have sat out, if they had not abetted, a German war against the East. But a Europe that had felt Nazi arms, seen Nazi ruthlessness, and had been scarred by Nazi atrocities from the Arctic Circle to the Mediterranean was not likely to follow Hitler anywhere. He was able to throw his East European satellites into the war, with disastrous results for them. He got no support anywhere else, except from the German people.

"God help us in this fight!" Hitler ended his message, much to the bitterness of the few thinking Germans who realized what this meant.

The first feeling inside Germany was not dread, but a sort of relief. There was even a sort of exhilaration, born of the carefully cultivated Nazi *hubris*. "Now, we fight our real enemy," many Germans said.

Almost all of them accepted without question Hitler's dictum that the peoples of the East were a "mass eternally fated to serve and obey." They took it for granted that the raw materials, land, and servile populations of Russia would form the base to assure permanent mastery of the world.

In Western Europe, German political reorganization had had some success. Germans were hated, but authoritarian governments had been formed, and they cooperated with Berlin.

But Germans envisioned a long period of second-class citizenship in the New Order for Frenchmen or Hollanders, with eventual equality by-and-by. They considered only eternal serfdom for the Slavs. This was an attitude guaranteed to attend the initial success of German arms in Russia with utter political failure, and it did.

The exuberance, as "four to six weeks" passed, and titanic battles continued, was to die as harshly as millions of Germans in the mud of Russia. Up to June 1941, the total of German dead, wounded, or missing in World War II was only two hundred thousand—a fantastically low figure, that showed the weakness of the Allies and the brilliance of German tactics.

The communiques from the Eastern front soon took a different tone. *Aus dem Führerhauptquartier gibt das Oberkommando der Wehrmacht bekannt* (From the Fuhrer's Headquarters, the High Command of the German Army now announces) began each pronouncement from Hitler's command post, and these were words that would touch every German family and come to haunt a German generation.

World War II was not decided in Europe by air and naval action, though the attention of Englishmen and Americans was most drawn to these theaters. The immense ground war —the Flanders Fields, Verduns, and Argonnes—of the second war were all in the East. For this reason, they did not impinge strongly on the Western consciousness, and the savagery of this mass combat was imperfectly understood.

Nazi Germany and Soviet Russia fought a genuine "war of the dinosaurs" with no holds barred on either side. But because Hitler chose to march East, the English-speaking countries were permitted to fight their much preferred "island war," with emphasis on sea and air, and with balanced forces. Neither Britain nor the United States raised a mass land army comparable to the German or Russian.

Between 1939-1945 the British raised only about forty land divisions. The United States organized approximately one hundred. These ground forces no matter how bolstered by sea and air power, could never have made a successful landing in France on D-Day in 1944 if Russia had not become the graveyard for the German Wehrmacht. Two things could have happened, if Russia and Nazi Germany had not gone to war: either the war would have been tragically more costly to the Western powers, with millions dead, or Hitler would have been permitted to remain in control of Fortress Europe. The "balanced" Western forces could never have defeated the massive German armies as they were organized in 1941. As it was, the Allies landed against a vastly weakened German army in June 1944, one that had already been thoroughly defeated in the East.

With a full understanding of British weakness vis-à-vis the German war machine, Winston Churchill, one of the earliest and most vehement spokesmen against Bolshevism, declared the Russians "co-belligerents" and extended an offer of British aid. The *Internationale* was even broadcast over the B.B.C. With great reluctance, Britain declared war on Finland, which had joined the German side. And the British, not immediately, but within a few months, agreed to let American Lend-Lease be diverted to the Russian front.

This was done not because the British distrust or fear of the Soviet state had ended, but because Hitler was the most pressing danger, and at the time Britain had no other allies in the world. The island empire had at last found a continental power with convergent military goals, if not a similar outlook.

The Russian-German war caught official Washington by surprise, again. No policy for this contingency had been planned, because the United States did not have a coherent, long-term policy toward the Continent—something Walter Lippmann and other analysts scored. Again, faced with this new situation, policy had to be put together hour by hour, day by day. The immediate action taken was no action at all.

There was no question of the United States going to war because of the new development, although Secretary of the

241

Navy Knox wanted to use the fleet now in the Atlantic, while Hitler's back was turned. The only important question was, would the United States aid Russia as it now was assisting Britain?

The question was put to Sumner Welles at a press conference. Welles made his own position clear: he was bitterly hostile to the U.S.S.R. and all it stood for. He also believed —as did the majority in the State Department—that the Russians would quickly be defeated and collapse, like France. The U.S.S.R. was eligible for Lend-Lease—or "Lenin-Lease" as one commentator put it—under the law, because the decision of who, what, when, and why had all been left to the President.

Welles's feelings were probably those of the American majority: a fervent wish that both sides would lose.

The new aspect of the war did not produce optimism, either in the Administration or the country at large. Conversely, this new Hitlerian adventure caused a deep pessimism and depression. The idea of German military superiority had been so well sold, and so deeply absorbed, that no one, either on official or public levels, expected the U.S.S.R. to last.

This was the considered viewpoint of *Time* and *The New York Times* and many other newspapers as well as the United States military staff, and the State Department. This pessimism did not stop with Russia; it extended to Britain. The British situation in the Atlantic had not improved, and it was worsening in the Middle East, with Rommel. A great deal of sophisticated opinion, both military and political, considered the British almost finished. In fact, one prominent United States general officer, returned from a tour of Britain, said as much in writing, with the concurrence of the staff. This report disturbed the President greatly.

Actually, the two things being confused were the British ability to hold and the British ability to win. The whole British war policy had to rest on a belief that the United States would come in, yet this could not be broached openly to every visiting American observer. By themselves, the British had no ability or any reason to hope they could win, but they had to put up a brave front, both for their own public and for the Americans. The trouble was, when American military officers held up professed British military assumptions to the light, they did not bear examination.

The British announced war strategy was to go on fighting to hold the Empire, control the seas, and to wait for the enemy's system to break up, as the Kaiser's had. This view, of course, had an apparent strategic idiocy. Hitler had immensely more resources to call upon than Imperial Germany had had, because he had overrun all Europe.

Europeans might go on short rations, but no German soldier would go hungry. Germany had certain important shortages, mainly oil, but the World War II blockade could never hurt Hitler as the 1914-1918 blockade had damaged the Imperial war effort. Further, in World War I, German armies had been engaged on two immense fronts and bled white. It was the massive Allied offensives, taken against the wishes of the British Cabinet in 1918, that broke Hindenburg's powers to resist, and made it immaterial what happened on the German home front.

In the second war, the British had not engaged the Germans at all, and their war strategy emphatically rejected any such engagement or unseemly continental brawl.

Leaving out the Russians, the British argument that they could win with air, sea, and economic power always had a hollow ring. American officers who left out sentiment, or hatred of Hitler, in their reports, told the truth as they saw it. They could also only proceed on the assumption that the United States would not engage, except perhaps in a limited way at sea. With this assumption, they saw no British victory in this war.

Upset by this pessimism in American ranks, Roosevelt fell

back on his preferred gambit: he dispatched Harry Hopkins back to Britain. The thing that worried F.D.R. the most was that Churchill was stripping the island defenses in an effort to bolster a Middle East situation rapidly turning sour. In doing this, Churchill had also overruled his own Imperial General Staff, which was prepared to let the Middle East go.

There was also depression in high British military circles, which were by no means unacquainted with strategy. These people felt their hands were tied by the deep-seated reluctance of the British nation to accept casualties in the millions again, as in World War I.

Hopkins was charged with four missions by the President:

1. Evaluate Lend-Lease efforts to Britain in the light of the new Russian situation.

2. Evaluate the United States staff's pessimistic reports on the British war strategy.

3. Discuss F.D.R.'s concern about continued British efforts in the Middle East.

4. Arrange a meeting between Roosevelt and the Prime Minister, to be held soon.

Averell Harriman, the Lend-Lease Coordinator, and many American officers of general or flag rank were in Britain at this time, July 1941. But F.D.R. trusted Hopkins' judgment.

Hopkins flew in, and again was treated with every courtesy. He met with the Imperial General Staff. He stated Roosevelt's point: United States military staffs were of the opinion that the Middle East was indefensible, and that the Atlantic was the decisive theater of the war. F.D.R. "believed in fighting the enemy wherever he could be found," but he was worried over the English ability to accept combat on too many fronts. In the United States military view, the Middle East held fourth priority. They were worried whether American munitions, now going to the British in the Middle East in quantity, might not be wasted.

The Imperial General Staff, and Churchill, convinced Hopkins that in both places the British could hold. They did not have to pretend with Hopkins about the need for the United States to get in the war. The British agreed the Atlantic was the decisive battleground, but they told Hopkins that island defenses were strong enough, under air cover, to resist invasion, and the war in the desert was not stripping the homeland of essential materials. Besides, it was the only front on which Germans could be fought, and Churchill was pressing for a vigorous British effort in this war.

Since Hopkins did not expect the British to defeat the Germans, only to hold on, he was satisfied. In late July, he sat with Churchill in the garden behind 10 Downing Street and mentioned "the President wanted a meeting in some lonely bay or other."

The Prime Minister, whose continuing hope was that Roosevelt would come to his aid, immediately agreed. The meeting was set to be held August 9, in Newfoundland, at Placentia Bay.

Hopkins then flew on to Russia via Norway and Sweden, on the second, and most historically decisive mission he was ever given. This was to evaluate the Russian war effort, and advise Roosevelt if the United States should aid the Soviet Union in its war.

In Moscow, Stalin was not only desperate for Anglo-American aid, but he evaluated Hopkins' ability and importance as well. Like Churchill, he spoke frankly. The historic Russian suspicion of foreigners, with the German invasion going on, was at its height, but Hopkins and the Russian regime were able to communicate at once.

Hopkins went to Russia with a deep bias that the destruction of Hitler took precedence over all else, and that it was in America's interest to assist any other nation committed to the same goal. Anglo-American weakness in arms made such a strategy almost unavoidable; the Anglo-American powers were not ready to fight Hitler's Germany, and would not be ready for some time to come. Even then, both nations showed deep reluctance: the British to engage in decisive combat, the Americans to get in the war at all.

In this light, any nation fighting Hitler at the moment was an almost automatic ally. Just as with the Nazi-Communist pact of 1939, ideology or world views had nothing to do with it; expediency called for and time demanded an immediate decision. It was in the Anglo-American interest to keep the Russians in the war, even if it meant diverting vital munitions to do so. But if the Russians were to lose soon, or to surrender or make a separate peace—a nagging suspicion in the West— then not only vital American war production, but irreplaceable time would have been wasted.

Hopkins' first problem was to decide how dedicated the Soviet Union was to its own commitment to oppose the Wehrmacht. His own keen vision, and the frankness with which the situation was explained to him, convinced Hopkins that the Russians could be counted on to remain in business, and that they would not be quickly or easily beaten. Hopkins was correct, but at this time he was almost the only influential American to adopt and argue such convictions.

The American view, from the United States, had been influenced by some misunderstandings and misapprehensions about the Soviet State. It was every bit as totalitarian, godless, drab, and tyrannical as the Sunday supplements said; Stalin's rule was in truth a reign of terror. But Russia, in military and industrial terms, was not quite the inefficient wasteland Americans pictured. The Russian people lacked butter, and maybe had no shoes, and their standard of living was the last thing Stalin or the Communist ruling circles, in this era, were interested in. But the Russians had immense quantities of planes, tanks, and guns, and millions of men under arms. There was tremendous inefficiency in Russia, in the pattern of all overbureaucratized states. This had been shown in Finland, and was shown again as German panzer armies began to swallow Russian field armies and army corps wholesale.

The Russian equipment was good, and the Russians not entirely deficient of modern skills. They were entirely proficient enough for modern war.

The Finnish war had pointed up some terrible weaknesses in troops and staffs, but Timoshenko and others had seen to it that they were largely corrected. The Russian army had a competent strategy of war, and on general officer levels, it was more than adequately led. And Russia had three generals the Germans had never faced before: General "Winter," General "Vast Spaces," and General "Numbers."

Above all, and most difficult to evaluate, was the problem of Russian morale. The Russians had no great love of their regime. Hundreds of towns and cities surrendered willingly to German soldiers at the first. But the German *hubris,* treating the Russians as an inferior race, and the deep latent patriotism for the Russian soil, soon altered this.

The story of the Russian campaign was this: Because the Russians had a deep stubborn peasant patriotism, and an industry and strategy geared for modern war, the Soviet Union could wallow in early confusion and defeat, reel back toward Moscow and the Don, lose an army equivalent to the army of France, suffer twenty millions dead in all, then take the offensive, and within four years destroy the greatest military machine the world had yet seen with a greater one.

Enough of this Hopkins envisioned. He was the only influential American, in the terrible summer of 1941, to see through the immediate disaster of large German advances, and argue that the Russians would hold. His—and F.D.R.'s—great strategic mistake, the belief that the attitude of the Russian rulers toward the Western world could be changed during and after the war, came later.

The question of whether the Russians would cooperate in

the postwar world was second to the question of whether there would be a postwar world other than Hitler's.

Hopkins flew back from Moscow to the meeting at Placentia Bay, where his view, once he had convinced the President, was to be decisive.

The meeting abroad the U.S.S. *Augusta* at Placentia Bay in August 1941, carried enormous implications. The President; the Chief of Staff; the Chief of Naval Operations; the "Assistant President," Hopkins; Averell Harriman, Lend-Lease Coordinator, and the admiral commanding the Atlantic Fleet, met and held conversations with the British Prime Minister and his military and naval staffs.

Roosevelt had two things in mind. One was to put the final touches on the North Atlantic strategy discussed with the British between January and March. The new United States Atlantic Fleet was about ready for extended operations. The other was, that if Franklin Roosevelt could not yet convince his public that he should lead them into what he considered a necessary war, he could at least establish for all the world to see where America stood.

Roosevelt could not yet give Churchill all he wished for— the United States Navy, the Air Force, and millions of American fighting men. But he could commit the power of American principle, for whatever it was worth, and this was what he did, while the uniformed officers held certain, secret tactical sessions in the wardrooms.

The Atlantic Charter, written by Roosevelt and Churchill at sea, was revealed to the public on August 14. It read, in part:

> ... The President of the United States and the Prime Minister ... have met at sea. ...
>
> They have agreed on the following declaration.
>
> First, their countries seek no aggrandizement, territorial or other.
>
> Second, they desire to see no territorial changes that do

not accord with the freely expressed wishes of the people concerned. . . .

Sixth, after the final destruction of the Nazi tyranny, they hope to see established a peace . . . which will afford assurance that all men in all lands may live out their lives in freedom from want and fear. . . .

The Atlantic Charter was a magnificent statement of principle. It had great propaganda value, which Churchill recognized. It implied the full cooperation of the United States with Great Britain, in the Atlantic and in the world, which Churchill accepted with delight. But the Charter, outlining and getting British approval for the Four Freedoms—of speech, religion, and from want and fear—that Roosevelt had already enumerated in his State of the Union message of 1941, was not a call to arms, or even an agenda of action.

And while it was the type of principle and declaration to which Americans responded, it also confused things—particularly aid to Russia. Russia enjoyed none of the Four Freedoms, then or later. Rather than making his emphasis on survival of the democratic powers, Roosevelt had already chosen to emphasize the ideological aspects of the war—democracy and freedom versus totalitarianism. If this was going to be that kind of war, then an Anglo-American-Russian alliance made no intellectual or moral sense. If World War II was merely another power struggle, this time on a global scale, then the Russian Alliance made such sense, just as when democratic France and England fought side by side with the autocratic Czarist regime.

But power struggle was the very concept the American public would not accept. Roosevelt felt he was forced to emphasize Anglo-American principle, and this, later, led to the official decision to try to clean up the Russian image, at least in American eyes. This was to cause trouble some years later because Stalin never thought the Atlantic Charter anything more than clever propaganda, and certainly never considered himself bound by it.

But whatever kind of war it was, the great decision in the middle of 1941 to extend aid to—and later, to make alliance with—Soviet Russia inevitably shaped the emergence of the postwar world. The decision was based not on ideology but Anglo-American weakness. The Anglo-American "Associated Powers" contained more people, more wealth, more resources than Nazi Germany; together they made more steel than all the rest of the world combined. The United States had begun spending fifty million dollars per day for defense, already topping the British figure. A one hundred billion dollar arms program was in the planning stage, with one hundred and twenty-five thousand warplanes to be produced by 1944. But still, in 1941, almost nothing was on the ground.

Nevertheless, American production of private automobiles was stretching toward five million units in 1941, the finest year in Detroit's history. This was a sense of values that shocked the British, and horrified almost all American returnees from the battle areas.

There had to be a Russian alliance, because the Anglo-American powers were too weak in arms to drive the Axis threat into the ground.

While a lot of nonsense, pro and con, was discussed on high levels about freedom of religion in the U.S.S.R., Russian domestic politics never entered into the strategic question.

Aid to Russia was formalized in Moscow that year in October. Lord Beaverbrook, the British production czar, W. Averell Harriman, and Molotov signed an agreement to "place at the disposal of the Soviet government practically every requirement for which the Soviet military and civil authorities have asked."

Actually, the Soviets did not ask for the moon. They wanted mainly machine tools, planes, and tanks. American industrial aid was important—but not decisive—to the Russian campaign. Much more decisive, to the postwar world, was the American decision to accept the Russian defense against Hitler as an alliance in fact and not a co-belligerency of convenience, since this led to later hesitancy and strategic errors.

The final decision on military aid as well as alliance was made by Roosevelt and Hopkins over the protests of both the United States military staff—which felt the Russians would be beaten, anyway—and the United States State Department, which had access to the secret protocols signed by the Nazis and Soviets in 1939 and later.

The State Department had had to endure two years of vituperation and insult from the Soviet Union's leaders while the Nazi-Communist détente lasted. They were aware of the cynicism and belief in power politics by the Russian regime, and from the secret protocols and the Russian actions in seizing foreign territory, they were convinced of Russian aggressive intentions.

In the exigencies of the moment, Roosevelt was right. In historic, long-term logic, the State Department was never wrong.

14.

Atlantic Escalation

... While men argued what form of campaign the United States should wage against Hitler, they refused to admit the patent fact that the United States was already in a modern-style, undeclared ... war—refused to admit that in a critical moment of history the United States had a part to play, would have to play it, was already playing it. Time magazine, February, 1941.

Our Navy is shooting Germans—German submarines and aircraft at sea. W. Averell Harriman, November, 1941.

... The shooting has started. And history has recorded who fired the first shot. President Franklin D. Roosevelt, Navy League Dinner, October, 1941.

All that will matter is who fired the last shot. Time magazine, November, 1941.

In order for the United States Navy to extend its patrols and operations further eastward, bases were needed on the other end of the line. The Neutrality Act prohibited the entrance of United States warships into British waters. To secure an operations base from which the Atlantic Fleet could take over the escort duty already promised to the British government, the Administration agreed upon a compromise: Iceland. The island lay in a strategic position athwart the vital northern convoy route from Halifax to Western Europe; it had a suitable port in Reykjavik. The British had occupied Iceland upon the fall of Norway and Denmark the year before.

There was no time to try to ram a change to the Neutrality Act through a balky Congress in the depressing summer of 1941. The gambit used was that the British announced they were going to evacuate the island, to use the troops there in the Middle East.

Of course, no British government in its right mind would have relinquished Iceland in 1941 if it had not known Washington's next move. Roosevelt called in the seven top Congressional leaders, briefed them on the British move, and told them the United States was going to occupy Iceland in the interests of national defense. The United States could not permit a possible German seizure by airborne Nazi troops, or the use of the island by German submarines. Roosevelt did not ask the Congressional leaders' opinion; he told them what the Administration was going to do. Faced with an accomplished fact, and the obvious importance of the island to hemispheric defense, no one objected.

A force of United States Marines, told in briefing it was headed for the Caribbean area, was subsequently landed in Reykjavik. There it came under the command of the British Major General Curtis; it seemed the British had not completely evacuated. Now, American ships in considerable numbers plied the Iceland run. This put United States forces well within the war zone delineated and declared by Nazi Germany. The occupation was made public at once, and was accepted calmly, though most qualified observers knew it was now inevitable that the German and American navies must come into conflict.

In the Atlantic, the question of "foreign war" and hemispheric defense was inextricably mixed, and this made things very difficult for the isolationists.

During the strategy talks at Placentia Bay in August, the commander in chief of the Atlantic Fleet worked out a new operational plan with the British Admiralty. Henceforth, the United States would take over all convoy duty for transatlantic shipping west of mid-ocean, on a line based on Iceland. The United States was ready to fulfill the promises made in Washington months before. To keep the letter of the law, ostensibly only American vessels were to be convoyed—but a clause in the operational plan read that "shipping of any nationality" might attach themselves to such convoys. United States ships were to darken lights at sea, and to go on war footing.

Actual convoy operations between North America and Iceland began in the summer of 1941. But nowhere in the operational orders issued to naval commanders was there any reference to what they should do if German or Italian submarines or bombers were sighted. This caused some very painful discussion, not only in Navy wardrooms, but on high levels.

Lindbergh and the America First Committee were now accusing the President of seeking "an aggressive war against other nations." It was not politic to order the Navy to shoot first.

On September 4, 1941, the *Greer* incident brought this matter into acute focus. The United States destroyer *Greer,* on a course for Iceland, received a radio message from a British aircraft that a submarine was in her area. *Greer* sounded general quarters, changed speed, and proceeded to zigzag—the standard defensive maneuver against submarine attack, while trying to detect the underwater boat on sonar.

The British plane circled the area, and queried the commander of the *Greer* if he planned to attack. The answer was negative; *Greer* had no orders or authority to attack. The British aircraft then proceeded to attack the submarine with depth charges, without effect, and flew away.

Now, a very logical accident occurred. The commander of the submarine, the German U-652, thought he was pursued by *Greer,* and he had no way of telling where the depth charges came from. According to his report to Admiral Dönitz, he had

254

no knowledge that the destroyer was American; he thought both plane and destroyer were British.

The *Greer's* actions, in any event, were hardly those of a neutral. The Germans had orders not to attack or provoke the United States Navy at this time. The U-652 maneuvered and about two hours later fired two torpedoes at the *Greer*. Both missed. *Greer* then dropped several depth charges with negative results; once fired on, the *Greer's* captain considered himself free to act in self-defense. The action then broke off; the submarine disappeared, and the *Greer* proceeded to Iceland.

Something like this was bound to happen, with German submarines, British naval forces, and American escorts all plying the same waters. It was impossible for United States destroyers to plow through this actual war zone without sooner or later being fired on, even if by mistake.

Any German U-boat captain who took too many pains to ascertain the nationality of every warship he sighted was likely to end up on the bottom. The German Navy held some pained discussions, too, but Hitler, in deep trouble in Russia now, refused to let the subs attack.

The fact that the *Greer* had been fired on first, however, created a sensation in the United States press. President Roosevelt took advantage of the affair; he branded it "piracy." Several prominent American newspapers compared the present situation with the troubles with the French in 1798, or the Barbary pirates a few years later. Then, in protection of the American flag on the high seas, United States naval forces fought a number of actions without the sanction of a declaration of war.

The New York Times and several other papers stated that the President had made clear his own sentiments: the Navy was to shoot. On September 12, Admiral King, CINC Atlantic Fleet, made this even more clear in writing: Operations orders issued to various naval stations stated that the United States naval mission included not only "escort but protection" of United States and foreign-flag shipping other than German or Italian. They were authorized to destroy "German and Italian naval, land, air forces encountered."

The orders were no longer search and patrol but search and destroy.

For a few weeks further action was avoided; the Germans were not anxious to sink an American vessel if it could be avoided.

First blood was spilled on October 17. Some four hundred miles south of Iceland, a German submarine "wolf pack" began one of the concerted, days-long attacks that were the U-boat tactics of the time, on a British convoy. The convoy was a slow one; it was forced to scatter, and the British escort vessels were unable to provide an adequate defense. The escort commander went on the air for help.

Five American destroyers, from one of the regular west-bound United States convoys steamed to the rescue. In the ensuing action, the destroyer *Kearny* received a torpedo in the side, but failed to sink. No one was killed, but several crewmen were hurt. The U.S.S. *Greer* escorted the damaged *Kearny* into Reykjavik.

This was not yet *de jure,* but it was *de facto* war.

The press and the President made a number of rather war-like statements. F.D.R. made a great point over "who had fired the first shot," and indicated this kind of "piracy" would be dealt with.

A few days later, the U.S.S. *Reuben James,* on escort duty with a destroyer flotilla approximately six hundred miles due west of Ireland, was struck without warning by a torpedo.

Reuben James, like all United States escort vessels at this time, was without radar and unable to detect the U-boats at their favorite tactic, surface attack under low visibility. The destroyer went down in five minutes, and as it sank, its depth charges exploded, killing many men struggling to get clear. This time more than one hundred American sailors died.

By late September, no informed American could be unaware that the country was engaged in an undeclared naval war with Nazi Germany. Few knew the actual background or the detailed orders at that time, but the headlines were clear. Shots were being fired. The significance of these actions was most apparent to the British Admiralty, whose members now understood that "American participation in the Battle of the Atlantic [was] a reality." For the first time, the Admiralty and British officers at sea felt confidence that the tide had turned and the battle for control of the sea would be won.

United States naval forces were now hunting subs all over the western half of the Atlantic. They were escorting British convoys to mid-ocean, thus halving the Admiralty's work. The joint war plans called for the United States to assume major responsibility in the Atlantic. But there was one thing in the way: the Neutrality Law of 1939 still stood on the statute books. Until that changed, the Anglo-American battle plan for the North Atlantic could not be fulfilled.

While Roosevelt tended to be more outspoken on the war in 1941 than in 1940—for example, while he let other parties carry the fight for the draft and aid to Britain the year before, he led the battle for Lend-Lease—it was still his way not to appear to be too far ahead of the public. He was too deeply wedded to consensus politics to be a Churchill, or to say anything immediately unpalatable to the people. But at the same time his vision was similar to Churchill's; he could see the handwriting on the wall.

After the fall of France there was never any question in his mind that the United States faced long-term danger, or that Britain must be aided in every way required. Harry Hopkins' missions abroad had not been to determine whether Britain should receive help, but to assure the President that such assistance would not be wasted.

Roosevelt always made his feelings apparent to the people. But where he confused them again and again was in his actions. He did not push for any action, or make any of his dramatic moves, until support for it seemed assured. He did not propose Lend-Lease until the tide of opinion for aid to Britain was overwhelming. Then, though all competent observers saw that Lend-Lease had to lead directly to convoying, he pretended to be against the latter. The United States was emotionally prepared for economic warfare with the Axis and declared it with Lend-Lease. Its people were not ready for a shooting war.

The public, for many long months, was gripped by a peculiar schizophrenia that supported all the acts that led the United States into war, but recoiled from the act of war itself. Roosevelt's considered policy was not to lead the people into a "President's war" but to try to convince them of the necessity of intervention step by step. He let events crowd the public, but did not try to push the people himself. At the same time, he moved to get his way secretly, or behind the scenes. Thus, both in 1940 and 1941 he made commitments of immense significance to the British—which must have eventually led to war—without revealing them to the public.

Each move F.D.R. made could be justified in terms of national defense. In retrospect, almost all of them were correct. But Roosevelt's refusal to accept a controversial war leadership, his consistent reluctance to implement his constantly stated views and principles with calls for action, created an unhealthy situation. It made his serious war moves seem casually taken, though in retrospect they were not. Roosevelt merely felt he dare not beat the drums for them.

Not only did events happen in such a way to crowd the public mind and push it into unpleasant realizations—Hitler's continued conquests, the *Bismarck* episode, which dramatized the Battle of the Atlantic, and the Germans' sinking of the *Robin Moor*—but the President, with the best of intentions, stacked the deck. By ordering United States naval forces into the declared Nazi war zone beyond Greenland, he made it inevitable that a clash would occur. By restricting the authority of the Atlantic Fleet to open fire while "searching and patrolling" he virtually assured that the other side would shoot first. The very nature of submarine warfare made it certain.

But Roosevelt did these things, which men like Stimson, Knox, and Forrestal had long demanded, because continued Anglo-American control of the North Atlantic was essential to American security. As F.D.R. said in a message to Congress, echoing the view of the United States military staffs, it would be sheer idiocy to accept a completely passive role, or to allow the other side to gain the strategic and geographical advantage.

Modern weapons and tactics no longer permitted the concept of static defense. This had been driven home painfully by the failure of the Maginot Line. But the immense problem of government, in a free society, was that the public shied away from a strategic view. The Cabinet could see long-term peril and the logic of an advanced defense. The people emotionally clung to territoriality, rejecting "foreign" war.

It was desperately hard to convince millions of Americans that a "foreign" war was the most successful kind of campaign the United States could wage. To permit the United States to be ringed, to allow the coasts of Eurasia to fall into the hands of hostile powers, was to surrender the strategic advantage of an "island" power. But millions of Americans argued it was more "moral" to wait until an invading armada appeared. This notion had its basis in a fundamental democratic rejection of the political foundations of war. The act of war itself, after the shattering experiences of 1914-1918, assumed immoral connotations in the liberal democratic mind.

War, for a status-quo democracy like Britain or the United States, was neither moral nor immoral. It could only be defensive.

The President's cautious way, then, of rearming the United States for an anticipated war in the name of "national defense," of continually proclaiming the moral issue of democracy against totalitarian armed aggression, and of making secret

259

moves in the field of strategic advanced defense, comforted many Americans, confused others, and worried many more.

One pattern—important for the future—had appeared: when the President took a dramatic step, or carried his arguments in strong terms to the people, they rallied in support. As Walter Lippmann discerned, the people were made of "better stuff." But after each limited success, F.D.R. never chose to press his luck. Momentum dribbled away. The government of the United States, by 1941, was not really drifting. It was on a considered collision course. But because the President himself did not state this in ringing terms every citizen could understand, the population remained divided and confused, and in large part, almost apathetic.

The nation's press was almost unanimous in pressing for stronger action. The *New York Herald Tribune,* as early as the summer of 1940, editorialized that "war now would be cheaper and less dangerous in the long run." *The New York Times* was concerned because the public was divided into "ostriches, war hawks, and mugwumps," the latter in the great majority, waiting to see how the chips would fall.

From the first, the "war-mongers" represented the most articulate and influential elements of American society. The "ostriches" represented considerable political and financial power. The fence-sitters or waiters had most of the votes. But seen in retrospect or from hindsight, while there were large bodies all across the nation opposed to Roosevelt's apparent policies, *there was no group or alliance anywhere with the power or numbers to overturn or derail or even influence the government.*

There was every evidence, that even hating war, the bulk of the American people were both reasonably tough and disciplined. They would have fought a President's war. But there can be no question that F.D.R. and his political, as opposed to his defense, advisers were afraid of political consequences in 1942 or 1944. They foresaw something of the problem that a later President, Truman, faced a decade later. But they failed to see something else: that American isolationism could not exist without a comfortable feeling of American security, and it would end when danger to the United States became clear. It was Washington's problem to make that danger clear. Instead, too much Administration opinion exaggerated the isolationist pressure, and at times was not able even to distinguish its component parts.

The pacifist segments of American opinion were vocal, but not politically powerful. It was not the nature of genuine pacifists to be activists.

The America Firsters, most vehemently opposed to Roosevelt's "interventions" always exhibited a strong seed of belligerency in their midst. With very little cultivation, this belligerency could have been fired and used. In fact, in later years, many members of America First (who studiously disassociated themselves from the defunct organization) were among those who most strongly adopted the advanced strategic view, of opposing potentially hostile situations where they appeared. There was a very thin line between "arming to the teeth" and the willingness to fight.

The business and financial interests that opposed war or intervention because of the fear of social or economic consequences rapidly became a minority. War did bring social change, but intelligent men could quickly see that the consequences of losing a war would be much worse.

The Communist and left-wing elements, never large, turned over completely once Russia had been attacked. The Communist line switched from opposing United States armaments to demands for immediate intervention. In either case, this opinion was vocal, but could not influence policy.

But by not stressing strategy, and letting the chips fall, the Administration developed support in the domestic liberal community because of the hideous image of Hitler. *Ironically, the conservative and business community in the United States, as opposed to the liberal and academic community, though slower to come over to interventionism in the 1930's and 1940's, made the change with a greater maturity than did the liberals.*

The conservatives accepted the concept of a world power; the liberals did not. The latter merely became convinced that Hitler must be destroyed.

Nothing showed this more clearly than certain *Fortune* magazine editorials in the fall of 1941. Just as the biographees in WHO'S WHO IN AMERICA were heavily in favor of intervention, the readers of media like *Fortune* tended to accept the fact "that the United States was already in an inescapable power struggle."

Fortune polls, regularly taken at this time, showed that this segment of the United States was overwhelmingly convinced the United States was menaced by Germany and ready to stop its march to power. *Seventy-six percent were ready to follow Roosevelt into the war that 70 percent said they did not "want."* Seventy-two percent thought Hitler was bent on world domination.

But *Fortune* stated that its readers' opinions were not firmed on which lands abroad they were prepared to defend. Only 51.6 percent were ready to send American boys to defend England, 59 percent to hold the Philippine Islands, 63 percent to repel invasion anywhere in Latin America.

A significant 21.7 percent thought the United States should dominate the world "in the interests of world peace." Only 6.9 percent wanted some kind of world union. This was diametrically opposed to liberal opinion, which was also more than 70 percent interventionist. The liberals wanted to fight Hitler, but then withdraw. *Fortune* concluded that the most rabid interventionists were interventionist only because they hated Hitler, and therefore, were still long-term isolationists.

These interventionists wanted to be isolationist again once Hitler was buried. *They "could not get it through their heads that America may never go home again. . . ."*

In the summer of 1941 returning newspaper correspondents were shocked because few people in the United States seemed to understand the savagery of the war in Europe. German—or for that matter, Soviet—mercilessness was not comprehended. The surface divisions of the people worried them even more. Liberals, conservatives, America Firsters, and warhawks were squabbling over everything. Millions still disliked both the British and the Russians. The old domestic ruptures over race, religion, and politics had not disappeared. Of course, this was part of the normal American scene, but the reporters were no longer geared to "normal" times.

With many Americans and Washington unsure of the national will—where 70 percent agreed Hitler was a menace but slightly more professed a reluctance to fight—the false estimates of American purpose by the Germans and Japanese were perfectly logical. *It was interesting, and significant, that by 1941 both the German and Japanese governments were completely aware of the tremendous perils to them inherent in American productive capacity, but halfway convinced that American domestic opinion would not permit the United States to be any more effective on the battlefield than France had been.*

With numerous American Congressmen preaching about the dangers of war, and America First and other groups taking full-page ads in newspapers and holding mass rallies across the nation, the totalitarians' confusion was understandable. This was a feature of American democracy they could not assess.

Ironically again, the policy of Nazi Germany toward the United States during the entire neutrality period was one of studied restraint. It was clearly never in the German interest to provoke the United States, either into aid or action. German planners never forgot the immense production impact of American industry in the 1918 war, or the fact that United States intervention as a belligerent in World War I broke Imperial Germany's back.

The threat from America to Nazi ambitions was always played down to the German people. The official German front was a kind of confidence mixed with a studied indifference, but behind the scenes the Nazi government was always deeply concerned. No nation, closely related to the British, and a part of the Western commercial hegemony, which was the greatest industrial and steelmaking country in the world, could be entirely ignored. The German policy, from 1939, was to win the European war by its existing superiority of arms before the United States could become involved.

The highly intelligent German Ambassador to the United States, Hans Dieckhoff, was not optimistic about the United States, despite its apparently passive role in world affairs. He wrote Berlin in 1937 that if Great Britain became involved in a total war ". . . we will have to expect that the weight of the United States of America will soon be thrown into the scale on the side of the British." He was to reiterate this ominous warning so many times that finally Berlin forced him to apologize for saying it.

Dieckhoff had to explain why the fact that approximately 15 percent of the United States population was of Germanic descent had no bearing. Dieckhoff analyzed this carefully and thoroughly for Berlin. He found that only four or five million Americans at the most were even "cognizant of their German origin" and that these were unorganizable. The average German-American was already of "old stock" since immigration from the Reich had practically ceased in 1870. Thus, German-Americans were for the most part not only assimilated, but they stemmed from those German elements which had had no German nationalism or were influenced by German liberalism. The greatest influx into America had been after the abortive European liberal revolutions of 1848; most Germans left the old country for political reasons and had never afterward identified with the emergent German Reich.

The letters and cables of Dieckhoff to the Wilhelmstrasse

often gave the impression of an intelligent man, given a task he knew was hopeless, forced to reason with a pack of fools. In the strongest terms he tried to tell Berlin that the idea of organization of German minorities or other fascists into storm troops—ten or twenty thousand armed men who could "render valuable service at the crucial moment"—was idiotic. "This conspiratorial child's play" was suitable for Danzig, the Sudetenland, or the Balkans, but not for the United States. The Justice Department would quickly infiltrate it, have all the rolls, and public knowledge of a storm troop would inflame American opinion.

He argued forcefully that the German government must completely disassociate itself from the "stupid and noisy activities of a handful of German-Americans," namely Fritz Kuhn's German-American Bund. Dieckhoff recognized these people as the misfits in American society that they were, and understood fully that the Bund's blatant imitation of Nazism irritated or sickened the vast majority of Americans. He made this appraisal and recommendation several years before Kuhn was finally arrested on charges of defrauding his own organization. In Dieckhoff's cutting descriptions of the Bund and other Nazi-type organizations one could almost—but not quite, for this was dangerous—read this diplomat's opinion of Germany's own, home-grown Nazis. However, the German Foreign Office agreed.

The German Ambassador cabled that the greatest opportunity for preventing United States aid to Britain lay with the isolationist groups. He came to this conclusion in 1937. He said bluntly that the isolationists could not be construed as pro-German. But they had the same goal as the German Foreign Ministry: American nonintervention in the coming war.

But he understood something about the isolationists that even Washington did not strongly believe: that *"if they should ever be frightened out of their lethargy, or if they should come to realize that their doctrinnaire conception cannot be carried out or that it benefits the foes of liberalism and democracy, the jump from isolationism would not be too big for them."*

Whatever the German Ambassador's efforts to neutralize the United States, he himself was undone by the infamous *Kristall-Nacht* in Germany in November 1938. Sparked by the assassination of a German diplomat in Paris by a Polish Jew, the Nazis began terrible reprisals and persecutions against German Jews. The atrocities and indignities perpetrated on German Jews shocked the civilized world, and as Dieckhoff wrote back bitterly: "The good prospects for a gradual spread of anti-Semitism have suffered a serious setback . . . even the most bitter [American] anti-Semites are anxious to dissociate themselves from methods of this kind."

President Roosevelt issued a statement condemning the Jewish persecutions in harsh terms, and recalled the United States Ambassador to Berlin, for "consultation." Hitler felt himself required to retaliate, and from that time on neither Germany nor the United States had an ambassador in residence.

The attaché in Washington, one Hans Thomsen, took over reporting on the American scene. As early as May 1939, he informed Berlin he was convinced that Roosevelt wanted war against Germany. When the arms embargo was repealed in late 1939, Thomsen, however, urged Berlin not to instigate sabotage against firms filling British orders. This kind of sabotage had been one of the factors that aroused United States opinion in World War I. Now, it would be promptly and extensively exploited by Roosevelt, interventionist circles, and enemy propaganda.

German propagandists never had any chance of penetrating the Administration from the first. They looked upon the American military with some hope, but were also thoroughly frustrated there.

The United States press was considered so hostile that there was no hope of getting it to print "German news." To circum-

266

vent this, the Germans used the Trans-Ocean Agency in New York—but it was known to be so closely controlled by the Nazi Embassy that it was never effective.

The only body of Americans the Germans could exploit were the isolationists and America First. The Germans even slipped funds to the peace bloc when they could. They had no hope in the election of 1940, because, as Thomsen reported, Willkie, although of pure German descent, "is unfortunate for us . . . one of those Republicans who see America's best defense in supporting England. . . ."

But the German Embassy was able to assist the isolationist plank in the Republican Party platform of 1940 by instigating the idea of "Americanism, preparedness, and peace" through full-page ads it paid for in *The New York Times*. Thomsen wrote Berlin smugly: *Nothing has leaked out about the assistance we rendered in this.*

The Democrats were not ignored. The German Embassy put up money to see that "several reliable isolationist Democrats" went to the Chicago convention in 1940 to get the pledge of nonparticipation in a European war. During the convention, the Embassy also paid for full-page ads in the *Chicago Tribune* similar to those run in *The New York Times*.

As Britain failed to fall, and the campaign in Russia began to look like an extended blood bath, German attitudes toward the United States were more desperate than arrogant. Admiral Dönitz, aware of the American preparations in the Atlantic, wanted to unleash his submarines in 1941. Hitler refused. Under the booming production miracle and the huge defense budgets, United States aircraft production was reaching a par with the German in 1941; it would greatly exceed it in 1942. The German Foreign Ministry had no doubt an American avalanche was coming; it only did not know when.

Hitler's best hope to keep the Americans occupied was Japan. But the psychological warfare and the threat of the

Tripartite Pact of 1940 did not work. Roosevelt was not diverted to the Far East.

When the shooting started in the North Atlantic, Hitler's policy was one, for him, of immense restraint. German subs were allowed "to protect themselves" but to instigate no war upon American shipping. On government order, the incidents and sinkings around Iceland in the fall of 1941 were ignored or passed over in the German press.

But meanwhile, what Dieckhoff and other Germans had always feared was slowly coming to pass. Not Roosevelt—who had always been hostile to them—but the pressure of events was visibly changing the American attitude toward the war.

By September, the huge armaments program was in full swing. Labor troubles, while endemic, were largely settled. Organized labor had won its fight. Ford and major steel plants were unionized, and on the other side, labor had mostly cleaned its own house of overt Communists. The index of consumer prices was rapidly rising: 100 in August 1939; 157 in August 1941; then 172.2 in September.

The Administration, not liking to move in peacetime, was showing a certain cowardice toward the use of wage or price controls. The public, after a long Depression, was confusing inflation with prosperity, and enjoying a great deal of both. Congress passed all "pork" bills, including some over F.D.R.'s veto.

Everyone knew taxes were going up; a steep rise was projected for 1942. But the most important swing, almost unnoticed after the long debate of many months, was the shift of opinion toward intervention.

The shots in the North Atlantic had been heard.

The American Legion at its convention in Milwaukee came out violently for action. It backed all of F.D.R.'s policies, and passed resolutions asking him to go much further.

Senator Bennett Clark and Congressman Fish, who had

come to plug for America First, were booed from the platform. Angry and humiliated, they left town.

Many Congressmen, returning home from the September recess were profoundly disturbed by the changes in the wind. Down South, almost every Congressman and Senator was a hero—they had been for intervention and against Hitler all along. Some of the last ditch isolationist columnists, like Raymond Clapper, changed their tunes. A poll of America First itself, and of some of Lindbergh's greatest admirers, revealed that 38 percent were resigned to the fact that Hitler would attack the United States if he won in Europe.

Outside the South there was no real war fever. The polls still showed the old dichotomy: an all-out effort "short of war." But they showed something new. For the first time, 70 percent of the public felt it was important to defeat Hitler—more important, in fact, than to stay out of the war.

One of the most sensitive barometers in the heartland of America showed the change in the wind. Representative Everett McKinley Dirksen, long isolationist and sometime favorite of the *Chicago Tribune,* the isolationist organ, member of the Old Guard who had usually opposed every move of F.D.R.—but one of the best and most efficient politicians who ever came down the pike—announced his "future support of F.D.R.'s policies."

This, like the mood of the nation, was not enthusiasm, but fatalistic acceptance. Lindbergh had lost; the President had won. But the decision was close, and nothing showed this more clearly than the results of the last two battles of the undeclared war.

General Marshall had asked for an extension of the draft law beginning in July. The army stood at one million four hundred thousand men, but only two of its divisions were filled with Regulars. Seventy-five to 90 percent of all officers in all divisions were Reservists or National Guardsmen. Like the draftees and enlisted reservists, they had been called up for only one year. All Reservists' service was limited to the Western Hemisphere.

If the conscripts and Reserve officers were released in 1941, under the 1940 law, the burgeoning army would once again melt away. The Navy was still expanding and was filled by volunteers. The original idea had been to train a million conscripts, then pass them into the ready reserve—but by 1941 the situation had changed. General Marshall, although he could not say so, did not believe there was going to be another year for training. Neither did F.D.R. The Army was still not combat-effective. It took two full years to train a modern division, no matter what armchair civilian experts said or wrote. Now, the Army was faced with seeing both trained cadres and half-trained staffs fade away, putting it back an entire year. The Administration went to Congress in the summer of 1941, asking it to extend the draftees' and Reservists' service eighteen more months.

Although Hitler seemed about to overrun all Russia, the situation was unsettled in the Middle East, the Battle of the Atlantic was in full swing, and a new hard note had just been sent to the Empire of Japan, this bill hit Congress very hard.

Even the most interventionist American was not really in favor of the draft. The fact that official American policy could no longer be implemented without selective service made little impression on a huge bloc of Congressmen. Here, the isolationists and all their allies made their next to last stand.

The Senate passed the extension by a vote of 45-30, with ten senators deliberately abstaining. Twenty-three negative votes came from isolationists, all of whom had at one time or another paid lip service to Fortress America.

But the real battle came in the House. Here a small majority rose against the Administration bill. One analyst examined the motives of each man or woman voting, and came up with the following odd alliance:

270

1. All pacifists.

2. Most Republicans—who had now made a dangerous, illogical decision to vote no in search of a popular issue to oppose the President, although Wendell Willkie and a majority of influential Republican citizens backed F.D.R. on foreign policy. Some Republicans did it to repudiate Willkie.

3. Congressmen who considered the bill a breaking of faith to men who had been promised one year, no more.

4. Democrats who had advised thousands of constituents to enlist and beat the draft and now were in political agony.

5. Fence-sitters uncertain how the public would feel in 1942.

6. Several New York Democrats angry with F.D.R.'s friendship with Republican Fiorello La Guardia.

7. Men of both parties who hated F.D.R.

8. Several members who thought the emergency was overrated.

9. Seventeen Irish-Americans who could never forgive Great Britain.

Only the most strenuous parliamentary action by Speaker Sam Rayburn and several Southern Democrats got the bill through. It failed the first time, then passed by one vote: 203 to 202.

The debate again divided the public, with public acrimony. Senator Wheeler mailed out one million post cards on his Congressional frank, urging recipients: "Write to President Roosevelt today that you are against our entry into the European war."

The cards were bought by America First, and inevitably—because mailing lists were used, and many names on mailing lists had just been drawn by selective service—many were forwarded to soldiers in uniform. There was an uproar in the press. Soldiers sent the cards to the War Department, asking, what the hell?

The press at this time was filled with draftees' and Guardsmen's grousing. There were minor mutinies here and there. The New York-New Jersey Forty-Fourth Division sent telegrams to Congress, wanting to go home. But most soldiers did nothing of the kind.

Secretary of War Stimson was deeply angered. He called the cards "subversive—if not treason."

The Senate berated Stimson thoroughly for this statement. Several prominent members of the club defended, not Wheeler's views, but Wheeler's right. No one defended Stimson, and he was forced to issue an apology to the Senate as a whole.

These cards showed a certain isolationist desperation to find a means that would now deter or turn the President from the "warmonger" course they were sure he was upon. But this kind of thing did Wheeler more damage, by far, than good.

Then Charles A. Lindbergh, equally desperate, made a speech that as much as the actual events, broke America First's back. Lindbergh's deal with America First, or with any other sponsor, was that he wrote his own speeches, said what he believed, allowed no one to edit him beforehand. At Des Moines, Iowa, on September 11, Lindbergh, with Senator Nye beside him, "warned the Jews."

He described American Jews as one of the "three groups that have been most important in pressing this country toward war." The others were the Administration and the British government. He advised all Jews to suppress their feelings against Germany, because if war came, "they will be blamed for it."

He then pinpointed a great danger to the "American nation" from Jewish influence in their "large ownership and influence in our motion pictures, our press, our radio and our government."

Many members of the America First Committee, some of whom were prominent American Jews, sat stunned. Whether Lindbergh—who was saying what many uninformed people believed—was merely betraying a latent anti-Semitism or had

272

succumbed to German propaganda that was constantly fed into America First was immaterial. His facts were wrong. American Jews did not dominate the press, radio, or government, nor were they as a body, although logically the most anti-Nazi group in America, so warlike as the South. But worse, Lindbergh had gone beyond the pale of American good taste and seemed to be trying to open up in America the very kind of argument that could bring Americans to each other's throats.

Thomas Dewey, a prominent Republican tending toward the isolationist stand, said this was "inexcusable." Resignations poured in, from many Americans who could only equate this kind of talk with Hitlerism.

The President now chose to use the re-echoing gunfire in the Atlantic and the subtle but real change in opinion to get free of the hampering Neutrality Act. Congress was called back into session. The Administration asked for three changes: the right to trade with the Allies, to permit United States merchantmen to arm, and to allow both naval and merchant shipping into the war zone. The Senate, in a fatalistic mood, passed the repeal on November 7.

In the House, the bloc that had almost scuttled the draft extension tried again. The bill passed by only 212-194, because of the defection of twenty-two Republicans from Party ranks. One hundred thirty-seven Republicans, fifty-seven Democrats voted no on November 13, 1941.

Immediately, United States ships began to be armed and readied for the England and Murmansk run.

The tide in the Atlantic, although there were bitter days to come, had turned. The battle lines, and battle plans, were already drawn. The events in the Pacific of a few weeks later made no essential changes.

15.

Ultimatum in the East

My Peruvian colleague told a member of my staff that he had heard from many sources including a Japanese source that the Japanese military forces planned, in the event of trouble with the United States, to attempt a surprise mass attack on Pearl Harbor using all their military facilities. He added that although the project seemed fantastic the fact that he had heard it from many sources prompted him to pass on the information. Ambassador Joseph C. Grew, Tokyo, to Washington, January 27, 1941.

The less said about Japanese-American relations, the better.... Saburo Kurusu, Special Emissary to Washington, November, 1941.

[The President] brought up the event that we were likely to be attacked perhaps [as soon as] next Monday, for the Japanese are notorious for making an attack without warning, and the question was what we should do. The question was how we should maneuver them into the position of firing the first shot without too much danger to ourselves. Henry L. Stimson, Secretary of War, November 25, 1941.

Looking backward, no responsible historian believes that the United States could have remained uninvolved in the European war. It was always impossible, after Munich, to do business with Hitler. The Nazi state had developed an hysterical drive

274

and a maniacal dynamism that could not be halted by any known form of diplomacy. Almost by reflex, the German nation kept expanding by force of arms. It could only be stopped by the force of arms.

Whatever happened in Europe itself, the advance of a powerful, armed, and historically hostile people along the coastlines of the Atlantic inevitably threatened American security. This was the salient circumstance that President Roosevelt, the Cabinet, and the United States military staff recognized long before the vast majority of the American people were willing to face it.

The fact that the United States took so long to recognize its stake in the existing world order and to make up its collective mind as to its role and responsibility for that order seems incredible.

No one ever credited the bulk of the American public with less than decent emotions—but few could credit it with historic vision. The people failed to see not only the nature of the German war, but the nature of the world itself.

While Hitler set forces in motion in Europe that no sort of negotiations and no American policy of appeasement could have stopped, the war that engulfed America from the East was a subtly different thing. It could be laid, once the war hysteria and war emotions had died down, to an almost tragic failure of diplomacy on both sides.

For forty years the United States took a very tough, almost belligerent stand against Japanese aspirations in Asia, but ironically, not until after Japan had been defeated in a bloody Pacific war did the United States give any real attention to legitimate Japanese needs. Even more ironically, in a very real sense the Japanese nation succeeded in World War II, for the terrible military failure did two things: it destroyed the European colonial regimes in Asia and thus the colonial exclusions against Japan, opening up a vital trade area from which it had always been barred; second, the war forced a realization in Washington and other European capitals that Japan had become a member of the industrial commercial world and must be allowed a partnership in it.

Neither idea had any currency whatever before Pearl Harbor, although it was the United States, as an act of dominant policy, that opened up Japan in the 1850's and set it on the road to modernization for commercial reasons.

Historically, the United States policy toward Europe was one of nonintervention, but this had never applied to the Pacific areas or the Far East. When the United States came into existence, Europe was a dangerous power center—but Asia was a power vacuum. The ancient Chinese empire crumbled rapidly in the nineteenth century, while all the European powers crowded around and in upon it like wolves, each seeking a dominant commercial interest.

The United States desired no flag hegemony in the Far East —the seizure of the Philippines from Spain in 1898 was uncharacteristic, a decision made by President McKinley after a "night of prayer"—but its clear and cold policy was that of preventing the hegemony of any other power. This policy was never expressed in so many words, but this was what the historic "Open Door" in China was all about.

The Open Door was not entirely pro-Chinese, as it was often characterized, nor did it build any real, historic friendship with the Chinese nation. The United States continually took the position of supporting a crumbling Chinese power against the demands of other nations—but Americans did not contemplate any right of the Chinese to "shut the door" themselves. The policy was to prevent any one nation—including the Chinese —from becoming dominant or assuming a real hegemony in the Far East, which it could then use to freeze out American interests.

Although many Americans never quite rationalized it, by its emergence on the California coast the United States became every bit as much a Pacific power as it was an Atlantic nation.

The United States faced Asia in exactly the same way it faced Europe, though distance and cultural differences made Asia seem much more remote. Therefore, Pacific strategy had to be, and was, basically the same as Atlantic strategy. It developed differently only because there was one major difference between the Pacific and Atlantic situations: off Asia there was no friendly Britain to bar the entrance of an unfriendly power into the Pacific.

Therefore, while the United States came to accept the British protection of the Atlantic approaches as "natural" or "historic" —to be taken for granted—and could espouse a policy of non-intervention in Europe, it had to become deeply involved in power politics in the Pacific. The British played the great game of "balance of power" in the West. The United States, through the Open Door, tried to forge its own balance of power in the East.

Again, as in the Atlantic, there was a certain unofficial understanding and alliance—when the United States built a powerful navy in the late nineteenth century this fleet was Pacific-based and Pacific-oriented. Because of generally compatible interests—the United States tacitly accepted the British Empire in Southeast Asia—the United States Fleet assumed the duty of protecting British interests in the East. Britain ruled the waves, but did not approach naval parity with the United States Fleet in Pacific waters. Britain had no need to do so.

By 1900, the United States had acquired certain possessions in the Pacific area—the Philippines, Guam, Hawaii, and other smaller islands—and thus the isolationism practiced toward Europe never applied eastward. This was a fact too many Americans tended to ignore: that the United States was already strategically and geopolitically involved in the Far East, and could not withdraw without exposing the Pacific coast.

In the early days of the Republic, the United States had developed important commercial interests and trade in China.

The forced opening of Japan by Commodore Perry was done to expand these interests and develop further American trade. In this sense, the American attitude toward the East was somewhat similar to the attitude toward Latin America. The United States did not want to plant its flag abroad, as the French and British were doing, nor did it necessarily want to dominate. It did want open trade under favorable conditions, and to assure that no other nation assumed domination of areas in which Americans had a commercial or strategic interest.

The American opening of Japan, with gunboats, for a long time seemed brilliantly successful. Japanese commercial ties, and American investment in Japan, soon greatly exceeded those in China. But Japan, by an amazingly farsighted effort of dominant policy, did not react as certain Latin American and other areas opened up to trade. The Japanese, deserting their former isolation, in two generations transformed their islands from a loosely knit, virtually pre-gunpowder feudal society into a coherent, organized, bureaucratic, modern industrial nation. The Japanese, of course, borrowed ideas heavily: naval organization from Britain, industrial processes from Germany, social titles and bureaucracy from France, and business techniques from the United States. They forged all this into a powerful, operating, successful whole, though with a certain amount of schizophrenia and dislocation due to too-rapid change.

But they also absorbed dominant cultural ideas from the West, in the last, great age of Atlantic imperialism. The Japanese situation was highly analogous to Britain's several hundred years before, but with one immense difference—there was no area of the globe left for the Japanese to colonize. Japan was a string of islands totally without resources such as petroleum or iron, and once it started to industrialize, unable to feed its own population. Japan, once it became industrial, logically had to have both markets and access to resources under favorable terms—but they found that all the older powers considered that the world was already made. There was no room for an expanding Japan in the great power club.

That the Japanese, becoming an organized, industrial nation when they did, would tend to behave as an imperialist power was utterly logical—every other modern power, in one way or another, was doing the same. The United States was expanding across and developing an immense virgin wilderness, replete with every kind of material wealth. France, Britain, and the other European states had either seized, or were seizing, colonies, resources, and markets in Asia and Africa. Czarist Russia was exploding eastward across Siberia, absorbing people and territories it could barely digest. The Japanese, on their islands, had nowhere to go but overseas. And everywhere, overseas, some other power had got there first.

The Dutch, British, French, and other powers excluded Japanese trade with their possessions, for obvious selfish reasons. The United States had no desire to open up its own vast internal markets to Japanese competition. When the industrial world went into economic crisis and deep Depression after World War I, these exclusions became severe.

In 1900, however, the United States, busily playing balance-of-power politics in the Far East, determined to allow no single power to achieve control, looked very favorably on Japan's emergence as a modern nation. Washington regarded Japan as a counterpoise to what was then considered the real menace in the Far East: Czarist Russia. Russia had poured material power into Siberia. It was pressing on India, and making the British very nervous. Russian influence was expanding into the Chinese province of Manchuria, winning concessions from China, dominating and occupying the northern half of Korea. Both the British government and President Theodore Roosevelt believed that Russia's expansion in the Far East must be stopped.

Because of this concern with Russia, when Japan went to war with the decaying Chinese Empire over the question of who should dominate Korea, and quickly established its position as the dominant Asian power, the West was not disturbed. When the Russian and Japanese interests in Korea clashed in 1904, and Japan fought Russia over the question of which power should dominate Korea and Manchuria, the United States openly supported Japan.

President Theodore Roosevelt materially assisted the Japanese in ending the war on favorable terms.

The Russo-Japanese war of 1905 made Japan a major Eastern power. It began to behave like one. It dominated Manchuria economically; Manchuria's vast stores of food, minerals, and timber were vital to the burgeoning Japanese industry. To secure a land bridge to Manchuria, Asia's richest province, Japan then annexed Korea. Korea was absorbed into the Japanese Empire, like Formosa had been after the Chinese war, and the native population was deprived of all national rights.

Not out of any intrinsic belief, but in its own interest, Japan joined the Allies in World War I. From this action Japan gained possession or a mandate over many islands in the Pacific which had belonged to Germany. The spoils, however, were slim, and far below Japanese expectations—for by now both the United States and Great Britain had become definitely uneasy about Japan's future policies.

The future course of Japanese commercial empire could only bring it into confrontation with the West. This was clearly seen, although Japanese needs in this new industrial world were not.

Japan's natural trading area was the Atlantic commercial world, but the wave of autarchy, high tariffs, and economic exclusions which swept that world and absolutely ensured the Great Depression, now virtually assured a dangerous internal combustion inside Japan.

Until the end of World War I, Japan's imperial policies had not been more aggressive, or more reckless, than the normal course of such powers as Britain or France. The Japanese

280

fought Russia for obvious reasons, and with the complete approval of the West. The economic domination of Manchuria, a spoils-rich but utterly backward area, was no worse than British exploitation of India. The Japanese seized Korea and Taiwan, but the French had seized Indo-China, and the Dutch still put down Indonesian dissidents by force. All nations, not excepting the United States, demanded humiliating concessions from China and pushed the Manchu regime around. Chinese sovereignty—which the Japanese understood—was more apparent than real, though the United States was the one power that made an effort to keep the Chinese government intact.

Through World War I, then, Japan sought commercial expansion and prestige in exactly the same way the other great powers did, with a big navy and by waging limited campaigns against "natives" in the less-developed world.

But in doing this, the Japanese developed a dynamic militarism that began to worry the West. Ironically, Japan was the only Asian nation that in any way matched the traditional warlike spirit of the Europeans. China and other Asian societies had long been dominated by the scholarly mandarin class; until industrialization, the ruling Japanese caste had been the *samurai,* or warriors.

The attitudes, outlook, and way of life of the *samurai* and the feudal princes above them in the unopened Japan of 1850 had been remarkably like those of the feudal classes of medieval Europe. Interminable internecine warfare had honed the martial spirit and developed a philosophy of arms. In a very real sense, the same kind of internal struggle between feudal warriors and a rising modern business class that had taken place in Europe many years before now was being fought in twentieth-century Japan. There was one immense difference. The modern *samurai* now possessed steel ships and aircraft instead of finely honed swords, in the event they tried to carry their philosophy of personal combat against the world.

As early as 1908, American military circles were openly

281

prophesying war with Imperial Japan. When the United States Army was again demobilized in 1919, and the ground forces disappeared, an immense fleet, fully equal to the Royal Navy, was still maintained in California. It could be pointed at no other nation but Japan. By 1924, the American military staffs had completed detailed war plans in contemplation of an engagement in the far Pacific.

But for a few years the tension seemed to ease. Japan's aggressive foreign policy became more moderate. One reason was that the immense economic progress of an industrial Japan had changed the domestic social and political scene. The dominant oligarchy and the warriors had steadily lost ground to a rising business and bureaucratic class, in a process that was similar to events centuries before in the West.

The business classes of Japan were similar to their counterparts in the West; in fact, they patterned themselves on them. Interested in profits and freedom for commercial enterprise, Japanese capitalists had no more love for high taxes or a large standing army than Sir Neville Chamberlain or Henry Ford. Because this class made a great deal of money in the new, emerging Japanese economy, and because they were generally better-educated than other Japanese—many went abroad— and better organized, the business and industrial classes tended to gain political dominance. They influenced the new, emerging bureaucracy which had been scorned by the original *samurai,* and they began to have an immense effect on national policy.

The original warlords of Japan had rightly understood their need of modern industry and modern techniques if Japan were to retain its sovereignty and emerge as an influential nation. They had not quite realized that the imposition of such factories and techniques on a feudal society would inevitably create a non-feudal class, which seemed likely to dominate the country by 1920.

The business interests vigorously urged a cutback in military preparations, and the end of a militaristic policy of expansion. Having been abroad, either for education or for the propagation of business, the commercial groups understood the real weakness of Japan compared to such industrial giants as the United States or Britain. Japan had made immense strides, but it had by no means caught up. The businessmen not only felt war with the West would be militarily disastrous, but they were also genuinely influenced by the attitudes of their counterparts across the world. War or other military action was bad business.

This group, influential in the bureaucracy and the cabinet, argued a policy of getting concessions from the other powers through diplomacy, and efforts to advance the nation through major efforts at peaceful trade.

In the 1920's it seemed they were going to be successful, and that they were going, from the top, to liberalize Japan. Japan reduced its ground divisions substantially, over the protests of the generals. It pulled its troops out of China, where, under extraterritorial treaties, they had stood for many years. Japan agreed to a naval limitation treaty with the United States and Great Britain that established a permanent Japanese inferiority in ships and arms.

In Japanese society itself there was also definite liberalization. The franchise was extended to all male citizens, and the warrior psychology of old Japan was increasingly demeaned among the educated classes.

But, tragically, a number of historical factors destroyed this emerging liberalism. One was a logical *samurai* reaction and counterattack, to turn the nation back into old paths and regain their old influence. Another was the fact that the worldwide Depression dealt severe damage to the business groups in Japan, just as it destroyed confidence in similar structures in America and Europe. The business classes lost power in both America and Japan, but in Japan there was no other alternative except a form of totalitarianism.

283

The final blow to the Japanese liberals' hopes was the fact that peaceful diplomacy gained nothing. Panicked by their own domestic economic troubles, none of the industrial or colonial nations dared extend the slightest concession to Japan. The same United States Administration that hoped for a liberalization of Japanese society under business influence also was instrumental in facing the Japanese with severe tariffs that drove them out of their hoped-for, natural trading areas.

For the best and most logical of domestic reasons, the industrial societies of the West informed Japan that it was a tough, competitive world, and they would have to live with it. In desperation, Japanese industry turned to making gimcrack goods and penny novelties—that did not compete with Western manufactures and that also created an unfair image of Japanese abilities—but this was not enough.

Japanese missions seeking trade concessions, or permission to make cameras or build ships for the advanced nations, met universal failure. This was utterly understandable; Western industry itself was at a standstill and millions of Americans and Europeans were unemployed. Japanese entry into the colonial trading areas of Asia was also denied; again, logically, because Japanese living standards and the desperation of its businessmen made them willing to undersell every industrial plant in the West.

Meanwhile, an enormous emotional counterattack on the Westernization and liberalization of Japan began. In what they considered pure self-defense, the officer groups of Japan went strongly into politics. These groups, mainly army officers, were almost wholly descended from the former rural *samurai* of Japan. Their fathers had been something similar to the old European knights and men-at-arms. Now, they were becoming increasingly useless and irrelevant in a modern society. Logically, they hated everything modern: money, capitalism, business, liberalism, and even Western clothes, which the business classes were adopting.

There were two officer groups, both ultranationalist and rural and provincial in background. One group was made up mostly of younger field officers. Its main intellectual thrust was to "purify" Japanese society by returning it to the old ways practiced before the foreign devils came from across the sea. This was of course a normal, but impossible, human phenomenon. These younger officers were prepared to destroy the present emerging capitalist system by violence, and they joined with certain civilian terrorist groups with similar aims.

The other officer group entering politics was called *Toseiha,* or the Control Group. This was an apt name, because its members wanted to control the emerging Japanese industrial society rather than destroy it. *Toseiha* members were also rural and feudal in background, but they generally came from a higher social strata than the younger officers. They were mostly colonels and generals, and their birth and earned positions gave them a wider—though just as nationalistic—viewpoint than the violent young terrorists.

These men regarded the *samurai* notions of returning Japan to its old, loose, pre-Perry feudal customs as complete nonsense. They were nationalists who wanted to increase Japanese power and prestige in the world, while they themselves controlled Japan. Their drive was not to destroy modern capitalism or the modern, liberalizing bureaucracy, but to assume command of both through a single political party in which senior military officers would retain a dominant role.

This was similar to European fascism, but it did not spring so much from economic failures as in Italy or Germany, or a fear of Bolshevism. Its basic roots were the fear of dispossession by an important social class, and the cultural schizophrenia resulting in any human society from too-rapid change.

Toseiha generals were not so bloodthirsty as the young *samurai.* They did not plot or condone armed revolt—but they did not mind at all if armed terrorists and fanatics, without

285

their direction, insisted upon wiping out certain of their enemies.

This terrorism—the assassination of liberal politicians by ultranationalist groups and societies—had not yet become completely disreputable in Japan. It stemmed from the long centuries of Japan's feudal age, in which, just as in medieval Europe, most political questions were settled by personal combat or the sword. Japan was infused with the warrior ethic. It took very little to convince many young fanatics that the answer to a policy they did not like was a thrust of a *samurai* sword. During the crucial period while liberals and traditionalists struggled for control of the nation, a Japanese premier, a former finance minister, and many other liberal dignitaries and leaders were struck down in a savage welter of blood.

With considerable skill, the experienced generals and colonels of the Control Group were able to use this terrorism both to kill off politicians they hated and to destroy the power of the opposing ultranational groups by arresting them and executing them afterward. Also, with considerable intelligence, the military group realized that Japan was too highly organized already, and too pluralistic socially for them to rule alone. They made alliances of convenience with certain great industrialists, such as the Mitsuis and the Mitsubishis, and joined with certain professional politicians as well. The generals themselves wanted to control policy, but for many years they preferred to stay in the background, out of public sight.

In this long battle, unfortunately, the United States, for the best of reasons, played most of its cards wrong.

It was to the United States' interest that the modern liberals win out in Japan, but few Americans could see that their success and the success of Japanese diplomacy was fatally intertwined. Nor did Washington strategists understand fully that military failure was the one thing that could destroy the power of the military groups in Japan, and denigrate the warrior myths.

What happened was that the United States, over the crucial years, handed Japan diplomatic defeat after defeat, with moral righteousness, but then failed to act at all when the Japanese generals precipitated a warlike move. In this way, Washington, from Hoover through F.D.R., tended to help destroy the liberal policy-makers while convincing the Japanese that the generals had the only answers. It is very probable that economic concessions to the Japanese could have prevented war, even late in the game. It is also reasonably certain that military pressure, earlier, would have ended the dangerous game before it fully began.

The decisive turn came with the Manchuria incident of 1931. Japan had dominated Manchuria economically since the turn of the century, but Manchuria was still officially a Chinese province. All Japanese wanted fuller control. But what occurred late in 1931 was not only ominous, but largely misunderstood in the West.

Local, ultranationalist army commanders of the *Toseiha* group in China provoked an incident between Chinese and Japanese soldiers on the ground. Then, acting not on orders from Tokyo but on their own initiative, Japanese commanders invaded Manchuria and by January 1932, had assumed complete control of the province. The move was believed by most Japanese historians to be an action taken by *Toseiha* to force the Tokyo government's hand, to fight a quick, successful war and hand the government spoils it would not dare repudiate.

But American observers were never sure about what had happened. Some felt that the Manchurian action had actually been ordered by the civilian Tokyo government, influenced by the generals. Other American opinion, in which President Hoover shared, felt that United States interference in the act would merely force the still-liberal Japanese regime to back up the generals. It was forcefully argued that United States

287

noninterference gave the civilians and liberals their best hope to prevail. But this view excluded Japanese psychology, and also gave the liberal groups credit for more strength than they possessed. Liberalism was a new patina on Japan; the traditional ethos was *samurai,* which some individuals in Washington, certain that all peoples everywhere were much alike, emphatically refused to understand.

What happened was that neither the United States nor the Tokyo regime called the generals' hands. Great Britain, with a keen eye in the Orient, at least, offered to oppose the Japanese seizure if Washington would make a common front. Henry L. Stimson, who was Hoover's Secretary of State, wanted to take up the British, give the Japanese a serious ultimatum: back down, or face sanctions, perhaps war. But the President, deep in his own woes in 1931-1932, adamantly refused. Hoover, who once said firmly that freedom in America did not depend on the outcome of struggles for material power between other states, now took the position that the United States could not, and had no business in trying, to act as a policeman halfway across the world.

> ... This is primarily a controversy between China and Japan. The United States has never set out to preserve peace among other nations by force, and so far as this part is concerned, we shall confine ourselves to friendly counsel.

This was, actually, a full retreat from Theodore Roosevelt's old policy, however mistaken, of trying to balance off the powers of the East. Then, the United States had been involved, seeing its own interest. Now, Washington collectively professed to see no American interest at all in a major shift of power in the Far East.

In this policy and action, incidentally, Franklin Roosevelt in those years concurred. His eyes were only opened years later, when the consequences of Western retreat became clear. Hoover's eyes, in all respect to a great and sincere American, were never opened. His brand of management and vision of foreign affairs never accepted the entry of the United States into anything so sordid as traditional power politics, preferring a form of purity and intellectuality instead.

"Friendly counsel" however failed to help the Chinese resist; it did not deter the Japanese. The Tokyo government, as the *Toseiha* guessed, did not dare repudiate the generals in the full flush of patriotic success. Stimson was only permitted to deliver a bitter note to the effect that the United States would not "recognize" the forcible change of government from China to Japan, and found it "morally" reprehensible. "Moral sanctions" were then applied—but no one, in Tokyo or Washington, quite knew what these meant.

The seizure of Manchuria was the first major territorial aggression to follow World War I. It revealed a deep weakness in the potential order-keeping powers: Britain would not move without the United States, and the United States disclaimed all responsibility. Both nations took this position with full support from their publics; very likely the publics in question would have supported no other policy. Here again a deepseated unwillingness of the democratic system to defend itself was revealed.

Most observers agree that a strong Anglo-American stand on Manchuria would have forced the Japanese government to recall its generals. The Japanese government was not prepared for war with the two industrial powers.

Japan was economically vulnerable, and worst of all, completely dependent upon Western sources for such necessities as metals, oil, and aviation gasoline. Economic sanctions would have hurt, and the civilian governmental structure of Japan, then and later, was positively terrified of the prospect of war with America. Had the *Toseiha* generals been balked, they would have lost face, never to be regained. They also would have learned a bitter lesson before millions of Japanese had to die. As it was, they emerged national heroes, much as

Hitler became a hero after his bloodless triumphs against a spineless Europe.

Japan consolidated its conquests in Manchuria, and meanwhile, the *Toseiha* slowly extended its penetration of the power structure. In February 1936, the radical *Kodoha,* or younger officers group, finally attempted its long-preached coup d'état. Under these firebrands, Japanese soldiers occupied part of Tokyo, seized and killed three high civilian officials. But the senior officers, quick to understand their advantage, moved with stunning effect. The revolt was put down with force. Thirteen *Kodoha* officers and four civilian terrorist leaders were executed. The *gumbatsu,* or military overlords, appeared to have saved the government. Actually, they had destroyed their rival group and took complete control of the Japanese government at the same time. Having "saved" the regime, the generals were now in charge.

The abortive revolt also convinced the *zaibatsu,* or large industrial oligarchists, to throw in with the generals. The alliance was complete when Prince Fumimaro Konoye, a scion of one of the noblest families, a relative of the figurehead Emperor, and a man acceptable in both business and military circles as well as a man who had chosen a political career, agreed to front for the new nationalist powers behind the throne.

Konoye agreed with the *gumbatsu* that Japan must embark upon an expansionist, imperialist career; peaceful trade and economic expansion through diplomatic persuasion of other powers simply was not working fast enough to feed the burgeoning island population. Already almost one hundred million Japanese were crowded into an area approximately the size of California, living on frugality and discipline and skills alone.

Konoye, however, was opposed to a war with the United States. He had no illusions whatever that the Japanese could win such a war. The Japanese Navy, which had not engaged in politics like the Army, agreed with the Premier. Men like the brilliant Vice Admiral Isoroku Yamamoto had a deep respect for the United States Fleet. Oddly, while the Japanese Army remained backward, traditional, and officered by rural types, the navy was a fully modern affair. Its top leaders were better educated than army men, and had a much clearer notion of the world. The navy continued concerned that the army would move in China, get Japan into a war with the United States, and force the navy to bear the burden of the war. And this is almost exactly what happened.

With the new nationalist regime in power in May 1937, the Japanese Army moved two months later. Japanese ground forces went on the offensive in North China. The announced purpose of this action was to carve out two new "autonomous" states in the region, Inner Mongolia and North China, to build a buffer against Soviet Communism; the Japanese regime called upon Chiang Kai-shek's Nationalist government and all Chinese to assist economically and politically in this mission. The actual result, of course, was to create new puppet states under direct Japanese control and to expand the Japanese empire.

Planning a short, decisive campaign, the Japanese misjudged Chinese temperament badly. The vast region of China had no effective modern government—Chiang Kai-shek himself could not shift government troops across many provinces without first securing permission from the local warlord. It had no modern arms that could match the Japanese in open combat. But China had a vast population, which coalesced in hatred of the invaders. Neither Chiang Kai-shek's government, which retreated inland to Chungking, nor the Chinese Communists, secure in far Yenan, acquiesced to Japanese demands. The "China Incident" of July 1937 dragged on into a drawnout, indecisive war.

The Japanese armies could march across China almost at will. They occupied most of north and central China, and seized the important sea ports on the south coast. But without acquiescence or surrender, they could not forge an effective control of China's peasant millions. Japan "conquered" China in a year—but somehow could neither end the war nor withdraw. After spending one hundred thousand men and billions of yen, the Japanese warlords seemed no closer to final victory than when they had begun.

Chiang Kai-shek hoped for aid from the United States and refused every Japanese offer to negotiate. However, the only assistance he got in those years was from the Russians.

Japan's aggressions in China again put Washington on the spot. By now, the full sympathy of the United States government and the public was with the Chinese. Not only the unprovoked nature of the attack, but Japanese atrocities—the rape of Nanking, the mass bombing of defenseless civilians—angered American opinion.

Facing massive popular resistance by the Chinese people, the Japanese adopted terroristic tactics. When the victorious Japanese field forces seized Nanking, the Nationalist capital, the conquerors permitted their troops to run wild, sacking the city. For several days there was no effort on the part of the Japanese commanders to restore order or enforce discipline. Maddened soldiers bayoneted thousands of civilians, including women and children, and a large part of the female population was brutally raped or molested. Thousands of panic-stricken Chinese tried to find refuge in some of the foreign compounds, but had to be driven away.

At the same time, the Japanese used their air force not as a tactical military instrument, but a terror weapon against defenseless Chinese villages and towns. The Chinese had neither an air force, a warning system, nor bomb shelters. Japanese bombers attacked remote towns in the path of the advancing armies as well as large cities. Thousands of panicked civilians were driven into the crowded streets and indiscriminately slaughtered by falling fragmentation bombs. In this way several hundred thousand Chinese civilian men, women, and children were killed. The military uselessness of such actions horrified Western military people as well as humanitarians because in the end they only intensified Chinese bitterness against the invader.

The Neutrality Acts, however, forced President Roosevelt into a painful decision: if he declared the existence of hostilities in the Far East, this would automatically bar all American assistance to either side, and it was felt that this would aid the Japanese more than the Chinese. Roosevelt deliberately chose not to see the war; the "China Incident" remained an incident, and a belligerency that was killing millions received no official recognition in Washington.

The President, however, by 1937 was no longer in sympathy with the Neutrality Acts. In October 1937 he made his famous "quarantine" speech. He condemned aggressive war as a "disease" and suggested that the carriers of the disease be quarantined in order to protect the human community as a whole. This was a trial balloon for action against spreading totalitarianism.

It collapsed. F.D.R. was criticized severely for trying to intervene in foreign wars; he picked up almost no support at all. Henry Stimson, now out of office, but expressing the same views, said that "Mr. Roosevelt seemed to conclude that the country was not ready for strong medicine." At any rate, the President continued the pattern of criticism of aggression while remaining politically inactive.

The warfare in China caused incidents between the United States and Japan in another way. The United States had private property in China and troops stationed there, and the Japanese invasion affected both. There were hundreds of incidents, as American property or United States citizens' rights were violated by Japanese soldiers. The most serious was the sinking of the United States gunboat *Panay* in December 1937.

The *Panay*, a clearly marked gunboat flying the Stars and Stripes on the Yangtze River, was deliberately attacked by a swarm of Japanese warplanes. The American crew, taken by surprise and unable at first to believe they were under fire, were not able to put up an effective resistance. Struck by bombs, and repeatedly strafed, the *Panay* went down. Some crewmen swam to safety on the river shore, but a number were killed and wounded.

The attack was unquestionably ordered by Japanese commanders, as part of the general policy of harassment of all Western presence in China. It was also widely believed, but never proven entirely, that the attack was a deliberate testing of American nerve—to see what reaction the United States would make to a violent provocation.

The reaction, for better or worse, was relatively mild. The government protested sharply, but without threats—the American public was angry, but not nearly angry enough to authorize the use of force in retaliation.

Having proved whatever they had set out to prove, the Japanese government promptly apologized for the sinking—it was impossible to deny the evidence—and paid several million dollars for the *Panay*. At the same time, United States diplomats in Asia reported to Hull, it was apparent that the Japanese were bent on eradicating the American presence in China, and that more incidents could be expected. Hull accepted this view. His dilemma, and Roosevelt's, was how to maintain American influence, or protect American interests in China short of authorizing force, which public opinion still would not accept.

In 1938, however, Washington instituted what was called a "moral embargo" against Japan. American industrialists were requested not to sell aircraft or aircraft parts to Japanese. However, while Tokyo protested this moral embargo, it did not hurt the Japanese war effort in China.

The Japanese vital needs were oil and scrap metals, of which Japan had none. The United States continued to sell Japan at least one-half of its total needs of these materials. Thus the

United States was materially assisting the Japanese war effort in China while using harsh words against it.

State Department political advisers wrote memoranda stating that "opposing Japan by use of words . . . would not halt the forward march of Japan's military machine," and that continuance along this line would sooner or later require Washington to accept a diplomatic defeat or "find itself forced to resort to arms."

Such reports were pigeonholed, for two reasons. One was that current trade treaties with Japan precluded oil or iron embargoes. The real reason nothing was done was that Washington feared that cutting off Japan's oil would lead to an open military takeover of the government, and an invasion of the Dutch East Indies to replace American with Indonesian oil. The threat of embargo, however, was retained as a diplomatic weapon. In the summer of 1939, at Congressional insistence, the government gave Japan notice that the trade treaties would be abrogated. But when the necessary six months' notice period expired, the actual sale of goods was not ended; oil and scrap iron continued to flow to Japan in the absence of any formal agreement.

In December 1938, Premier Prince Konoye took steps that should have clarified the Japanese aims in Asia. He proclaimed the creation of the "Greater East Asia Co-Prosperity Sphere," which could only be seen as a New Order for Asia under Japanese hegemony. This was an open announcement that Japan intended to eradicate all Western influence. The proclamation, printed in most of the United States media, noticeably did not exclude the Dutch East Indies or other Western colonial areas.

The moral embargo and war of words continued for two years. Then, the German conquest of western Europe altered the entire balance power. In Japanese eyes, France, Holland, and Britain were removed as effective Asian powers; they were now unable to protect themselves in the Far East. The awesome menace of Germany, with German power lapping at the shores of the Atlantic, suddenly seemed likely to draw American attention and action toward Europe. The Japanese warlords began to dream dreams they had formerly suppressed. If Germany destroyed the structure of Atlantic civilization, dazzling opportunities would be opened up to Japan.

Recognizing a common interest, Germany, Italy, and Japan signed the Tripartite Pact in September 1940. The United States had become the balance of world power, even if the public did not recognize the fact and Washington hesitated to implement it. By the Tripartite Pact Germany and Japan each cynically hoped to engage the other with America, and thus take the potential threat of United States power off its own back.

The Pact, however, hardened F.D.R.'s Cabinet against Japan. The realization came that the Asian and European conflicts were not merely isolated incidents, but events in a major assault against the Anglo-American concepts of world order. Japan now began to exert pressure against the embattled Allies. Japanese troops occupied French Indo-China, to close off a source of aid to the Chinese. They pressured Thailand into a neutrality treaty. They forced Great Britain to close the Burma Road, over which war materials were trickling into China.

The French rulers of Indo-China—finding it impossible to get any aid or support from the emasculated French regime in Vichy—appealed to the United States for assistance to prevent the Japanese occupation. After some deliberation, Washington rejected the request. American strategic interests in Indo-China did not seem to exist, and since Japanese forces were expanding overland from China, there seemed to be no effective means of stopping them.

American policy in the Pacific region was geared to the Pacific Fleet; the United States had no effective land forces in the area, nor any policy to use such forces. In fact, it was considered American policy not to commit ground troops in Asia. Unable to fight the overwhelming power of the Japanese Imperial Army, the French colonial authorities in Hanoi surrendered. Here began the overthrow of French power in this area, which was to have far-reaching effects.

The British, with almost all their military power concentrated in the Atlantic or Mediterranean, urgently requested Washington to pressure the Japanese to drop their demands over the Burma Road. Again, Washington demurred. The British closed the road—but on Churchill's orders reopened it some months later.

All this provoked heated controversy inside the Cabinet. Morgenthau, Stimson, and Hopkins were among those urging tough measures against the Japanese, now. They argued that Japan would not go to war, but would back down if put to a firm test. The State Department, under Hull and Sumner Welles, were of the opinion that delicate diplomacy was preferable: a hard stand would force the Japanese to attack the Indies as a source of oil.

Again, halfway measures were taken. On July 25, 1940, F.D.R. ordered a "licensing system" for petroleum products and iron and steel scrap. In effect, however, only aviation gasoline was placed on the prohibited list, and the flow of war goods to Japan continued.

The increasing hostility between Washington and Tokyo also caused some viewing with alarm inside the United States. While opinion was firm against Japanese aggressions, there was much sentiment that the United States really had no responsibility for stopping it. Walter Lippmann was an influential spokesman for this view. In early 1940 he wrote an article condemning Congress (especially Senator Vandenberg of Michigan) for its actions in ending the United States-Japanese trade agreements of 1911. He argued that this was a step toward war. It "put the United States in the position of challenging a great power." Of course, the United States was doing exactly that, though slowly and hesitantly.

In Lippmann's view, Japan seemed likely to dominate the

297

Far East anyway—and it was better to acquiesce, in such an event, than to take America into a foreign war, especially one in which it had only strategic, not territorial interests.

Ironically, the American investment in Japan, in those years, vastly exceeded the United States investment in China or any other area of the Far East.

There were other disputes. President Roosevelt determined to use his trump card to overawe Japan—the United States Fleet, stationed in California. He ordered the name of the fleet changed to the "Pacific Fleet" and moved it from the West Coast to Hawaii, both obvious moves in a game of war nerves. Admiral J. O. Richardson, naval commander in the Pacific, protested the move. He argued that to station the fleet at Pearl Harbor was logistically inadvisable; he was not interested in diplomatic chess but in the safety and operations of the fleet itself. But Richardson was removed from command, and the changes went through.

However, the secret agreements to assist the British in the Battle of the Atlantic, and the creation of the Atlantic Fleet in early 1941, materially weakened the power of the naval forces at Pearl Harbor. Ships and personnel were drained off to the Atlantic. This left the Pacific Fleet actually inferior to Japanese naval forces. This was fully understood in military circles but was not bruited about publicly.

Now, at the beginning of 1941, the Japanese government decided to embark upon two concurrent courses of action: to try to avoid actual war by diplomacy while trying to get the United States to accede to Japanese ambitions, and to plan for war in case the other approach failed. In simplest terms, the Japanese requested the United States to permit them a free hand to reorganize China under their hegemony, and to extend their domination over all East Asia excluding the Philippines but including the Dutch East Indies, or Indonesia.

In the event the United States failed to agree, Admiral Isoroku Yamamoto—whose Navy respected the United States'

298

power far more than the provincial generals who had only seen China—was ordered to begin a staff study for a carrier strike against Hawaii. The plans were complete by summer, and actual preparations began.

All Japanese war planning was based on the premise that war would come before the end of 1941. The Japanese military, even in their exaltation and folly, understood that time was running out for them. Japanese Intelligence reported the increasing military strength of the United States. By 1942 the naval imbalance in the Pacific, due to the siphoning off of strength to the Atlantic, would be restored. The Philippines— a threatening bulwark across the Japanese line of communications to the Indies—were expected to receive sufficient United States personnel and air power by the end of 1942 to make them impervious.

The purpose of the Japanese strike was simple: to seize and hold the territories included in Konoye's Greater East Asia Co-Prosperity Sphere. The prime target was the East Indies, with its oil. In 1941 the United States finally stopped shipments of petroleum to Japan, and all Japanese planners knew that by the fall of 1941 Japan would be consuming its reserves. Singapore and the Philippines—British and American bastions— had to be captured to protect the oil lifeline to the East Indies. Meanwhile, the Pacific Fleet at Pearl Harbor had to be immobilized so that it could not interfere.

The Japanese dream was both aggressive and defensive. The seizure of foreign territories was aggressive, but once East Asia had been taken, the Japanese had no intentions of going further. They planned a defensive line across the Pacific to keep the United States and Britain at bay—and they expected, in view of the forces, techniques, and apparent wills of the two nations in 1941, to be able to do so. It never entered Japanese heads to attack the continental United States, or to expand beyond Asia.

The war had to be short, or Japan would fail. No Japanese

naval expert—and there were some very good ones—had any illusion that Japan, which could produce at most about two hundred aircraft per month, could withstand a protracted war of attrition with the United States.

A very interesting corollary of this view was the one also current in Japanese top levels at the time: if Japan struck, it might be doomed; but if Japan did not go to war and win, it was doomed, anyway, as a great power. Without further access to resources and markets, the Japanese industrial machine was at the point of decay. The Japanese saw themselves as increasingly at the mercy of Anglo-American world power and hostile populations which had never shown any understanding of genuine Japanese needs in the modern world. Japan was in the position Britain would have been in, if it had had no empire and found most of the world's ports closed to its manufactured goods.

At almost the same time that Japanese staffs began to plan military action, British and American staffs were meeting, secretly in Washington, more openly in the Far East. Here, a basic Anglo-American-Dutch strategy was devised. It was entirely defensive.

The details of this planning, which extended through most of 1941, and the disagreements which left both Americans and British without a real coordinated plan of action as late as December, were not important. What was important, then and in retrospect, was that the United States military staff wanted to avoid war in the Pacific, or at least delay it so long as possible. An agreement of enormous strategic importance had been reached that Hitler was the greater foe, and that the war in Europe must have priority. General Marshall expressed the views of United States planners to the President.

A major war with Japan would reduce the effort in the Atlantic; Singapore in American eyes was vulnerable; and the Philippines, only incorporated into United States defense plans in early 1941, inadequately garrisoned. Marshall wanted to build up the Philippines with a powerful air and submarine force. This would make any Japanese strike southward toward their vital oil too hazardous to be undertaken. Marshall said, succinctly, as relations deteriorated, that "until powerful United forces have been built up in the Far East, it would take some very clever diplomacy to save the situation." The War and Navy Departments actually asked the President to avoid any ultimatum to Japan, and to try to make some agreement that would "tide the situation over" for "several months."

Marshall emphasized the importance of gaining time; a Japanese strike in 1941 could only result in defeats or losses for the Western powers. If such time were gained, he had no fear of eventually containing and overawing Japanese power. He and Admiral Stark, the Chief of Naval Operations, briefed Roosevelt on November 5, 1941, that the only plans they had for opposing Japan were to hold the Philippines, Malaya, and the Indies by purely defensive action.

Actually, there were no plans to involve the Pacific Fleet in a strike against the Japanese Navy in case it moved southward. The United States forces were inferior, and the logistical support required to operate in East Asian waters was not yet available. Ironically, the Japanese staff took the President's transfer of the fleet to Hawaii far more seriously than did Marshall or Stark. They had no intention of using the United States fleet against Japan immediately in case of war—*which was one very important reason why American thinking never envisioned a Japanese effort to knock that fleet out of action.*

There were many leaks about the Japanese plans, including the strike planned for Pearl Harbor. No competent American military officer really credited them—*for a strike on Pearl Harbor, in American eyes, made no strategic or tactical sense.*

In fact, it was far from decided whether the United States would declare war—or merely engage in another undeclared naval action in the Pacific, like the one in the Atlantic—if

Japan moved aggressively against the European colonial regimes.

But time was the one thing now rapidly running out.

In Tokyo, Konoye, who was still adamant against risking a war with the United States, was up against increasing opposition from Foreign Minister Yosuke Matsuoka and others, especially after Germany invaded and seemed on the verge of defeating the U.S.S.R. The dazzling success of German arms throughout 1941 fascinated and excited the Japanese militarists. The end of the old order that had never allowed Japan a major place in the scheme of things seemed near; the militarists felt that in 1941 the time would come, and pass, to strike.

Matsuoka, who was very pro-Nazi, argued for an immediate attack on Russian Siberia to remove the old Japanese rival in Asia. Japanese-Soviet hostility was historic and profound, dating from Czarist times. In the late 1930's the two empires had fought several severe border clashes along the Manchurian-Siberian frontier. And one of the major drawbacks, to the Japanese, of risking a war with America and Britain, was the possibility that the U.S.S.R. would attack in Manchuria while the Japanese were engaged in the Pacific. The best Japanese ground forces were stationed in North China, and actually they would remain there through the end of World War II.

The idea of attacking Siberia was rejected by majority opinion among Japan's rulers. The decisive reason was the feeling that Hitler would destroy the U.S.S.R. without help and Siberia would fall to Japan without the expenditure of blood. Also, the generals and expansionists rightly saw that the United States, not the U.S.S.R., was the main obstacle to Japanese ambitions for a co-prosperity sphere. In July 1941, the ruling clique adopted a firm stand to carry out the provisions of the Greater East Asia Co-Prosperity Sphere, which meant Japanese hegemony of the Far East. This decision was announced to the Emperor, who acquiesced.

Prince Konoye and a respectable number of men in the Japanese foreign service still hoped to avoid war. Both the war and peace parties were afflicted by a deep pessimism—some of Japan's top naval leaders, who knew the American and British navies intimately, were far from sanguine—but Konoye did not give up easily.

Konoye, however, was never in real command; he had always been something of a figurehead for the ruling clique. His one insuperable problem was that he was never able to get any concessions from the Anglo-American powers by diplomacy—*while the adventurists secured gain after gain, without retaliation by those powers.* Washington, until 1941, refused to accede Japan anything in the way of trade or territorial concessions—but it also refused to use force to block any military move the Japanese began. This not only confused many Japanese, but it played directly into the militarists' hands.

Washington's approach was both moralistic and impractical, stern and unrealistic at the same time. The United States was under no obligation to grant concessions to the Japanese—but on the other hand, refusing to strengthen the Japanese moderates through concessions and at the same time refusing to take action against the military adventurists could only lead to genuine crisis.

The real turn in the road that led to Pearl Harbor came in July 1941. Japanese war plans were still just that—plans; Yamamoto was far from enthusiastic about implementing them. But in July, after the Cabinet decision to go ahead with the Co-Prosperity Sphere, the Japanese Army took over all of Indo-China and absorbed the region into the Empire.

Japanese troops had been stationed in northern Indo-China since 1940, as part of a war move against the Chinese. The United States had refused to take action—urged by the French colonial regime—when the Japanese garrison moved in. In fact, Roosevelt advised Ambassador Nomura that he would accept a "neutralization" of Indo-China on the "Swiss order."

But if Japan actually absorbed the area, F.D.R. said he would impose full economic sanctions.

Based on past history, it is obvious that the Japanese regime did not believe him.

Indo-China, the later Vietnam, posed a thorny problem for both the Japanese and the United States. After the initial Japanese garrisoning, American planners became more aware of the region's strategic importance. The possession of Indo-China, with its long coastline and areas like Camhrahn Bay (where the Japanese fleet that attacked Singapore eventually assembled) by any hostile power posed a genuine threat to the Western position in Malaya and the Indies. Without Indo-China, it was vastly more difficult for Japanese power to influence the south. This was belatedly seen.

To Japan, however, Indo-China was important for two reasons: one was that it would be far more difficult to pacify South China unless the Indo-Chinese border were sealed off; second, a Japanese strike at Indonesian oil would be enormously difficult without the use of Indo-China as a staging area.

Immediately after the Japanese Army moved in Indo-China, Roosevelt issued an executive order freezing all Japanese assets in the United States. This was the most severe form of economic warfare. Immediately afterward, Great Britain and all the nations of the Commonwealth did the same. The action came as a great shock to Tokyo, as Ambassador Grew reported.

Nomura, in Washington, was profoundly impressed by F.D.R.'s attitude and quick intervention. He cabled Tokyo that Washington "meant business," and urgently requested that some Japanese "appeasement measures" be taken. Nomura, though he was a loyal Japanese who supported his country's ambitions, had no illusions about a war with the powerful United States. In reply, he received a long, indefinite cable stating that Japan required raw materials, needed Indo-China, and had to break the "chain of encirclement" the Anglo-Saxon powers were drawing around her. The foreign minister also stated that "economic relations" were so "horribly strained" they could not be endured much longer. This last was perfectly true.

Now, Nomura and Konoye approached F.D.R. with the idea of a summit conference between the President and Premier, to iron out differences at the highest level. The offer provoked heated argument in Washington circles. One faction believed Konoye was sincere, and that he needed the prestige of such a meeting to hold his office. Ambassador Grew held this view. He cabled that Konoye would fall from office if he could not get some encouragement. Should this happen he would certainly be replaced by a military junta that would lack his qualms for beginning a war with the United States. Grew also wrote that the Japanese would sacrifice the Tripartite Pact if they could make any kind of deal.

Grew's view was not popular. Hopkins, Morgenthau, and most of the State Department felt that it made no difference whether Konoye held his post or not; that Japan was already "half-beaten" by its failure to conquer China and by the Anglo-American economic squeeze; and that Japan would back down rather than start a war. President Roosevelt endorsed this position, and denied the Nomura-Konoye request for a meeting.

A summit meeting, at this late date, could not have solved the Japanese-American dilemma. Konoye had to ask for too much; Roosevelt was in no position or mood to give him anything. The last-ditch Japanese demands were three:

1. The stopping of Anglo-American aid to Chiang Kai-shek,
2. The halting of hostile moves against Japan, including further reinforcements or fortifications in the Pacific,
3. Full cooperation by the Western powers in Japan's search for raw materials and markets. The Japanese asked that the colonial exclusions be lifted, and that Japanese goods be

allowed to enter American markets under favorable circumstances.

In return for these concessions, Konoye was prepared to agree to the following:

1. Not to use Indo-China as a base for any military operations except against Chiang Kai-shek.
2. To withdraw Japanese troops from China after the China Incident had been "settled."
3. To guarantee the neutrality of the Philippines.

The minimum American demands, by the summer of 1941, however, were as follows:

1. Immediate evacuation of both China and Indo-China by all Japanese troops, and the relinquishment of all Japanese privileges and concessions won in both areas.
2. Formal renunciation of the Tripartite Pact.
3. A multilateral nonaggression pact between Japan and all its neighbors.

The only concessions the United States was prepared to grant, after the above had been carried out, were to "negotiate" the question of most-favored-nation trading status for Japan, and to place raw silk on the free trade list.

Thus the American position was moralistic and legalistic rather than coldly practical, and it now tended toward an over-reaction to Japanese aggressions which had been let go by the board earlier. Japan was considered a lawbreaker, and therefore its past crimes were not negotiable. The demand for evacuation of China without regard to Japanese humiliation was hardly realistic. However, in American eyes all these demands were enforceable because of the extremely vulnerable Japanese economic situation. It was well known that the island could not long exist without raw materials, especially petroleum, from the Western powers.

It could have served no useful purpose for Roosevelt and Konoye to meet, since the positions of each country were transmitted to the other diplomatically, and neither was willing to give ground. Nomura argued with Hull that the United States had presented a virtual ultimatum in applying sanctions, and that for the Japanese to accept it meant that Japan would have henceforth to live on Anglo-American economic sufferance, and to face a continual economic crisis. This argument was essentially correct, but it won no sympathy from Washington, where there was now a strong reaction against Japanese aggressions in Asia, but no real understanding or acceptance of Japan's genuine economic needs.

In a very real sense, Japan had now gotten herself into an untenable position through her military adventurism, although that adventurism never approached the totality of Hitler's.

Conceivably, Japan might still have been turned from war by the granting of the economic considerations that were, ironically enough, granted after Japan's total defeat. These included opening up of the European colonial preserves in Asia, and also the American market to Japanese manufactures. But in the past climate of the Great Depression in America, and the sourness of the rape of Nanking, F.D.R. could not even consider this.

Noticeably, the United States took a much harder stand against Japan in 1941 than it ever took against Germany, even after F.D.R. ordered American warships to shoot in the Atlantic. Roosevelt could not embark upon an open defiance of Germany because of the large and vocal opinion opposed to measures that might lead to a European war. No virtual ultimatums went to Hitler, and unlike the Anglo-American staff conferences held in the Pacific, the Atlantic strategy meetings were kept secret from the public. But oddly, there was immense support for a hard line against the Japanese, even from America First. Senator Wheeler stated he was "100 percent behind" the President where Japan was concerned. The isolationist majority never felt isolationist toward the Far East, or rather, had stopped being so by 1941.

Although there was a vast cynicism toward a European war based on 1917-1918 experience, and an equal fear of the consequences to America in engaging the mighty German war machine, there was something like an actual belligerency throughout the United States toward Japan. The reasons were both historic and psychological.

While American policy had long been one of withdrawal or indifference to European politics, the public realized the United States had long been committed in Asia. United States troops had been stationed in China since the Boxer Rebellion at the turn of the century. The Philippines were annexed in the Spanish-American War, and this possession automatically made the United States an Asian power. Hawaii, Alaska, Guam, and other Pacific interests kept the nation involved to the west in a way it had never really been immersed in Europe.

Furthermore, while there was a deep fear of, and grudging respect for the German military efficiency, the feeling of the average American toward Japan was more nearly contempt. Only the United States military staff actually recognized the fact that the United States would be inferior in Pacific power through the end of 1942. The economic and industrial deficiencies of Japan were too thoroughly understood, while the superb navy, and above all, carrier attack forces of the Japanese Empire, were given too little credit. It was widely understood that Japan lacked oil, but not that the Japanese Navy gave the Empire the means of seizing oil in one quick campaign.

Finally, there were two more factors behind public belligerency. One was that the people seemed more willing to accept a strategic role in Asia than in Europe; Japan's demands to exclude the United States from China and close the Open Door angered millions who were perfectly agreeable to permitting Hitler to exclude the United States from the European continent. The other factor, hardest to express honestly, was that

308

many of the groups in the United States who were most isolationist in sentiment toward Great Britain were also hostile to the Japanese on ethnic or racial grounds. To many minds, the "Yellow Peril" was no myth.

It was highly ironic, almost paradoxical, that during the last six months of 1941 General Marshall, Admiral Stark, and the military staffs were urging caution and diplomatic concessions, while the State Department and Cabinet and most of the public backed a get-tough policy. Civilian opinion was much more sanguine over the prospects of an air and naval war in the Pacific than the military, while it remained impervious to the urgent need for an eventual land war in Europe.

Thus, the Administration had to wheedle, compromise, and deal under the table to achieve its war preparations against Germany, while Roosevelt could take a firm stand and let war come in the Pacific with at worst, public apathy and at best, wide support.

There was almost complete recognition in the nation by the autumn of 1941 that the United States had "called" Japan in the Pacific, but even as America First was mounting some of its most hysterical attacks on the Administration, there seemed to be no great concern. The two most widespread feelings were that: 1. the Japanese would not fight; 2. if they did, they would be defeated within six months.

A form of undeclared war had already begun in Asia. This centered around the colorful and unusual military organization called the American Volunteer Group, or A.V.G., which became universally known as the Flying Tigers.

To assist Chiang Kai-shek's Nationalist China, which was desperately short of any kind of air power, the United States government in close collaboration with the British, organized several squadrons of fighter aircraft to fight over China. The A.V.G. was composed of American citizens, commanded by an American, flying United States planes, and paid by American appropriations or credits transmitted through the Chinese. Almost all the pilots and ground crews who volunteered for the A.V.G. were members of the regular United States forces—Army, Navy, or Marines.

Officers and men were recruited informally at American bases. They were promised high pay, bonuses, a chance to retain their commissions, and above all, an opportunity to fight. The chief recruiter was a "retired Air Corps captain." Inevitably, the offer drew a certain number of misfits, brawlers, and men who could not take the doldrums and disciplines of peacetime military life. But a high proportion of these same men possessed the famous "killer instinct" of the true combat pilot, and they included men such as General Claire Chennault, Colonel "Tex" Hill, and the Marine ace "Pappy" Boyington—some of the finest fighter pilots World War II produced.

The pilots, of course, could not fight for a foreign power, even as civilians. This had long been forbidden by United States law. But a certain official chicanery was permitted. Members of the armed forces were allowed to "resign," but the resignations were not published. The papers were merely filed in Washington, and with each resignation was filed an agreement stating the resigner was to have full reinstatement of his commission or rate if: 1. he survived and returned; or 2. the United States entered the war.

The A.V.G. was assembled in San Francisco from cities and bases in various parts of the country. Members were issued new official passports—usually designating them as "members of the clergy"—and shipped to Burma via Netherlands-registry freighters. At Rangoon, the British authorities turned lend-lease P-40 Tomahawk fighters over to them. They eventually arrived in South China.

The A.V.G.'s problems were monumental, ranging from command—they were all officially civilians—to relations with the British and Chinese, often thorny, and fantastic logistic

310

tangles. The Japanese were thoroughly aware of their activities, for accounts were openly published in the American press.

The gaudy name "Flying Tigers" came originally from the tigers' teeth painted on the nacelles of the P-40's—Boyington wrote wryly that this art work was supposed to frighten the veteran Japanese flyers—but the nickname was soon justified by their exploits in aerial combat.

Two things happened. One, Colonel Chennault, an Air Forces officer whose career had been marked by controversy because he openly refused to adopt the official Air Forces policy that bombers could live in the air without fighter cover, was undoubtedly the best air-fighter tactician produced by the United States in World War II. Second, his men, who had never been easy to keep around in peacetime, quickly proved they could out-fly and outfight superior Japanese numbers and better aircraft. They raised utter havoc with Japanese bombers who, until that time, had been unopposed over China's skies. New fighters were thrown against them, such as the Nakajima, which was superior to the P-40. When some flyers, like "Tex" Hill, protested these Japanese planes were too hot to handle, Chennault remained calm and unmoved.

By clever tactics, he refused combat and destroyed the better machines through surprise attacks on the ground. In time, Chennault's tactics and ideas proved out. Eventually, and without fanfare, they became the basis for American fighter tactics in World War II, though Chennault, both by reason of his stormy personality and his outspoken loyalty to Chiang Kai-shek, remained embroiled in controversy all his life.

After Pearl Harbor, the A.V.G. fought over Burma. Some of the men were incorporated into the Air Forces in the China-Burma-India theater; others returned to their former services in the Pacific. A final, somewhat bitter, note ended the story for the survivors, however. Many of the flyers who volunteered for combat before the declaration of war lost rank or precedence by not remaining at home. While they were destroying enemy aircraft at fantastic ratios over China and Burma, as civilians, they missed out on rapid promotion at the start of the war.

In 1954, Colonel Hill, who became Chennault's deputy, offered to lead a new American Volunteer Group to Indo-China to assist the French at Dien Bien Phu. But the days of "Flying Tigers" were over; Washington frigidly declined the offer.

The pattern for Pearl Harbor was thus set irrevocably in July. Konoye, who refused to implement the Yamamoto plan or precipitate a war with the United States, eventually was pushed out of office in October 1941. He was replaced by Lieutenant General Hideki Tojo, a known warmonger, who formed a war cabinet made up primarily of military men. Tojo was described in United States Intelligence files as a man of unshakeable convictions and determination, who "had little or no patience for other people's arguments or views." The provincial Japanese war lords behind him were spoiling for a trial at arms.

Admiral Nomura in Washington was not a member of the war party, and he did not completely understand the picture in Tokyo. However, he was pessimistic about coming events, and asked to resign. He was ordered to remain at his post, and to work with Saburo Kurusu, who was now sent from Japan with no new instructions, but with orders to assist the Ambassador in further negotiations.

Neither Nomura nor Kurusu knew why the latter was sent. However, if there were to be any fruitful new offers, the choice of Kurusu made sense. Unlike Nomura, he spoke excellent English; he had an American wife; and he was regarded as reasonably pro-American.

Neither Kurusu nor Nomura knew the war plans of the Tojo Cabinet. They did know, however, that the adventurist spirit was reaching a peak in Tokyo, and both were opposed to this and deeply concerned.

With Special Emissary Kurusu in America, continuing talks that were recognized on both sides as going nowhere, the Tojo Cabinet held a final policy session. Here a decision was made to let Nomura and Kurusu make one last effort to get United States concessions—but if there was no change in the United States position by November 25, a war resolution was to be placed before the Emperor.

Now, virtually no one in the Japanese Foreign Office knew about the Yamamoto plan, or that a strike on American territory was being prepared. But all Japanese diplomats knew of the November 25 deadline, and it was thought that at that time Japan would move into Thailand, or strike at Singapore or the Dutch East Indies. Ironically, American Intelligence agreed with this view. Some Japanese took great risks to transmit their fears to the Americans, and in one case, Ambassador Grew was furnished with hints of the actual strike plans. Grew faithfully transmitted these home, where they were not taken seriously.

Grew cabled in November that the Japanese Cabinet was in a mood to commit "national hara-kiri" rather than remain vulnerable to American sanctions, and he further advised that any move might come with "dangerous and dramatic suddenness."

Washington knew of the November 25 "deadline" directly. The Japanese diplomatic code had been broken, and all messages between Washington and Tokyo were being intercepted and handed to the President. Also, Kurusu tried to make Roosevelt aware of his own anxiety that Japan was going to declare war, or take some violent action in the Far East. Kurusu kept receiving cables reading "the fate of our Empire hangs by a slender thread of a few days" but no cable ever contained any specific information about what the Japanese government planned to do, only vague warnings, spurring Kurusu to keep trying.

Tojo, of course, was simply stalling, until all military preparations were complete.

313

The November 25 deadline was now extended to November 29. Foreign Minister Togo warned Kurusu and Nomura, however, that the new date could not be extended. *After that, things are automatically going to happen.* This message again did not specify what things were going to happen. It also was intercepted by United States Intelligence.

The reason the President remained so calm during this period was a simple one. President and Cabinet had now conferred and agreed that apparently a conflict was inevitable with Japan. Hopkins said that the war was going to come out of the East. Everyone was fully prepared to accept it.

In a meeting in November with Hopkins, Secretary of War Stimson, and the military chiefs, Roosevelt made the statement that *it was likely the Japanese would strike somewhere without warning, but the major problem of the United States government was to maneuver them into firing the first shot.* In other words, the United States was ready to fight, but it was vitally important that the other side be allowed to strike the first blow.

Neither the President nor any military chief had any thought that the Japanese would strike directly at American territory or United States forces. In fact, there was no firm decision as to what action the United States might take if the war merely extended in East Asia. Roosevelt was prepared to let Thailand go, but to begin aiding the Dutch and British by shooting—possibly without a formal declaration of war, in case they should become engaged.

Very early in the morning of November 27, Secretary of State Hull telephoned General Marshall, the Chief of Staff. "These fellows mean business and you will have to watch out."

Then he called Henry Stimson and told the War Secretary: "I have washed my hands of it and it is now in the hands of you and Knox—the Army and the Navy."

The War and Navy Departments now sent out a warning to all installations on the West Coast, Hawaii, and in the Philippines. The message began: *Consider this a war warning.* It pointed out the dangers of Japanese action beginning on a Saturday or Sunday. It was not the first message; during 1941 a number of more informal warnings had gone out.

These messages read differently in retrospect than they did to contemporaries of that time. No American officer, including Marshall, dreamed of a carrier strike on Hawaii or an attack on the Philippines. Intelligence knew that Japanese fleet units had put to sea, but it was confidently expected they were sailing south, to the Indies. In Hawaii, General Short, the Army commander, on receiving the warning did the worst possible thing he could do: he massed his aircraft on the ground at Hickam Field. The greatest danger Short could envision was Japanese sabotage, and massed planes, under ground guard, would be less vulnerable than scattered at fields throughout the islands.

American military planners had adopted the idea of an advanced defense in the Atlantic, but never credited the Japanese with evolving the same concept. Just as American war plans in the Atlantic were a form of defense—the United States had no designs or ambitions whatever toward Hitler's Europe—the Japanese stroke at Pearl Harbor was *defensive*. The carrier attack was not, and was never meant to be, a prelude to an invasion. It was designed and executed merely to prevent the United States Pacific Fleet from interfering—in a declared or undeclared war—with Japanese conquests in the Indies. Just as it never occurred to American military chiefs that it could happen, it never occurred to Japanese that such a strike would be the worst strategic blunder they could make against a nation like the United States.

The story of how Kurusu and Nomura—whom history has cleared of any real duplicity—bungled the last hours is well known. The Japanese emissaries were ordered to stall for time, then deliver a certain message precisely at a certain hour on December 7. This message reiterated Japan's differences with the United States, and indicated that Japan was going to take hostile action. But the two Japanese in Washington, not aware

315

of the carrier strike, could not know how important timing was, nor could they know that the message was intercepted, and that Cordell Hull had it in his hands when they appeared for their appointment with him on the afternoon of December 7.

The Tojo plan was to have the diplomats deliver what was, in effect, a war note, a few minutes *before* Japanese planes attacked American soil. A move of this kind, while not the highest ethics, was still well within the rules of war. But keeping Kurusu and Nomura in the dark as to the real situation allowed them to bungle the timing; they arrived at Hull's office to deliver their note after the attack had commenced, and after Hull was already aware of it, by telephone from Hawaii. This resulted in the most horrible propaganda failure imaginable. It convinced the entire American people that the Japanese government planned a strike while still officially negotiating, which, if one split hairs, was not the case.

President Roosevelt was handed the note Nomura planned to deliver some hours before Nomura and Kurusu were to meet Hull. He read it carefully and said to Harry Hopkins, who stood nearby, "This means war."

Hopkins, overheard by a naval officer who had brought the message to the White House, told F.D.R. that the United States should avoid being surprised, that it ought to strike the first blow. The intercept of the Japanese cable had given the United States a priceless advantage.

But Roosevelt said, "No, we can't do that. We are a democracy and a peaceful people," or words very similar.

Harry Hopkins was the perfect realist, quick to see the real situation, quick to grasp advantages. But Roosevelt was a realist, too, and something Harry Hopkins never was—a brilliant political leader. Hopkins had never been elected to high office, and he had long before arrived at a state where he did not care what the public understood or wanted. In the hours prior to Pearl Harbor F.D.R. was certainly aware that the United States was going to war with Japan—in a few hours, or a few days, or a few weeks. He had made up his mind to that war—and the war against Germany—long before.

But Roosevelt desperately wanted a war with popular support. The country had to go into battle as a united people, with emotional isolationism turned inside out into emotional belligerency. At all costs—his whole policy had shown this—he had to avoid a President's war.

There were not only the political dangers to himself, his Party, and his programs if he should get entangled in a war of policy without popular support. There was a very real danger to the nation. Divided peoples had never been very successful at winning desperate wars. France had declared war on Germany, at a time when most of her population wanted no such war, because of an attack on Poland. The French had waged war utterly without conviction, although the strategic danger was or should have been plain.

Great Britain had gone to war with Hitler in the same way, and only the English Channel and a tiny R.A.F. saved them until they finally understood the massive German peril. It was surely in Roosevelt's power to engage the nation in war by executive action—he could order United States forces to shoot, and probably, against Japan, this would have produced a different reaction than it had from Germany, for Japan was clearly in an exalted mood and ready for desperate adventure. But if it were known that Roosevelt made the first move, toward a war that 80 percent of the American people still opposed, no one—not even the nation's most powerful President —could be sure of their reaction.

All during November and December 1941, many newspapers had urged the President to declare war against the entire Axis. But there was as yet no precedent for Roosevelt to ask for this kind of action. He could not formally declare war himself; this power was reserved to the Congress. As a constitutional safeguard, this fact was an immense factor in millions of American minds. Many Americans might not regard conflict by executive action as legal.

Under the new-found powers that had been discovered to be "inherent" in his office during the long crisis, F.D.R. could commit United States arms; Congress could not stop him. When he had ordered the Navy to shoot in the Atlantic there was no effective way his Congressional critics could oppose him. But F.D.R. was fully aware that, in his own mind, he had not even been able to go this far until it had been made to seem the Germans had shot first. And as yet the Atlantic war was clandestine, not much seen or understood, with very few men involved.

Of course, faced with the Japanese crisis, F.D.R. could have immediately gone to Congress with a war resolution. But he had secured repeal of the Neutrality Acts by a thin margin, and a delay or failure on a war resolution would have been utterly disastrous. Neither house would have given him a quick declaration in 1941; every Congressional leader made him aware of this. There would have been lengthy debate, most probably a filibuster in the Senate by Wheeler and his cohorts, and the resulting controversy and bitterness would have kept the nation divided even in the event of an enemy attack.

F.D.R. knew that no section of the country, outside of the South, was emotionally ready to accept a deliberate United States act of war, even in the nation's paramount interest.

But Roosevelt knew that almost 100 percent of the American people had indicated in the polls that the nation was ready to fight if first attacked. He had to let the other side strike the first telling blow. That he had any notion of how serious that first blow would be, or that he deliberately let Pearl Harbor happen is, on the evidence, nonsense. The best military minds among his advisers had never even suggested the possibility of a Pearl Harbor. If F.D.R. had had prescience of the destruction of the Pacific Fleet, no one who knew him ever doubted that he would have struck at the Japanese at sea, come what may.

And after all, despite the bloodshed in Hawaii, the President's course was proved correct. Roosevelt was right. Unity came only after Pearl Harbor—after the Japanese had flown out of the sun in a sneak attack and left behind blazing wreckage and more than a thousand dead Americans.

Pearl Harbor, of course, was a bitter lesson. Many people have written about it, and so described it. But almost no one has written that the real strategic lessons should have been learned long before.

Conclusion

There are those ... who ask me and other veterans ... "What did it get you?" People who ask that question "What did it get you?" forget one thing ... the thing they forget is that liberty and freedom and democracy are so very precious that you do not fight to win them once—and then stop. Liberty and freedom and democracy are prizes awarded only to those people who fight to win them and then keep fighting eternally to hold them. Sergeant Alvin C. York.

Was it a mistake for the United States to enter World War I? Yes: 64 percent. From a Gallup poll taken in 1937.

Those who support the pacifist ideal inevitably support efforts to conquer the world to the fullest! Adolf Hitler.

Every military and political strategist, and every potential enemy of the United States, is aware that the Japanese assault on Pearl Harbor was one of the greatest national blunders ever made. Admiral Yamamoto, who planned it and executed it, was thinking along purely military lines: he respected and feared the United States Pacific Fleet, and he wanted it out of the way.

Japan had to fight the coming war with the hardware it had on hand; it lacked the industrial capacity and raw materials to build more. But the United States was under no such handicap. The fleet units sunk or damaged at Pearl Harbor were replaced in months. By an extremely fortunate coincidence, the United States' three attack carriers were not at anchor on Sunday, December 7. Two had gone to discharge planes to reinforce American island outposts; one had returned to California for repairs.

The waves of Japanese bombers and torpedo planes sank the main battle line of the United States Navy or else battered it into temporary uselessness; they left 2,280 American servicemen dead. But they destroyed a fleet that the United States had never intended to use to prevent them from seizing Southeast Asia—their strategic goal. If Pearl Harbor had not been bombed, the Japanese could still have taken every one of their objectives in the Pacific and the Indies without interference. No American naval planner would have dreamed of dispatching the Pacific Fleet across the ocean, without logistical support and within range of land-based Japanese aircraft, in the early months of 1942. The plans on the books on December 7, 1941 so state.

Actually, the Japanese made a real tactical error by attacking ships, and not facilities. If the harbor and docks and yards at Pearl Harbor, not the replaceable ships, had been destroyed instead, the United States war effort in the Pacific would have been delayed many more months. The Japanese Navy in 1941 was very good. Its fleet air arm was superb—probably, on December 7, 1941, the best in the world. But the haunting fear of a navy and its commanders—who had never wanted a Pacific war—that they were second best led to a preventive strike that enjoyed only limited success, and aroused the very tiger that Japanese with a world view had always feared.

The Japanese Army with its *samurai* ethic feared nothing— but it was the Japanese Navy that had to defend the Empire and that died in that defense.

The real blunder of Pearl Harbor, with its horror, its shock, and its background of treachery, was that no other act could possibly have pulled the American people so immediately and emotionally into total war. Almost all Americans were outraged, almost none felt there was any longer a question as to peace or war. Americans had seen bombs fall on Frenchmen, Dutchmen, Poles, Britons, and Chinese—but these were in pictures, or newsreels, and seemed unreal, far away. America had seemed immune from a messy world, somehow above it all. But on December 7, 1941, the American public realized with cold shock that the choice of peace or war was seldom unilateral, and that their own opinion in the matter was not necessarily decisive.

The shock was followed by a roaring anger, then a deep determination. Intellectually, most Americans had always sensed the danger; emotionally they had rejected it. Now, as German Ambassador Dieckhoff had predicted, the most bitter isolationists did not find the leap from noninvolvement to belligerency hard to take.

In Washington, Roosevelt conferred with the Cabinet while the reports on the damage and casualties were still coming in. These were classified at once, but enough seeped through so that all Americans realized the Hawaiian forces had been savagely mauled. The President's purpose was now to put a war message before the Congress, and he discussed its contents. All agreed on war.

Secretary Hull wanted to review the whole story of Japanese-American relations, in an attempt to prove the United States was both moral and right in its stands. With keen instinct, F.D.R. brushed aside this idea. He felt that a simple call to arms would be more effective. On December 8 he delivered his "day of infamy" speech to the Congress and the nation. The Senate voted unanimously for war. The House had one dissenting vote, from a woman Representative of pacifist conviction. War was declared against Japan.

But, although few Americans paid any attention at the time, since they were still bemused and angry over the Japanese sneak attack, this declaration left the United States at peace

322

with Nazi Germany. Roosevelt, the Cabinet, and the entire policy-making staff of the government had agreed that Germany was the greater danger and the principal foe. The real attention—and the real shooting war—was in the Atlantic, not the Pacific, on December 6. The question F.D.R. now pondered was, should the Congress be asked for a declaration of war against the European Axis?

The warhawks of the Cabinet all said yes. But there was no immediate agreement on how and when, and Roosevelt, again following his instinct, preferred to wait. In traditional terms, the United States did not actually have grounds for war against the Germans. One of the ironies of the situation was that, for more than a year, the United States government had been far more belligerent toward the Nazis than the Nazis had been toward it. It had conspired against, acted against, aided the enemies of, and finally set out to sink the vessels of a Germany that was—for the moment—deliberately trying to avoid war. The United States had done all these things against a vicious power in its own dominant interest—but the President hesitated at the possible odium that might accrue if the United States began what might seem to be an aggressive war. The undeclared war in the Atlantic went on for several days after Pearl Harbor, while the Japanese and the Allies were now fully engaged in the Pacific.

Roosevelt did have one thing he was relying on: the intercepts of the Japanese coded messages had given him a feeling that the Germans would act first.

The fact was not made public, but the Administration knew that the Japanese had struck in the Pacific without either consulting or notifying the German government. The Pearl Harbor attack came as a surprise to Hitler as well as F.D.R. But immediately following the strike, the Japanese regime formally invoked the Tripartite Pact, and asked Berlin to declare war on the United States. These communications were intercepted by "Magic"—the code name for the operation by which Japanese cables were intercepted and decoded—and cannily, Roosevelt decided it would be best to wait.

Hitler was delighted with the Japanese attack. He did not know the full extent of the British-American strategy decisions. He was immediately hopeful that the United States would be distracted by a Pacific war. On December 11, at Hitler's insistence, Germany charged the United States with repeated, open acts of belligerency in the Atlantic and declared a formal state of war. Italy did the same. If Hitler had not acted in this way, the Administration would still have been faced with a serious quandary—but now there was nothing for the Congress to debate.

Both houses passed a joint resolution that a state of war had been "thrust" upon the United States. The Senate was unanimous; the House took no record vote.

The President's hands were freed at last.

The long, crucial period between 1939-1941 pointed up a number of salient facts. During these months the United States crossed a new frontier almost without public realization. The actual frontier was passed long before Pearl Harbor.

The United States was not, as many Americans assumed, a great, uninvolved, peaceful nation minding its own business on Sunday, December 7, 1941. It was a country that had already begun to mobilize for war. It had a one hundred billion dollar arms program already far advanced. It had already defined, planned, and coordinated its future war strategy on the highest levels. It had revamped not only its armed forces, but its entire defense concept and strategy. The new strategy accepted belligerency, as dictated by geopolitical expediency. The new strategy was devised in a vacuum of public knowledge—although Administration spokesmen tried to popularize it—and throughout in a vacuum of popular support. The Administration had begun an actual limited war against the Axis, through executive action.

324

By 1940 the United States had actively violated the precepts of neutrality under international law by giving government-to-government assistance to belligerent Britain. The transfer of United States military equipment to the Allies in 1940 was not a legitimate neutral act. The enactment of Lend-Lease, by any definition, was a hostile move. The assumption of convoying in the Atlantic and the orders to fire on Axis vessels was an act of active war. All of these actions, and the Axis response to them, showed that the concept and prosecution of war between nations had entered new dimensions, particularly for the heretofore legal-minded United States.

Certain damage had been done to traditional American attitudes and practices. The legitimizing of the war by the Japanese attack on Pearl Harbor did not wholly retrieve what had gone before. Enormous, significant precedents had been set. The expanding concept of the President as the Commander in Chief—without sharply defined limits to the powers of this office—forever changed the role of the President from a requester of legislation to an executive who could commit American power abroad.

It was established that the President could participate in multilateral strategy decisions with other powers, make secret commitments of a far-reaching nature, and even order the armed forces into limited, undeclared belligerency. President Roosevelt felt, in the dominant interests of the nation, that the will of Congress, and by extension, the people, was frequently best avoided. Again and again, more than any President up to his time, he employed "inherent" powers and executive orders which bypassed Congressional action. It was established that the Congress had no effective means to halt a strong President who was willing to use these powers in a judicious manner.

It was shown that the Congress, which could be effective where there was a domestic concensus, could not be effective in the fields of foreign policy—where there was no longer a sharp delineation between the states of peace and war. The

American system of government did not envision an extensive entrance into the field of international power politics. Because of the exigencies of these politics, in a rapidly changing world, changes in the structure of the United States government had to be made. Roosevelt, with a genuine feeling for and appreciation for all forms of power, made them freely.

There was probably, in any event, no other choice, for the period pointed out certain defensive weaknesses in the democratic system and the attitudes of the democratic public. One illustration of this was the twenty years of agitation against the act of war itself that followed 1918. War—or any form of active belligerency—in itself, in world politics was neither moral nor immoral. Only its purposes were one or the other. War, for any genuine democracy, had both dangers and limits. It had to be defensive, that is, war could not assure any indefinite or vague political goal such as "ensuring peace" or fostering "international justice." Such goals, by definition, were beyond the purview of armed force. What the use of arms could do, and sometimes must do, was to defend lands, territories, and ways of life against external attack.

Hitler was not a true phenomenon, but merely a historical figure in a long chain of adventurers and revisionists. Repelled by the hideous sacrifice and indecisive ending of the first world war, almost all democratic peoples chose a form of self-deception: that the bloody and horrible results of armed violence could be prevented by a unilateral effort on their part. Hitler understood this attitude fully, just as he sensed that the abhorrence of war had progressed into a real fear of war, and he played upon both fears and attitudes to remake the world in his own favor.

In retrospect, from any angle and from any sensible philosophy, the decision of the democracies for unilateral disarmament, and to allow the avowed enemies of democratic order to erect an armed hegemony was disastrous.

Democratic publics, during the period of Hitler's rise,

showed no historic vision, no great fund of common sense, no fundamental understanding of the modern world. This made the need for leadership in democratic states a matter of urgency. The publics preferred managers rather than leaders; and England and France and America all enjoyed too much of management—with Hoovers, Chamberlains, and the French bureaucracy—in government. Managers could only implement the popular will; true leaders had to forge it, and advance in front of it.

Yet, under sound leadership, democracies showed that they could be more vigorous than nations accustomed to autocratic rule. Fascism could not escape massive bureaucracy and palace politics. Britain, under Churchill, proved that a democracy could match and excel the efforts of a totalitarian power. The United States, later, did the same.

The vital balance democracy had to attain was one of retaining personal liberty, but at the same time finding the personal discipline to follow competent leadership in foreign affairs. This was made extremely difficult because few people in any country, the democracies included, had any deep or continuing interest in events abroad. Meanwhile, popular opinion in every democracy showed itself hostile to the idea of sacrifice, involvement, or a continuing struggle. In the United States, the tragedy of England's hesitancy, the folly of wishful thinking, and the belief that war could be avoided by an effort of will, was almost repeated.

In a very real sense, the United States avoided great damage not by its own efforts but because of the stubborn defense of a friendly power. If Britain had surrendered in 1940, the subsequent history of the United States would have been quite different. If the Nazis and the U.S.S.R. had not gone to war when they did, the United States would have been faced with an immensely grimmer picture. The twenty million Russian dead of World War II might instead have been American.

Even as late as December 6, 1941, there was no indication

that a majority of the public had gained wisdom, in spite of two years of the spectacle of armed aggression and global war. The concept of defensive strategy evolved by the best minds in Washington tended to be emphatically rejected by the public. The American people continued to think territorially, verbally admitting, but emotionally refusing the idea that modern techniques and weapons had shrunk the world. The idea of *foreign war* still was met with prejudice, despite General Marshall's patient explanation that the United States could never fight a successful war on its own soil. Any defense predicated on a defense of the homeland alone was a defense taken in too narrow form, and implemented too late.

The public also indicated no acceptance of historic logic, or the true logic of power relationships between the nations and peoples. The notion that the "world was made" persisted. Yet this assumption, firmly held, was not strong enough to lead to the conviction that the "world as made" must eternally be defended. As late as 1941, the United States people were not really determined to fight for *a* peace—they wanted peace instead.

Ironically, the people who supported the Administration's undeclared war did so more from hatred of the enemy than from any understanding of strategic relationships. This presaged, sooner or later, the emergence of a new, liberal isolationism to replace the disillusion with "power politics" of the 1920's. All future foes would not be so hateable as Adolf Hitler, or the sneak attackers at Pearl Harbor.

By historic logic, in 1941 both the U.S.S.R. and Nazi Germany, not one or the other, had to be opposed. Both were basically revisionists; both powers hated the Anglo-American world as it had emerged. *But the weakness of the Anglo-Saxon powers forced a decision to make an alliance with the Russians.* Out of this decision, and this alliance, inevitably came certain enormous dangers for the postwar world. The map, and power relationships of 1945, were inevitably made in 1941.

Yet the very weakness at arms of the democratic powers was historically ridiculous. The English-speaking nations numbered two hundred million people against only seventy million Germans. They had more wealth, more able-bodied men, more resources, and more skills, than the Germans—even after conquering Europe—could command. Together, Britain and America made more steel—the vital ingredient of power—and controlled more oil than all the rest of the world combined. In 1940, the United States alone forged 66,993,000 tons of steel. The Nazi state produced only twenty-eight million. Yet German power held the democracies with their backs to the wall. It was no wonder that during this period many men despaired of the democratic system, or that the notion that totalitarianism was more efficient took hold.

The danger proved that democracies could not rally around ideas or systems or legislatures but only around a symbol of leadership. In Britain it was Churchill; in America it had to be the President. No other official had a truly national office; no other official, even Cabinet officers, could get the national attention. Secretaries Knox and Stimson clearly enunciated national policies for months—yet no one paid attention, or heard them, until the President spoke. The vast majority of Americans—who voted, and who made their political power felt—rarely read the so-called influential columnists, and never the carefully prepared speeches printed almost solely in papers such as *The New York Times*. They remained concerned with the here and now of their existence, rarely with historic happenings overseas.

In this atmosphere, without precedents, the President had to feel his way. There was no real rationale, and no immediate example for Roosevelt's war role. Roosevelt was forced, or felt he was forced, to create precedents and to increase Presidential powers. He felt it necessary to prepare the country for war and lead it into active participation and an undeclared

329

belligerency while all the time pretending to be for continued peace.

There is no question, from the evidence, that by 1940 Roosevelt realized that the global struggle was a necessary war for the United States. He never quite dared to admit it. He played his role skillfully, and with eventual success. But his initial hesitation in 1939, and his allowing a "peace bloc" to form around certain Senators, permitted opinion to develop in favor of neutrality. At first, in September 1939, there was no desire to enter the war, but there was throughout the population a far higher percentage who were resigned to entrance than eight months later. In the fall of 1939, about 40 percent of all Americans thought the United States would get in the war. By June 1940—when the need was acute—only 7.7 percent agreed that belligerency was a sensible course. Some of F.D.R.'s hesitancy, and refusal to speak out, was a political mistake.

His real failure—and only failure during the whole time— was his inability to form a true consensus in favor of the use of American power abroad. He still lacked any such firm consensus when the bombs fell on Hawaii. It might have been far better, and far healthier for the future politics of the United States, if the Japanese bombs had never fallen, and the public had been forced into a realization of strategy through Presidential leadership.

One immensely striking fact that emerged by 1941 was that when the President spoke, or argued, or revealed a dramatic action nationally, there was an immediate rallying around. He was the symbol of the nation, and in extremis even men who hated his politics would not repudiate him. When he seemed to drift, opposition hardened.

Another fact that presaged potential trouble was the difficulty of forging a genuine two-party foreign policy. It proved impossible for the Republican Party—despite the fact that no dominant body of Republican opinion was really isolationist

330

in 1941—not to try to use the issues of "peace," military service, and personal sacrifice for political advantage.

There was no real understanding in many quarters by intelligent men that the world power and the world position of the United States could no longer afford external policies subject to the whim of internal politics. Yet many people could not distinguish between a consistent foreign policy and dictatorship. Foreign policy, in the dominant interests of the nation, could not be allowed to waver or change because of shifts of domestic political power. Many observers said this could not be prevented—but it was the primary factor that destroyed France and almost destroyed Britain.

Meanwhile, the Washington Administration showed no great courage in the face of opposition. *The Administration, even when it felt compelled to do so for reasons of dominant strategy, never took an act in open defiance of majority opinion.* Decisions were made, and action implemented, that had public disapproval—or at least, no approval. But these were invariably made in secret. Looking backward, the Administration was much too fearful; it paid too much attention to scattered criticism. It could not really identify or classify the isolationist opposition, and it did not squarely face the fact that the opposition could in no way have halted or prevented any Presidential act—if the act were strongly pushed.

To take such action was frequently discussed on Cabinet level, but never implemented on Presidential level. Roosevelt was fond of the trial balloon—but he preferred to let his Cabinet officers or other spokesmen send it up, when he himself would have been the only effective spokesman.

President Roosevelt was perhaps too fond of popularity, or even office, to lead the horses to water, let alone to make them drink. His problem was that, in the United States, elections were based on popular polls—but foreign policy could not be, without the greatest danger. The Presidential challenge was not to implement public opinion where there was no vision, but

331

to form it, and to force the public to rally behind him in crisis.

A truly great President and American would have no concern for what might happen to him personally once he had committed the nation on an irrevocable course, anymore than a soldier charging up a hill.

Yet the President could not be blamed for a certain hesitancy. In his time there was no core of conviction, even in Washington, about the true role of the United States in the world. Such a conviction might have told the Administration, and the people, when and where to fight. There was no conviction that the United States should take, or use, power. There was a reluctance to accept responsibility, and a real fear of the odium inevitably associated with world power. Roosevelt's clear vision could see the dangers inherent for modern democratic civilization in the twentieth century—but it was beyond the powers of any one man to make the United States public know who it was, what it was, what it wanted in the world, and where it was, like it or not, going.

The dubious, bitter years between September 1939 and December 1941 showed that somewhere, somehow, such a conviction about the United States had to be found. The next Pearl Harbor, in an age of increasingly hideous weaponry, might not be survivable.

Government by consent could not be translated forever to mean government by the Gallup Poll.

Index

335

336

337

338

341

DATE DUE